DATE DUE

Super Girls, Gangstas, Freeters, and Xenomaniacs

GENDER AND GLOBALIZATION

Susan S. Wadley, *Series Editor*

Other titles from Gender and Globalization

Bodies That Remember: Women's Indigenous Knowledge and Cosmopolitanism in South Asian Poetry
 Anita Anantharam

Family, Gender, and Law in a Globalizing Middle East and South Asia
 Kenneth M. Cuno and Manisha Desai, eds.

From Patriarchy to Empowerment: Women's Participation, Movements, and Rights in the Middle East, North Africa, and South Asia
 Valentine M. Moghadam, ed.

Hijab and the Republic: Uncovering the French Headscarf Debate
 Bronwyn Winter

Imperial Citizen: Marriage and Citizenship in the Ottoman Frontier Provinces of Iraq
 Karen M. Kern

La Chulla Vida: Gender, Migration, and the Family in Andean Ecuador and New York City
 Jason Pribilsky

Making Miss India Miss World: Constructing Gender, Power, and the Nation in Postliberalization India
 Susan Dewey

Policing Egyptian Women: Sex, Law, and Medicine in Khedival Egypt
 Liat Kozma

Transforming Faith: The Story of Al-Huda and Islamic Revivalism among Urban Pakistani Women
 Sadaf Ahmad

Super Girls, Gangstas, Freeters, and Xenomaniacs

GENDER AND MODERNITY IN GLOBAL YOUTH CULTURES

EDITED BY

SUSAN DEWEY AND KAREN J. BRISON

SYRACUSE UNIVERSITY PRESS

For a listing of books published and distributed by Syracuse University Press, visit our
Web site at SyracuseUniversityPress.syr.edu.

ISBN (cloth): 978-0-8156-3274-0

Library of Congress Cataloging-in-Publication Data
Super girls, gangstas, freeters, and xenomaniacs : gender and modernity in global youth
cultures / edited by Susan Dewey and Karen J. Brison. — 1st ed.
      p. cm. — (Gender and globalization)
    Includes bibliographical references and index.
    ISBN 978-0-8156-3274-0 (cloth : alk. paper) 1. Youth—Cross-cultural studies.
2. Youth—Social conditions.   3. Young women—Cross-cultural studies.
4. Civilization, Modern—21st century.   I. Dewey, Susan.   II. Brison, Karen J.
    HQ796.S897 2012
    305.235—dc23   2012015459

Manufactured in the United States of America

Contents

Contributors

Julie Soleil Archambault is a lecturer in African anthropology at the University of Oxford. She has been conducting research on mobile phone practices among youth in southern Mozambique since 2006 and received her PhD in anthropology from the School of Oriental and African Studies (SOAS), University of London, in 2010. Her research has been funded by the Social Sciences and Humanities Research Council of Canada, as well as by the Overseas Research Student Scheme, UK. She received her MSc and her BSc in Anthropology from the University of Montreal, Canada.

Fiona Beals's PhD in education focused on the discourses used in constructions of youth crime in policy, research, and media. She posed that an alternative discourse could be framed around youth crime that focuses on resistance in moments of liminality. This work has recently been published as a monograph. In other published research, Fiona has looked at the gendered constructions of women prisoners and how discourses of femininity can be asserted as actions of resistance within the environment of the prison—an environment that strips gender away in a process of "rehabilitation" and "punishment." Fiona has a key interest in empowering young people to engage in resistance through social media and has begun to write community-centered resources (for youth and youth workers) to both enable social action and bring academic theory into the streets of Aotearoa–New Zealand.

Karen J. Brison is a professor of anthropology at Union College in Schenectady, New York. She received her PhD in cultural anthropology from the University of California, San Diego (1988). She conducted anthropological research on gender, cultural identity, and childhood in Papua New Guinea from 1984 to 1986 and published a book, *Just Talk* (1992), and numerous articles based on that research. In 1997 she began doing research on children's construction of gender and ethnic identity in play in Rakiraki, Fiji, and she continued that research in 1999–2000 and 2003 and published a second book, *Our Wealth Is Loving Each Other* (2007), as well as articles in journals such as *Ethos* and *Ethnology*. In 2005 she began comparative research on children's ethnic and gender identity in kindergartens and in Pentecostal churches in Suva, Fiji. Her research has been supported by National Science Foundation grants.

Miranda Christou is a lecturer in sociology of education at the University of Cyprus (EdD, Harvard University, 2002). Her work concentrates on the role of educational systems in shaping questions of history and collective memory, the gendered processes of defining the nation, and the pedagogical function of the media in representations of human pain and suffering.

Lindi Conover will graduate from DePauw University with a BA in anthropology and women's studies. Her interests broadly concern the ways people negotiate institutions, with a particular eye on women and children. She has conducted research on child sex tourism in Goa, India, supported by a DePauw University Howes Grant.

Emma E. Cook is a PhD candidate in the Department of Anthropology at SOAS, University of London, where she is completing her dissertation, titled "Failing Freeters: Young Men, Masculinity, and Adulthood in Japan." Her current research interests include youth, gender, notions of selfhood, and the role of Japanese popular culture in identity construction. Her research has been funded by the Japan Foundation, the Federation for Women Graduates (UK), and the Meiji Jingu studentship (SOAS).

Susan Dewey is assistant professor of gender and women's studies at the University of Wyoming. She is the author of three books that analyze the tense dynamics that characterize relationships between postadolescents and "modern" institutions: *Making Miss India Miss World: Constructing Gender, Power, and the Nation in Postliberalization India* (Syracuse University Press, 2008), *Hollow Bodies: Institutional Responses to Sex Trafficking in Armenia, Bosnia, and India* (2008), and *Neon Wasteland: On Love, Motherhood, and Sex Work in a Rust Belt Town* (forthcoming). Susan has also published scholarly articles on related subjects in the journals *Ethnography and Education, American Ethnologist,* and the *Journal of South Asian Popular Culture.* Her research has been funded by nationally competitive grants from Fulbright-Hays and the National Science Foundation.

Joseph Esser holds a PhD from the Department of Anthropology at the University of Minnesota. His dissertation is based on his research among deported gang members returning to their Pacific island country of origin. His research interests revolve around issues of gender, youth culture, and transnationalism within the Pacific.

Shikha Jhingan is teaching at the Department of Journalism, Lady Shri Ram College, University of Delhi. She is a doctoral candidate in cinema studies at the School of Arts and Aesthetics, Jawaharlal Nehru University. Her research work focuses on performance, practices, and circulation of the female voice in Hindi film songs. She has published journal articles on this topic in *Seminar* and *Bioscope: South Asian Screen Studies*.

Jacquelyn A. Lewis-Harris is the director of the Center for Human Origin and Cultural Diversity and presently holds the title of assistant professor in both anthropology and the College of Education at the University of Missouri, St. Louis. Lewis-Harris has her doctorate and master's in anthropology from Washington University, St. Louis, Missouri. She has lived and worked in the Pacific, Papua New Guinea, as well as Liberia, West Africa, for thirty years. She currently consults for several national and international museums as an independent curator. She has also published numerous articles and catalogs on Pacific art and cultures and African American and West African cultures in relation to identity, art, and contemporary society.

Bronwyn Wood is a doctoral candidate at the Faculty of Education at Victoria University of Wellington, New Zealand. She is currently researching aspects of youth agency and social action in relation to the social studies curriculum in New Zealand. Her research interests include citizenship, youth sociology, geographies of youth, and curriculum studies.

Hui Faye Xiao is assistant professor in the Department of East Asian Languages and Cultures at the University of Kansas. Her special areas of interest include Chinese literature and popular culture, film studies, and gender studies. Her recent publications have appeared in the *Journal of Contemporary China, Journal of Chinese Cinemas, Chinese Films in Focus II, Globalization and Chineseness: Postcolonial Readings of Contemporary Culture,* and *From Camera Lens to Critical Lens: A Collection of Best Essays on Film Adaptation.* Currently she is working on a book project titled "Chinese-Style Divorces: Narratives of Gender, Class, and Family in Post-Reform Chinese Literature and Culture."

Sayumi Yamakawa holds a PhD (University of Manchester, 2009) in social anthropology with a specialization in Namibia and southern Africa. Her PhD research, funded by the Mie International Exchange Foundation, explored the aspirations, expectations, and challenges faced by young Owambo people in northern Namibia in relation to their understanding of tradition, culture, and Owamboness. She also conducted her master's research in Namibia and produced a thesis titled "Adolescent Sexuality in Namibia: An Analysis on Sexual-Health Knowledge, Attitude, and Practice among Secondary School Learners in Katutura" (University of Namibia, 2002). Her recent publications include "The Interrelationship of *Ohango* Ritual, Gender, and Youth Status among the Owambo of North-Central Namibia," in *Unravelling Taboos: Gender and Sexuality in Namibia* (2007).

Super Girls, Gangstas, Freeters, and Xenomaniacs

Introduction

Cross-Cultural Visions of Youth and Modernity

KAREN J. BRISON AND SUSAN DEWEY

Standing near an informal housing settlement in southern Mozambique, a teenage girl shades her mobile phone from the sun as she dials the number of a male admirer. She is calling to ask him if he will buy her family's bread for the day. "The way it happens these days," a male acquaintance of this young woman explained to anthropologist Julie Soleil Archambault, "women are the ones who gain more and the men who spend more." Both the female caller and her suitor regularly make use of mobile phone technology, which has only recently become available in Mozambique, in ways that mirror gendered gift-giving obligations otherwise sorely tested by years of war and economic uncertainty. Yet many Mozambican youth complain that the ubiquity of mobile phones has also increased the frequency of multiple-partner relationships among young women, who benefit from these alliances in the form of gifts and support. This sort of profound cultural ambivalence toward a pervasive albeit newly arrived technology is evident in multiple arenas of Mozambican life, prompting one young man to lament to Archambault, "Nowadays, relationships are more commercialized."

Buddha, a Tongan-born adolescent male, reflects upon the path that led him to an American prison by employing ancient Pacific oral histories of interisland battles to explain how gang membership helped him to define his ethnic identity as a teenage migrant. The difficulties inherent for young men like Buddha who live in hostile Los Angeles neighborhoods have resulted in the formation of Crip-affiliated gangs, such as the Tonga Crip Gangsters, composed entirely of South Pacific islanders who quickly became known for violent criminal activity. Buddha attributes the eagerness with which so many young men joined such organizations to a host of factors: poverty; parents working multiple low-wage, low-prestige jobs with little hope of upward mobility due to their status as undocumented migrants; and, perhaps most significantly, a sense of severe disconnection from both Tongan culture and American educational institutions. "So I created my own identity of what I thought makes me Tongan," Buddha recounted to anthropologist Joseph Esser. "A Tongan is a warrior. . . . [W]e don't bow down to nobody. I'm not scared of nobody." Buddha and his predominantly adolescent peers make a powerful statement about masculinity in migrant youth diasporas through their autochthonous interpretations of American inner-city disaffection and reified Tongan history.

"I don't think that I will ever get to vote [for] a president in this lifetime, so I'll choose a girl that I like," noted a teenage fan of the enormously popular Chinese version of *American Idol, Super Girl,* which selects its youthful winners by tallying text-message votes sent via viewers' mobile phones. This statement was part of a flurry of Internet-based activity circulating around viewers' obsession with the *Super Girl* contestant least favored by the show's organizers: Li Yuchun, an androgynous young woman rumored to be a lesbian. Li Yuchun's democratic rise to superstardom in a country undergoing unprecedented socioeconomic change raises questions not only about young people's understandings of acceptable norms regarding gender and sexual expression, but also about the boundaries of state authority in China.

Feminist scholars Kathy E. Ferguson and Monique Mironesco have noted that "every global is somebody's local, but not everybody's local is equally authoritative or desired" (2008, 339). In the three opening anecdotes, and in the chapters that follow, we witness young people actively engaged in projects of gendered meaning making throughout the world. Drawing on transnational "techno," "media," "youth," and other "scapes" (Appadurai 1996; Maira and Soep 2005), youth (as locally defined) craft new identities for themselves that are strongly gendered to make sense of very local lives.

Anthropologists Jennifer Cole and Deborah Durham (2007) suggest that the impact of transnational economic, political, and cultural flows is felt only as mediated through relations between generations and within families. In other words, individuals feel the impact of global flows in numerous ways, including through changes in relationships between young and old that are brought about by migration that separates children from aging parents and via mass schooling that impinges on socialization of youth. Conversely, the force of global flows in individual lives differs according to the way families and communities react.

This volume endorses Cole and Durham's (2007) insights into the mediating impact of generation and family, while additionally arguing that gender relations are themselves key mediators in cross-cultural constructions of youth. As the opening examples clearly demonstrate, youth often have desires and aspirations defined by gender and respond to diverse economic, political, and cultural flows with their own attempts at redefining marriage, sexuality, and appropriate gendered behavior.

But as Ferguson and Mironesco (2008) stress, young people are themselves keenly aware that they operate on an uneven global terrain whereupon some people's *imaginaires* (Marshall-Fratani 1998) are much less authoritative and more constrained than are others. Like Buddha and the teenage girls in China and Mozambique, young people everywhere struggle to redefine gendered and ethnic identities in dialogue with transnational images of the modern youth that stress individual agency and self-cultivation. But they are all clearly aware of a gap between these images and local possibilities.

It is important to note that the relatively recent emergence of childhood and adolescence as special phases of life requiring rather lengthy periods free from work and other "adult" responsibilities (e.g., Aries 1965) coincided with the rise of industrial capitalism in Europe and the United States. Colonial administrators exported these ideas about childhood and adolescence by promoting mass education and other "reforms" in gender roles and family life (Anderson-Levitt 2003; Comaroff and Comaroff 1991). More recently, neoliberal economic policies and structural adjustment plans in Africa and Latin America have brought with them nongovernmental organizations (NGOs) and educational policies designed to enhance "youth agency" (Durham 2005).

Indeed, discourses on agency and the rights of young people emanate from international organizations most obviously in the form of national legislation prohibiting child labor. These notions, however, conflict both with local social expectations and often with an economic reality that makes children's work necessary for family or, in some instances, individual survival (Kovats-Bernat 2008; Montgomery 2001; Offit 2010). In many countries, such realities are further compounded by the contraction of the formal labor sector through reduced government employment under structural adjustment plans, the elimination of many stable career paths via global economic restructuring, and huge numbers of children orphaned by AIDS (Durham 2005).

Young people also operate within local hierarchies based on age and gender. The term *youth* as a transnational category embodied in mass media, and institutions such as schools and NGOs, is increasingly defined as a liminal state accorded license for experimentation. But youth generally have limited agency since they are often bracketed as unfinished adults not to be taken seriously (Durham 2005; Beals and Wood, this volume). Thus, youth are at the forefront of imagining new kinds of identities and communities because they are defined as liminal. They are also often the targets of transnational mass media and corporations that cultivate the idea of "teens" as consumers (Diversi 2006; Liechty 1995; Quinn 2005), and by international NGOs and educational systems promoting youth agency (Durham 2005; Liechty 2002). Nonetheless, the cultural productions of young people are often relegated to the realm of "just play" (Durham 2005) by elders who want to circumscribe attempts to rewrite gender-, age-, and family-based roles (see both Cook and Yamakawa, this volume). Likewise, males and females occupy different niches in local societies. Liechty (2002), for example, shows how Nepalese girls have less access to popular culture and more limited scope to redefine identities than do their brothers.

It is all too tempting to analyze our opening ethnographic examples of young Mozambicans' patterns of mobile phone use and Tongan American gang membership as part of an outdated model demonstrating how "change" is neatly encapsulated within "tradition." Yet such an analysis would fail to account for the complexities evident in each example. Why, for instance, did urban Chinese youth almost unanimously elect an androgynous figure so ill-favored by the authorities featured on a popular television show? Does their youthful rejection of the feminine beauty characteristic of most Chinese pop singers simply signal a shift in acceptable appearance norms for young women, or is it a much more subversive rejection of a state project that demands ideological uniformity and obedience from its citizens? In asking such questions, we hope to provide nuanced answers to what these gendered modernities might mean for young people, who must simultaneously make sense of their own lives in the context of adult expectations and within a world very different from that of their parents' youth.

Accordingly, chapters in this volume emphasize the historical and cultural relativity of youth while remaining attentive to the reality that such ideologies are now spread via schools, mass media, children's literature, international organizations, and popular culture. The analyses in each of the chapters carefully examine how these complex processes have helped to create a global scenario in which young people increasingly emphasize their right to self-expression through consumerism, experimentation with various forms of gender and cultural affinities, and, above all, the right to make choices on their own terms.

Youth Agency on the Global Stage:
Why Youth? Whose Modernity?

There has been an explosion of scholarly interest in youth cultures in the past fifteen years, particularly on the question of how young people shape, and are shaped by, the experiences of globalization in late modernity (see, for example, Allison 2006; Cole and Durham 2007; Condry 2006; Hansen et al. 2008; Honwana and de Boeck 2005; Liechty 2002; Maira and Soep 2005; Stephens 1995; M. White 1994; and Wulff 1995b). Children and youth become both "makers" and "breakers" in late modernity (Honwana and de Boeck 2005), valorized as the hope of the future but also seen as increasingly problematic and dangerous. This notion may be related to the fact that a significant percentage of the population in Africa (41 percent), Asia (28 percent), Latin America and the Caribbean (30 percent), and Oceania (25 percent) is now under fifteen years of age (United Nations Statistics Division 2006). This demographic explosion has coincided with a contraction in economic opportunities and in social services following the advent of structural adjustment policies of the 1980s. Throughout the world, young people have encountered increased difficulties in moving from school to economic self-sufficiency, leading to increasing pressure to do well in school and attempts by young people themselves to postpone markers of adulthood such as marriage and a steady career (see Cook, this volume). Young people attempt to redefine kin-, gender-, and age-based relationships (Durham 2007) and simultaneously demand political attention by virtue of their numbers, giving rise to widespread fear of youth violence (Mains 2007).

These socioeconomic shifts have been accompanied by the spread of new communicative technologies such as cell phones and the Internet, which are widely available and free of centralized control, allowing young people new opportunities to define identities and mobilize populations (Comaroff and Comaroff 2005). More generally, however, the recent interest in youth culture stems from a sense that youth, as part of an emerging transnational category, are at the forefront of creating heterogeneous modernities as they appropriate global images and ideologies to fashion new senses of self and society.

Both *youth* and *modernity* are by their very nature vague and polysemous terms. In one commonly used sense, "modernity" and particularly the period of "late modernity" that geographer David Harvey (2006) traces to the early 1970s, is a state of global capitalism marked by more flexible systems of production, geographical mobility of capital, and neoliberal economic policies. Late modernity also brings distinct challenges to national sovereignty as transnational relationships dominate both commercial and cultural flows. Local communities face unique dilemmas in the late-modern system, which requires workers to be increasingly mobile, often via long-distance migration, and an explosion of mass media and travel creates "time-space compression," exposing people to multiple life possibilities (Stephens 1995, 19). At the same time, the gap between the rich and the poor has increased, so many come to imagine their lives in terms that they can never achieve in reality.

Late modernity, in this first sense of the term, involves semiautonomous flows such as mass media, technology, and religion. In a now classic work, Appadurai (1996) argues that the many flows of late modernity offer increased scope for individuals to "imagine" new kinds of identities and communities. Late modernity, then, does not lead to homogeneity, or consistent movement toward so-called Euro-American values, but instead creates a proliferation of identities and communities, many centered outside of Europe and North America. Examples of this phenomenon include "youthscapes" (Maira and Soep 2005), whereby "youth" from around the world utilize mass media to construct a similar identity as youth emphasizing individual choice and expression of self through consumption. Notably, however, such youthscapes are influenced as much by Japanese and Bollywood productions as by Hollywood (Allison 2006; Larkin 2008; both Xiao and Jhingan, this volume).

In a second, overlapping, and commonly used sense of the term, "modernity" is an imagined condition whereby increased individual agency leads to greater prosperity (J. Ferguson 1999; Liechty 2002; Rofel 1999). Appadurai argues that modernity involves the stark reality that "for many societies, modernity is an elsewhere" (1996, 10). "Modernity" in this sense is a privileged *imaginaire* with which people all over the world must grapple. The image of the "Western" or "modern" society may be mythical, but it is firmly embedded not only in Euro-American scholarship of the 1950s and 1960s and in international mass media but also in the policies of governments and international agencies shaped by modernization theory and more recently by neoliberalism (J. Ferguson 1999). Indeed, part of the reason that terms like *modernity* are so seductive and enduring is because they so neatly encapsulate the way in which everyday life is shaped by both institutional codes and individual desires for mobility within them. Moreover, there is a gap between the imagined modern state of being and ability to attain that lifestyle in many areas of the world wherein economies cannot offer the stable life trajectories upon which educated youths could once depend (Durham 2007; Liechty 2002).

In response to this crisis, people everywhere fashion their own versions of "modernity." In this third sense, scholars use "modernity" to refer to the way people define self and society so as to suggest they have their own way of being "modern" (Piot 1999). Rofel (1999) and Liechty (2002), among many others, show how people craft senses of self and society drawing on an *imaginaire* of the modern society but adapting these *imaginaires* to justify and encompass their own positions both vis-à-vis an outer world that defines them as "traditional" and "undeveloped" and in relation to other groups in their own countries. In a similar vein, Brison (2003, this volume) and Besnier (2004) show how in some Pacific island societies, high-ranking adults claim that their own traits are naturally "modern," thus both justifying their continued high status at home and validating "traditional" Pacific island ranking systems to transnational organizations by portraying chiefly elites as having the same goals as international NGO workers.

The chapters in this volume draw on these overlapping senses of modernity, each analyzing the lives of people who are dealing with a world shaped by late modernity in the form of local economic changes generated by mobile and transnational capital and neoliberal economic policies (Archambault, Yamakawa, Cook, Dewey and Conover, Christou) multiple semi-autonomous transnational "flows" in the form of mass media (Xiao, Jhingan, Brison), new communicative technologies such as cell phones and the Internet (Archambault, Lewis-Harris, Xiao, Beals and Wood), world religions (Brison), and migration (Lewis-Harris, Esser). Most of the chapters examine individuals who grapple with modernity, in the second sense, as an imagined state highlighting individual agency and self-cultivation through consumption. And all of the chapters show how individuals, distinctively positioned in particular societies, define their own versions of modernity, in the third sense, in dialogue with modernity both as an imagined state and as a real institutional system.

As Cole and Durham (2007) suggest, the impact of late modernity, as an economic and political reality, and as an imagined state, is mediated everywhere through changes in relationships between generations and in families. This point is particularly evident in the way that late modernity has problematized "youth" and "childhood." "Youth," like modernity, is a concept so fluid and contingent that Durham (2000, 116) suggests that it should be considered a "shifter," that is, a linguistic category that draws meaning from particular contexts where it is used. Many societies traditionally contained no adolescent or youth category (e.g., Bucholtz 2002; M. White 1994), and everywhere the ages and characteristics of youth are locally defined, with many African and Pacific societies considering people in their forties and fifties as youth (Bucholtz 2002; Durham 2007).

Recently, however, youth has taken on a new reality as a transnational category defining adolescence and young adulthood as a liminal phase with special license for exploration, including the construction of a unique "self" through questioning of parents and other authoritative adults and consumption of international mass media and products (Maira and Soep 2005, xxiii). Mark Liechty (2002), for example, argues that "teen" or "adolescent" categories emerged over the past two decades in Nepal as a result of the extended period of education necessary for aspiring middle-class professionals (see also M. White 1994).

According to Liechty, local and international entrepreneurs develop the new youth market by cultivating the idea of the teen years as a period devoted to finding and expressing self through fashion, music, and other forms of consumption. Nepalese families who aspire to membership in a transnational middle class, in turn, emphasize self-cultivation in youth to stake their position in Nepalese society relative to traditional elites and less educated workers.

Maira and Soep (2005, xvi), propose the term *youthscape* to capture the ways that youth, as an emerging transnational category, are similarly positioned relative to cultural, technological, economic, religious, and other scapes across nations. Youth, they argue, is not a cross-cultural psychological stage but instead a category created by parents, peers, "juvenile justice systems, social welfare and labor policies, military apparatuses, marketing schemes, and media and entertainment industries" (Wyn and White 1997, cited in Maira and Soep 2005, xviii).

Youth are "makers" at the forefront of reimagining modernities because they are "forced to make themselves mobile, flexible and fluid transnational capital, yet [are} still capable of drawing upon disparate histories, principles and values" (Lipsitz 2001, 20, cited in Maira and Soep 2005, xix). Specifically, youth are central to defining modernity because: (1) they attend schools that follow international philosophies and institutional patterns while promoting "modern" citizenship as locally defined (e.g., Coe 2005; Stambach 2000); (2) their lives are saturated by mass media, prompting identification with international gendered youth communities such as athletes, rock stars, and beauty queens; (3) they are often targeted by institutions, including Pentecostal churches and other religious organizations, as well as by NGOs with distinct international ideologies; and (4) they are often taken by parents across international boundaries, where they are "sutured" (Maira and Soep 2005) into nations, schools, and neighborhoods.

The contemporary scholarly and popular preoccupation with youth highlights and enhances the role children and adolescents have always played in redefining their worlds.[1] Anthropologists and sociologists (see, for instance, Adler 1998; Caputo 1995; Corsaro 1985, 1997; Fine 1987; Goodwin 1991; Lanclos 2003; Schwartzman 1979; and Toren 1990)

---

1. As with other areas of the field, anthropology has gone through phases vis-à-vis ways of thinking about childhood and youth, and these changes have been well-documented and analyzed elsewhere (Hirschfeld 2002; A. James 2007; Levine 2007). Literature on this subject has expanded exponentially from initial discussions of the cultural relativity of childhood and youth (Kessen 1983) to studies of the serious importance of play and other child-centric elements of life in structuring children's worldviews (Brison 1999; Goldman 1998; Lancy 1996; Morton 1996; Reynolds 1995).

argue that children and youth develop patterns of behavior and views of the world that differ from the patterns and views of adults, arguing that "children's peer groups create their own culture by selecting and rejecting various aspects of adult culture and making cultural innovations of their own" (Adler 1998, 206). Through peer culture, "children not only reproduce but also challenge and transform the world of adults so as to achieve self-control and a measure of autonomy" (ibid., 207).

The creative potential of child and youth cultures increases with the distance between the worlds inhabited by children and adults. The gap between child and adult worlds has increased in many if not most areas of the world with the spread of mass schooling that removes children from the daily round of adult activities (Wulff 1995b). The increased cross-cultural upheaval produced by warfare, radical socioeconomic changes, and migration means that children inhabit worlds significantly different from their parents.

Historically, scholars have conceptualized children and youth as marginal actors whose agency is confined to resisting adults and their institutions (e.g., Willis 1977). More recent works, however (e.g., Condry 2006; Wulff 1995b, 6), suggest moving beyond an emphasis on dominance and resistance to examine the many ways that particular individuals in very specific situations appropriate a variety of images and ideologies in order to shape new identities and make sense of their lives. The mass media itself are hardly monolithic and provide a variety of ways of means to conceptualize youth that are, in part, established through a dialogue between consumers and producers (Mallan and Pearce 2003, xii). In his study of the hip-hop music industry in Japan, Ian Condry (2006) found that hip-hop culture was not controlled by the recording industry but resulted from an interplay of artists, recording studios, and fans.

The chapters of this volume focus on the interactions of particular people in particular situations to show that children and youth, like adults, are not a monolithic group, and youth experiences differ significantly according to gender, class, and ethnicity, resulting in a variety of ways of imagining identities (Mallan and Pearce 2003, ix). Even superficial examination of the growing literature on "youth culture" quickly reveals that such cultures are generally gendered and that males and females often have very different preoccupations. Research presented in this volume foregrounds this dimension by recognizing that youth cultures are gendered in ways that are specific to particular ethnic groups and social classes. Analyses of youth culture in Japan have, for example, revealed gendered preoccupations engaged in by teenage girls experimenting with "cutismo" (Condry 2006), characterized by its combination of older Japanese idealized models of helpless, innocent, naive femininity with new modes of female power (Allison 2006). At the same time, males grapple with alienation from a future as salarymen (Cook, this volume).

More generally, Besnier (2002, 2004) and others (Dewey 2008b; Gal 1979; Meyerhoff 2003) have shown that gender and globalization are intertwined categories such that definitions of gender always implicate the way modernity and tradition are imagined and vice versa. As classic linguistic studies have shown (Trudgill 1983), the associations of service-oriented professions with femininity often lead males to reject the symbolic trappings of modernity, such as speaking English (Brison, this volume). Conversely, women may see institutions of modernity such as beauty pageants as ways of enhancing their autonomy within local society (Dewey 2008b). Thus, modernity, tradition, and gender are intertwined categories that are in turn redefined in relation to each other.

Defining Gendered Modernities

It is no coincidence that the anthropology of childhood and adolescence followed closely on the heels of gender's establishment as a worthwhile category of scholarly analysis. Feminist theory is extremely familiar with discourses of control and domination, and it is thus unsurprising that its incorporation into the academic canon has encouraged a reanalysis of how children and youth experience the world. Gender, like childhood, is a culturally constructed category that could equally be regarded as a "shifter," with content always defined in particular cultural and social contexts. And, like childhood and youth, very local gender categories are now defined in dialogue with pervasive transnational ideologies.

Many definitions of modernity in the social sciences emphasize individual choice and human agency, and thus modernity's advent (if that period can ever truly be marked anywhere in the world) is bound to problematize and push gender norms. This situation is further complicated by the contradictory meanings ascribed to localized modernities that, following Shoma Munshi, are "not 'real' but [rather] potential subject position[s]"

(2001, 6). Munshi's thoughts on the gendered nature of modernities help to explain why many of the chapters in this volume feature young people who embrace these transnational flows in seemingly self-defeating ways. She notes that while what she terms "the 'Asian modern woman'" may be little more than a seductive mirage, "her image interacts with so many other social forces that compete for space in female imagination, that historically and cross-culturally she continues to be a powerful dream or female fantasy" (ibid.).

The gap between imagined identities and real possibilities is particularly significant for young people as they begin to map out their place as gendered beings in an interconnected world that increasingly promotes the illusion of social mobility to the marginalized through consumption practices. Yet ideology also plays a critical role in the construction of gendered identities, and accordingly, we envision each of the chapter's particular geographical focus as a site for the analysis of the cross-cultural meaning-making projects that are an intrinsic part of modernity for innumerable individuals. Modernity's advent has coincided with the rise of global "rights" discourse in ways that encourage women and other subaltern communities to empower themselves, albeit on terms often defined from outside their immediate surroundings.

Anthropologists have recently begun to document how such macrodiscourses are increasingly used by populations outside these geographical regions in ways that illuminate gendered points of tension in local communities. Jyoti Puri (2008) underscores the paradoxes inherent in this process in her research on the use of "global gay" identities by relatively privileged South Asian homosexuals, who consequently receive religious conservatives' criticisms of so-called Western influence. Elissa Helms (2003) similarly observes how gendered norms that position women as inherently peaceful have been reinscribed by activist groups to facilitate the participation of young women in the construction of Bosnia-Herzegovina's sociopolitical future. In both these cases, we see the incorporation of so-called global ideas in ways that privilege local systems of gendered power and oppression and result in the inevitable creation of changes to the original meanings ascribed to such discourse.

Such global inequalities are presented in sobering relief in recent works on young people living in poverty that detail the striking role youth play in informal economies, adult decision-making processes, and even state discourse. J. Christopher Kovats-Bernat's (2008) work on street children in Haiti clearly demonstrates the elaborate strategies of subterfuge young girls enact to avoid sexual assault, while boys engage in macabre nocturnal activities known as *läge domi* (the sleeping wars) in which they maim or kill their rivals with concrete blocks or razor blades as they sleep in coveted hidden areas. Such behavior is strikingly gendered because it violently parodies broader norms regarding public space as dangerous to females because of its potential for male violence. That it takes place among Haiti's most marginal citizens makes it all the more notable.

Thomas Offit's (2010) research with child laborers in Guatemala City also uncovers sharp delineations in gender roles among the young urban workers he studied. Depicting minors who work in the informal sector as conscious decision makers who actively plan for their futures and develop skills that would be unobtainable through formal education, Offit demonstrates how feminized forms of labor such as food production are delegated to young girls, while boys engage in entrepreneurial activities. Leigh Campoamor (2008) finds that child laborers in Peru have a clear understanding of how to appeal to adult sympathies, with acceptable "performances" of a pitiable condition enacted very differently by boys and girls.

The unsettling reality of child labor is further complicated by anxieties about young people's sexuality and ability to consent. In her pathbreaking cross-cultural work on child sex tourism, Julia O'Connell Davidson (2005) suggests that the level of international concern regarding the phenomenon functions as a sort of metaphor for the acknowledgment of unequal sociopolitical relations that currently structure the world.

The same might be argued of migration, as several studies indicate that children are a powerful organizing force in constructing their parents' understandings of appropriate gendered economic roles for men and women. Rhacel Salazar Parreñas (2005) observes that migrant Filipina mothers are expected to grieve and express profound sorrow for their absence when they contact their children by phone. In the context of Ecuador, Jason Pribilsky (2007) notes the prevalence of *nervios,* an anxiety-related condition manifested predominantly among young boys whose fathers have emigrated to the United States.

Children and young people clearly function as indicators, creators, and perpetuators of gendered inequalities, which are themselves central aspects of late modernity. Indeed, sociologist Zygmunt Bauman believes that globalization manifests itself through a widening sense of polarization between the minority who have freedom of mobility and choice and the majority who do not. He notes that this condition has in no small part been prompted by the growth of neoliberalism, an economic and moral philosophy in which Bauman notes that "the responsibilities for resolving the quandaries generated by vexingly volatile and constantly changing circumstances is shifted onto the shoulders of individuals—who are now expected to be 'free choosers' and to bear in full the consequences of their choices" (2007, 3–4). Bauman essentially argues that neoliberalism's deceptively seductive offer of increased individual choice comes at a heavy price, in which individuals find themselves increasingly vulnerable. This situation is particularly true of those who already inhabit the margins of social life because of their gender, poverty, or youth.

Bauman argues that an increased sense of insecurity worldwide combines with the declining ability of nations to effect positive change in individual lives, and in doing so creates a seemingly chaotic condition that does little more than cleverly disguise the interests of the powerful. Although Bauman writes in the context of western Europe and North America, parallels clearly exist in the lives of individuals discussed throughout the following chapters, in areas as diverse as Japan, Mozambique, Namibia, India, and Fiji as well as many diasporic and migrant communities.

This point raises one of the central key themes to be probed throughout this volume: the question of whether *modernity* as scholars use the word is simply a cautious synonym for what many interlocutors would call *Western,* a term that has a long and complex history that varies from place to place. We cannot deny that the two terms share an intimate connection in many, if not most, sites. As one of us has documented elsewhere in her work on young women and social mobility at the Miss India beauty pageant, the term *Western* is used in urban Indian parlance in ways that are inseparable from localized beliefs about appropriate gendered conduct, as part of "a constellation of behavior and beliefs related to the individual choice and independence associated with . . . Western Europe and North America [and include] . . . a (superficial) sense of male-female equality, English language education, and the acceptance of the right to individual choice and pleasure" (Dewey 2008b, 3–4).

This association of modernity with individual choice is cross-cultural in nature and is now well-trodden terrain in anthropological research, particularly in postcolonial societies increasingly saturated with media and consumer commodities informed (but not completely shaped by) North American and western European cultural trends. Anthropologists working throughout the world have noted these intimate linkages between the gendered concepts of modernity, popular culture, and individual social mobility (Burke 1996; Gerke 2000; C. Jones 2003; Kemper 2001; LiPuma 2000). Yet these linkages do not always take place on terms originating in the Western Hemisphere; Brian Larkin's (2008) work on Nigeria, for instance, demonstrates how Hindi films have played a key role in shaping how Hausa men envision ideal romantic partnerships. Bob W. White (2008) similarly notes the complex connections between popular culture, specifically in the form of music, and politics in Mobuto's Zaire in ways that focus upon individual young people's strategies for upward mobility in one of the most troubled regions of Africa.

Studies of Indian popular culture dramatically illustrate the power of media to both shape and reflect young people's understanding of gendered norms and ideals. Patricia Uberoi (2001) comments upon how women's magazines help to shape popular conceptions of appropriate courtship behavior in a society where the vast majority of marriages are arranged by parents. Rachel Dwyer (2000) has also noted that young girls avidly read film fan magazines reporting on the dramatic love lives (both real and imagined) of Hindi film stars because actresses' relative independence allows readers to discuss the heterosexual relationships that are impossible in their own lives.

Although often invoked to explain the worldwide phenomenon of such popular cultural forms, Benedict Anderson's now iconic notion of "imagined communities" (1983) only partially explains the symmetry uniting many of the chapters' foci on individual agency. It is inadequate, for instance, to suggest that teenagers in Mozambique fetishize mobile phones simply because doing so positions them as part of a global consumer economy; clearly, their use sometimes amounts to survival through the networks of support they help to nourish. These networks clearly build upon and create new gendered practices, as we see in the case of Mozambique's configuration of gift-giving obligations through mobile phones.

In this regard, Kelly and Kaplan's (2001) concept of "represented communities," in which divergent modernities stem from the experience of decolonization, is infinitely more apt in describing many of the disruptions evident in the following descriptions of young people's notions of gendered modernity. Although Kelly and Kaplan do not explicitly address gender in their work, it could be argued that women are perhaps the ultimate represented community because they are so often vaunted as symbols of national honor. This symbolization is cross-cultural in nature, and, as Appadurai has observed, it is imperative that we "recognize that the capability to imagine regions and worlds is now itself a globalized phenomenon. . . . [D]ue to the activities of migrants, media, capital, tourism and so forth, the means for imagining areas is now itself globally distributed" (2001, 8).

Such acknowledgments of modernity's universalized specificities are precisely why our volume focuses on the everyday meanings of gendered modernity for youth. In her book *Other Modernities,* Lisa Rofel presents an extremely nuanced analysis of how both state agents and individual actors in China have consistently used gender as a central organizing element of patriotic discourse. Rofel's compelling argument follows several generations of women workers in a silk factory to document how the meanings and images ascribed to being a "modern Chinese woman" have dramatically changed in recent decades from an unadorned Maoist figure in the dedicated service of the people to a contemporary hyperfeminine ideal. "Modernity," she notes, "feeds on the idea of overcoming the past. In creating a self-portrait as a triumphal march through time, it gathers up the memories of the past into tidy linear narratives that act as mythical guides to that overcoming" (1999, 153). Yet, as Rofel cautions us, "that which has been taken as homogenous and called 'modernity' . . . obscures a range of practices. For memories are reordered but not erased by the introduction of new epistemes" (ibid., 260).

This definition of modernity is particularly theoretically seductive for those scholars who write about young people, a group best known in anthropology as the subjects of liminal rites of passage accorded precarious status as not-quite adults. It is thus unsurprising, if we follow Rofel's logic, that young people cross-culturally seek to define their gender identities as becoming-men and almost-women in ways that emphasize their adult subjectivity, particularly in terms of the right to self-direction. Yet in the chapters that follow, we see that this self-direction takes place on terms that reinterpret adult understandings of the world on youth terms. It is notable that many youth do so as part of the globalized notion of youth and youth culture rather than because of some "natural" adolescent urge to seek out the unfamiliar. Hence, we see "the boy's hut becomes the hood" for Tongan migrant boys to inner-city America, just as young Owambo women in Namibia embrace their mothers' gender roles even as they experiment with wage labor and higher education.

Given the contentious nature of late modernity, it is thus unsurprising that gendered modernity means quite different things in each of the featured studies but nearly always relates to individual young people's desire to define a special sort of identity for themselves. Each chapter accordingly elaborates on the means by which youth mediate gendered modernities in ways inseparable from their status as future citizen-subjects, liminal adults, and sexual beings. Brison, Cook, Christou, and Beals and Wood all detail how children and young people use their liminal status as a means to carve out an individual identity as independent actors through their use of cultural vehicles as disparate as consumer spending, religion, part-time work, and activism. Yamakawa, Esser, Jhingan, and Lewis-Harris speak to the ways in which adolescents use rather stylized forms of hypermasculinity and femininity as distinctive forms of self-identity. Archambault, Dewey and Conover, and Xiao discuss how sexual expression among young people is a point of serious cultural tension in diverse cultural areas, while highlighting the transformative powers youth are often accorded by both adults and themselves.

Synopsis of Key Themes

Youth as a Transnational Construct

The chapters that follow consistently reveal "youth" as a key contested category in transnational struggles with modernity. Ideas about children and youth are integral to national and regional attempts to define self relative to former colonizers and wealthier nations. Dewey and Conover, for example, show how pervasive fears that local children are being sexually exploited by international tourists lead to discourses focusing on the innocent and vulnerable child as a metaphor for expressing discontent with the inequalities structuring life in Goa, an area long dependent on international tourism. Many ethnic Goans depict modernity as a condition of decay subverting normative ethnic Goan age and gender norms, and hence the authors argue that popular discourse on child sex tourism depicts children's innocent bodies as a sort of metaphorical stage for the enactment of economic inequalities that organize life in Goa. This chapter demonstrate how struggles to define localized modernities can lead to constructions of youth and children that draw upon North American and western European images of the malleable, vulnerable child. Cypriots, as portrayed by Christou, similarly view youth as a symbol of modernity's corrosive potential. Youth, according to elders who have endured the civil war and its associated deprivations, are soft and overly concerned with imported consumer goods that destroy local autonomy and traditions.

Chapters in this volume also demonstrate how children, adolescents, and young adults themselves appropriate transnational constructions of youth as a liminal phase with special license for autonomy, individual choice, and self-expression through consumption. Youth, however, are always gendered, and males and females, positioned differently in each situation, exploit the liminality of youth in different ways that redefine not only generational relations but also gendered roles and relations.

Cook, for example, shows how young Japanese males postpone leaving home and entering the full-time workforce into their late twenties as "freeters" (part-time workers), in order to explore life choices based on personal fulfillment and self-expression, qualities seen to be lacking in the prototypical life of the "salaryman." These young men's choices are incongruent with norms for Japanese masculinity and have become the subject of considerable cultural debate, as they directly contest state-defined notions of male adult responsibilities for company loyalty and head-of-household status.

Likewise, Archambault shows how young men in Mozambique, cut off from job opportunities, use cell phones to establish themselves as autonomous males, with the ability to provide for girlfriends through footing the bill for cell phone calls. Young women, at the same time, gain control over relationships while appearing to be traditional dependent females through "biping" boyfriends, a move that requires the male to return, and pay for, the call. Yamakawa similarly shows how young Namibian women postpone marriage in favor of independent motherhood, leaving their children with their matrilineages while pursuing a "youth" phase in which they live away from home, earning just enough money for their own room, cooking stove, and jeans, the equipment of a "modern" female.

Brison illustrates how rural indigenous Fijian boys and girls both eschew identifying with the local community, where young people are subordinate, to imagine themselves as parts of transnational religious and media communities offering greater autonomy. Brison, however, describes very different strategies for imagining new identities among Fijian boys and girls, leading to differences in aspirations as expressed in commitment to education and in language use. Lewis-Harris and Esser also demonstrate that gender profoundly influences strategies, as Tongan boys in Los Angeles gangs draw on warrior images, while Papua New Guinean girls in Australia redefine kinship in ways that increase the prominence of ties through females. Beals and Wood similarly document young people's creation of both virtual (and, occasionally, physical) spaces for youth resistance to adult political and economic dominance, thereby giving young people "a sense of being in the now (active agents) rather than being in the future (becoming agents)." Christou likewise notes how Greek Cypriot youth, envisioned as both the promise of the nation and the obstacle to the nation's continued existence, are caught between the presumed opposition between the citizen-shopper and the citizen-warrior.

The chapters also reveal that as quickly as transnational constructions of youth are appropriated, they are also rapidly localized. Yamakawa, for instance, shows how autonomous female youth who get jobs become income-generating women whose social adulthood is defined through their economic powers rather than their status as wives. But Yamakawa shows that such women are accepted as full adults only to the extent that they realize traditional obligations to contribute to their matrilineage. The looming presence of neoliberal ideals is inescapable in nearly all of these accounts both in the construction of youth as a time of autonomy and exploration and in the distinct gap between the aspirations of youth and their ability to achieve the lifestyle to which they aspire.

Imaginaires of Modernity

A second theme emerging from the chapters is the appropriation of new communicative technologies to claim new kinds of agency. As Archambault shows, the cell phone allows Mozambican youth to exert new kinds of control over their social networks and senses of self. In doing so, young women become involved in multiple-partner relationships in order to garner material support through mobile phones, which function as "both a practical and a discursive tool to navigate the uncertainties of everyday life" in which postwar, postsocialist poverty has redefined gender norms.

Similarly, Beals and Wood demonstrate how New Zealand youth have made use of the Internet to exert new kinds of political influence, although their attempts to advocate for higher wages are hampered by adult views of youth as foolish, selfish, and easily manipulated by others. The use of the Internet to craft new kinds of gendered cultural identities is also a prominent theme in Lewis-Harris's chapter, which shows Papua New Guinean youth in Australia using Internet social networking sites to create cyber-clans, a new form of lineage-based identity that enhances young people's sense of being embedded in cultural communities while not significantly impinging on individual agency.

Xiao, Jhingan, and Brison all show how youth appropriate mass-media productions to define new positions for themselves in society. Jhingan documents how young Indian women engage in the remaking of the gendered self through beauty culture and conspicuous consumption on *Indian Idol,* a tantalizing televised spectacle. She attributes the show's success partly to its use of the real-life stories of young women from small towns who achieve otherwise impossible social mobility through participation in the extremely popular and heavily advertised show. Televised singing competitions in India originally followed Bollywood in focusing on the voice of the singer, but young contestants pushed for the ability to dance onstage so that they could display fashionable images and dances, a move potentially empowering young women performers, who gain more control over their personae.

Xiao documents a similar phenomenon in a chapter that describes how young Chinese girls pushed to stardom a young androgynous female, rumored to be a lesbian, in a televised singing competition. Xiao speculates that the fascination with androgynous females and young homosexual males (as portrayed in popular Japanese *manga*) expresses desires to rethink polarized gender roles in China. Following this focus on popular culture, Brison shows how children in Fiji draw on Hollywood action movies and televised rugby matches to construct images of themselves as powerful, autonomous young men, occupying a world of young males far removed from the localized community where they are subordinate to senior males.

These chapters all highlight the decentralized character of contemporary global *imaginaires* as young people in various areas of the world turn to Bollywood (Jhingan), Brazil (Archambault), and the global Pentecostal rhetoric (Brison) that is increasingly shaped by the global South (A. Anderson 2001), as well as to images of a Pacific cultural identity (Brison, Esser, Lewis-Harris). If youth are at the forefront of redefining local modernities, it is evident, as Appadurai (1996) argues, that contemporary "modernization" is by no means dominated by Euro-American ideologies and institutions.

Borders and the Limits of Youth

We clearly see youth both limited and empowered by their liminal social position cross-culturally, and it is self-evident that this liminality becomes compounded by their distance from centers of power and privilege. For instance, this volume's accounts by Archambault and Yamakawa of young African women who tentatively embrace consumer identities, only to realize that their poverty significantly limits their self-expression in this mode, poignantly underscore that clear boundaries of privilege continue to demarcate young people's lives. Conover and Dewey, Lewis-Harris, and Esser all testify to the means by which the physical movements of people through migration and tourism have shaped concerns about youth as well as the identities available to them.

Esser, for instance, explores how young Tongan American men negotiate poverty and a tenuous migrant identity through gang membership, which offers "an important platform for youth to voice their shared experiences, negotiate culture and ethnicity, and actively define identity and community" through enacting a racialized, hypermasculine identity. Lewis-Harris observes similar patterns among Australian–Papua New Guineans, who describe themselves as embracing their Melanesian heritage in order to create a sense of unity and cohesion in a social environment strongly marked by negatively racialized Australian stereotypes about Pacific islanders.

The limits of youth, as we shall see, are thus powerful indicators of the cultures in which they are defined and, in turn, define themselves. The following chapters encourage us to come to terms with the reality that, for most young people, the seductive allure of localized modernities is symptomatic of their struggles to exert agency in a profoundly unequal world.

PART ONE

Gender and Generation

1

Mobile Phones and the "Commercialization" of Relationships

Expressions of Masculinity in Southern Mozambique

JULIE SOLEIL ARCHAMBAULT

"Nowadays, relationships are more commercialized," explained Antonio, a twenty-two-year-old Mozambican who had recently broken up with his girlfriend. "If you don't phone back when a girl sends you a *bip,* she'll run to another guy." As he recalled the events that led to their breakup, Antonio used mobile phone etiquette as an idiom to express his understanding of contemporary gender relations. In Mozambique, many people have passed "from no phone to [mobile] phone" (Orlove 2005, 699), and the recent integration of telecommunication into everyday life has opened up new spaces and possibilities. In Inhambane, mobile phones act as tangible and conspicuous proof of membership in what my young informants referred to as "the globalized world." With ever-increasing ownership, however, phones have also become indispensable (communication) tools used to navigate—in gender-specific ways—the uncertainties of everyday life (see Vigh 2006). Despite generating great enthusiasm, however, the phone is also understood to challenge power relations between men and women, as well as between generations. Indeed, although few would do without their phone, many are rather ambivalent in their evaluation of this new technology. In this chapter, I look into the integration of mobile phones into courtship practices among young adults in Inhambane, southern Mozambique. I argue that while reproducing gendered ideals, mobile phone etiquette acts as a new register to express and address the reconfiguration of gender relations and the redrawing of ideas of masculinity already under way. I hope to show how the recent spread of mobile phones is both reflective and constitutive of broader social transformations.

25

Being a Young Adult in Postsocialist, Postwar Mozambique

Inhambane is a small provincial capital of just over fifty-seven thousand inhabitants situated on the Indian Ocean in southern Mozambique. In the periurban areas of Inhambane, where most of my research was set, most of the houses are made out of braided palm leaves and woven reeds. Aged between nineteen and twenty-nine, few of the young adults I worked with had founded independent households, and most were living with their parents, often in women-headed households. Some were attending high school, others had recently graduated, a handful had a regular source of income from employment, and many were "not doing anything," but all aspired to a similar lifestyle in which the consumption of modern consumer goods figured prominently. Most of my informants were also at a crossroads concerning education, intimate relationships, household formation, and livelihood strategies.

These young adults were born in troubled times marked by a protracted civil war raging in the countryside and Frelimo's failing socialist modernization project (Geffray 1990; Roesch 1992).[1] Like their parents, who experienced postindependence euphoria (Isaacman 1978), today's youth have similar expectations that come from a new beginning, in their case consolidated peace and, perhaps more important, postsocialist neoliberalization (West 2005). Youth are also faced with a harsh reality, albeit a considerably less brutal one as the implementation of structural adjustment, state retrenchment, and economic liberalization has, in many cases, translated into deepening poverty amid growing disparity (Hanlon 2007; Newitt 2002; Pfeiffer 2002). I often heard people in Inhambane complain more specifically about growing disparity and how it enhanced economic hardship. As one woman in her forties said, "Now living conditions are worse, except for those who have [money and/or access to resources]. There is always change in everything, but life is more difficult nowadays than it was when I was growing up. Back then there was money, but there were no goods. We had nothing to eat, we had to queue, but it was more equal." She used her fingers to illustrate current social differentiation: "Each finger

1. Frelimo started out as a liberation front that orchestrated the war of independence (1962–75) from Portuguese rule and is the political party in power since independence in 1975.

is of a different length, just like there are some who have and some who don't." Indeed, as detailed below, although more than fifteen years have passed since the signature of the peace accords, only a few have reaped the benefits of the postwar economy.

The challenges of being a young adult tend to be compounded in contexts of rapid social change and increasing disparity like the one in postsocialist, postwar Mozambique (see Bucholtz 2002). In fact, African youth have been described as a "lost generation" (O'Brien 1996; Mbembe 1988; Ndebele 1995), a view also echoed on the international scene where "the 'problem' of youth is constructed as one of the great challenges of the twenty-first century" (Honwana and de Boeck 2005, ix; see also Abbink 2004, 2). Insofar as many dwell on the unfortunate plight of youth, recent studies emphasize the ambivalent position of young people. In this view, youth are seen as victims *and* perpetrators of atrocities (Abbink 2004; de Boeck and Honwana 2005). Beyond underscoring the cross-cultural variability of childhood and adolescence, many also represent youth not only as subjects shaped by society, or as adults *en devenir,* but also as agents shaping society (Amit-Tali and Wulff 1995; Bucholtz 2002; de Boeck and Honwana 2005; Durham 2004; Gable 2000; Rasmussen 2000). Youth is therefore understood as a historically constructed and contested category (Rasmussen 2000, 142) in which individuals "seek to inhabit, escape or move within . . . in meaningful ways" (Christiansen, Utas, and Vigh 2006). These theoretical developments have been greatly inspired by research set in sub-Saharan Africa, where youth ambivalence, epitomized by child soldiers (Stephens 1995, 19), is particularly striking. The scope of this approach is, however, much wider as it proposes a refined rethinking of agency (Durham 2000), which adds fine distinction to our understanding of conflict, by severing ties with an otherwise pervasive Gluckmanesque perspective (de Boeck and Honwana 2005, 6). I hope to show that exploring gender relations through experiences with and discourses on mobile phones offers an original avenue for getting a sense of what being a young adult in an uncertain socioeconomic environment can mean.

Between Aspirations, Expectations, and Possibilities

Henri Alexandre Junod, the Swiss missionary and first ethnographer of the region, stated at the turn of the twentieth century that, in southern Mozambique, masculinity rested on a man's ability to support his dependents. At the time, the region served as a labor reserve for the South African mining industry. Labor migration played a crucial socioeconomic role in the reproduction of local communities and helped households acquire consumer goods, like blankets and bicycles (Arnfred 2001, 36; see also Felgate 1982; and First, Forjaz, and Manghezi 1998). It also enabled young men to secure for themselves the means to acquire wives, instead of having to depend on their elders. Working in the mines was seen as proof of maleness and has been described as a rite of passage into manhood (Harries 1982, 158, quoted by Marshall 1993, 60; see also Sheldon 2002, 3). Also important was the idea that living up to mainstream ideas about masculinity was a process that took men to distant places, often for the better part of the year, leaving the women in charge of the agricultural work.

Still today, men are believed to have better access to money and things than women. For example, I came across a secondhand clothing store that featured a sign that read "30 MTn [meticais, the Mozambican currency unit] for any woman's item and 40 MTn for any men's item." When I asked about the price difference, the clerk explained that it was simply because "men make more money than women." In order to address inequities in terms of access to income, women are expected to rely on social networks. In many households, women also engage in urban agriculture and petty trade, while some work as domestic servants. And so although female opportunities in the formal economic sphere remain limited, the economic contribution of women appears heightened by the difficulties young men face in making a living. The importance of female economic initiative nevertheless remains poorly acknowledged.

If the ideal of the autonomous man providing for his dependent women and children still holds currency, the socioeconomic context has undergone important transformations, therefore making it increasingly difficult for contemporary young men to live up to these expectations. To start, the terms of the labor agreements between Mozambique and South Africa were seriously altered following independence, and the number of migrant laborers was drastically cut (Roesch 1992, 465). The civil war (1977–92) that broke out shortly after independence then had tremendous socioeconomic implications. Although the armed conflict never reached the center of Inhambane, the war nevertheless caused a severe disruption of daily life. With the escalation of the war in the late 1980s, agricultural production was interrupted in many places because of insecurity in the countryside, and a large portion of state resources had to be allocated for defense. Structural adjustments implemented in the second half of the 1980s then resulted in a sharp rise in prices (Hanlon 1996, 93) that further quelled consumption (Alexander 1997; M. Hall and Young 1997). The rural exodus brought on by the war also increased pressure on urban centers like Inhambane, where residents now face having to juggle limited employment opportunities, the rising cost of living, and "modern" life-style aspirations. What is more, work migration does not have the same appeal for educated urban youth who now covet working for the government or for an NGO.

Attending high school has become an integral part of most youths' lives. In just over a decade, three complete high schools as well as a faculty of tourism have opened in Inhambane. Education does not, however, guarantee formal employment, and even high school graduates face limited opportunities. Having studied, these youth are also reluctant to accept low-status jobs, and many prefer "not doing anything" to being seen digging latrines or pushing carts. "Not doing anything" is often understood as a euphemism for more lucrative options like petty crime and drug trafficking. In fact, most of my male informants, and a few of my female ones, had spent some time in jail, almost all of them for petty theft, often involving mobile phones.

Women remain responsible for the domestic sphere, but they are also redrawing the boundaries that relegate them to the household, and men complain that as their control over women's movements is waning, so is their control over female sexuality. Generalized high school attendance has also provided young women with increased freedom of movement, and although it is still early to determine how education will shape Inhambane women's access to formal employment, the effects of going to school every day are more readily observable. Temporarily freed from the surveillance of male kin, young women can now encounter new opportunities "along the way." There are in fact a number of songs that discuss older men trying to seduce young women on their way to school by offering them a lift or something to eat.

Like other women her age, Sandra, a nineteen-year-old who lives with her mother and two older brothers, wakes up at the crack of dawn to sweep the yard before heading for school. She tends to do household chores in the afternoons, namely, fetching water at the public tap down the road and cooking the evening meal, while sometimes braiding hair to get pocket money. When she was seventeen, Sandra started hanging out at a nearby bar to watch the Brazilian soap operas (*novela*) that run every evening. One thing led to another, and, every now and then, Sandra would only return home the following morning. At first, her brothers were infuriated and warned that if she continued behaving this way, she would never marry. They tried to educate her by beating her, but to no avail, and Sandra continued going out at night and eventually got pregnant. In women headed households, the elder son usually acts as the authority figure. Most of these young men are, however, unemployed, many are still studying, and few have the means to back up their authority.

Parents blamed economic hardship for what they perceived as a generalized loss of morality. They agreed that youth no longer had respect and lamented parental loss of control over their children. One mother, whose daughters lived with their three young children as dependents in her household, said:

> Youth accuse us of being witches, but what makes them talk this way is poverty. Youth insult us and kill us. They wake up in the morning and see that, again, there is nothing to eat. They ask us for food, and they don't believe us when we say that we don't have any. Girls go around having sex with any men who will give them money. They have to search outside as there is nothing at home. I made them and raised them, and now instead of helping me, they come home with more children. . . . In the past, youth used to respect their parents because there used to be food. Now that parents struggle to feed their children, the children don't see why they should respect their parents. Maybe it's also because we don't know how to educate them. But the problem is not just with my kids; it's with everyone's kids. Kids make and break [*fazem e disfazem*].

In recent years, the number of marriages in Inhambane has decreased, while the average age of marriage has risen steadily. Data I compiled at the Civil Registry in Inhambane revealed that just after independence in 1975, the average age of first marriage was 27.23 for men and 21.70 for women. Since then, it has risen progressively to reach 34.4 for men and 28.7 for women in 2006. Between 2000 and 2006, there were on average

60.1 civil marriages performed, a sharp drop from the 81.5 average marriages per year of the 1990s and the 91.6 of the 1980s, despite the latter being the war years.

Yet even those individuals who do form more stable unions tend to bypass the formalities of marriage. Given the high costs of weddings (Arnfred 2001, 35), many couples spend years, even decades, living together before getting married. Being a wife or a husband has since been locally redefined to include people living in such unions (see also Gage and Bledsoe 1994). The Portuguese word *mulher* is quite convenient for that matter as it can mean either "wife" or "woman." As such, when a man says *"minha mulher"* (my wife/woman), he is referring to the woman who lives with him without having to specify whether they are married. In any case, the fact of residing with a man confers to a woman similar obligations, regardless of the formality of the union. Acquiring a wife has therefore become easier, as men are given additional time to comply with the general formalities. Still for many, the daily costs of supporting dependents are prohibitive. None of the young men I worked with who were still living with their parents could foresee the day they would move out and form an independent household. Unlike their female peers who rarely made it past their twentieth birthday without getting pregnant, a number of young men were successfully delaying having children. They commonly gave lack of financial stability and school attendance as the rationale behind this decision.

Instead, youth engage in intimate relationships known as *namoro,* which can be loosely translated as "boyfriend/girlfriend" and is a relatively new phenomenon that started to be debated in the press in the 1980s (Arnfred 2001, 13). *Namorar* is seen as a modern and transitory relationship that stems from current socioeconomic dynamics and is inspired by foreign models. As a mother in her fifties jokingly commented, back in her youth, *"namorar* only lasted two minutes, as young girls would marry soon after being presented their future husband, unlike in today's day and age when girls can delay marriage and get a chance to enjoy *namorar."* In Inhambane, there is a lot of talk about what it means, or rather what it should mean, to *namorar.* Most would agree it is meant to be a time during which a couple gets to know each other better before getting married and that it should be a relatively serious relationship based on respect (S. Manuel 2008). *Namorados* should also be discreet about their relationship until the man in question has the desire and the means to formally introduce himself to the woman's family. Things often do not go according to plan, however, as many conceive before even thinking of the formalities, while others simply split up. There is also a sense that the relationship between *namorados* should be an exclusive one, despite the double standard that allows men to have multiple partners.

One of the rationales behind men having different partners is summed up in the slang term *somar*. In one young man's words, "*Somar* means going with many women and telling people about it so that they won't go there. You tell them: 'I've been there' [*Eu já passei d'ai*]. . . . *Somar* is also about trying women out to see how they feel." Some suggested that girls were often the ones to entice other women's boyfriends. As Flavia, a nineteen-year-old student explained, "You see a guy who comes every day to pick up his girlfriend after school, and he buys her nice clothes, nice things to eat, so you start thinking, 'Maybe he could do all those nice things for me too.' So you go after him. Men are weak; they fall straight away [*caiem logo*]!" Women involved with womanizers see *somar* as a means men have to keep them in check, by showing them that they are replaceable. In a popular song by the Mozambican artist Ziqo titled *Casa dois* (Second house), the husband warns his wife not to get upset with him and threatens to go to the *casa dois* if she does. In this song, *casa dois* is used broadly to refer to any woman a man might have relations with, other than his first wife or main girlfriend. And so, as the song illustrates, men can use the double standard that they enjoy as a means to control women. What the song does not mention, however, is that women are themselves increasingly involved with more than one partner.

Despite being undermined on many fronts, the hegemonic model that expects men to be materially independent prevails (see Heald 1999). To this effect, Vigh reminds us that although "there will always be a relative discrepancy between the ideal and the real, the *culturally prescribed* and the *socially possible* . . . , there is a difference between having a schism that can be socially and culturally incorporated, and one that is so pervading that it leads to conflict" (2006, 41). In Inhambane, the "schism" has not reached such dramatic proportions; it is, however, engendering more discreet renegotiations of gender relations. And since men are now finding it increasingly difficult to live up to these socioeconomic ideals, sexuality has come to play a more central role in the expressions of masculinity (S. Manuel 2008; see also Silberschmidt 2004).

In short, mobile phones come at a time when intimate relationships and the modalities of household formation are being redefined. As I show below, mobile phone communication is, in turn, understood to accentuate these changes. I now turn to the allocation of the costs of communication along gender lines, before exploring the debates surrounding this very specific dimension of courtship via the phone.

Phone Etiquette in Inhambane: Reversing the Charges and Reproducing Gendered Ideals

Very few houses in Inhambane have landlines, especially in periurban areas, and most of the youth I worked with went from no phone to mobile phone. In fact, mobile phones were commonly compared to letters, not to fixed phones. When mCel, Mozambique's first mobile phone company, started operating in the country in 1997, network coverage was limited to Maputo, the capital. It was only after mCel implemented its prepaid service, and expanded its network, that mobile phone use started spreading throughout the country. A high proportion of youth in the city of Inhambane became users in 2004, at a time when Vodacom, Mozambique's second operator, had just entered the market and was offering innovative and competitive services. Indeed, Vodacom conquered many for whom the 50 meticais mCel top-up was prohibitive, by offering a 20 MTn (US$1) top-up. Vodacom also appeared at a critical time when handsets were becoming increasingly available and affordable. One could buy a secondhand bottom-range phone with 150 MTn (US$5), approximately three days of work for an unskilled laborer. Once these technical hurdles were addressed, membership rose drastically. For example, according to a survey I conducted, 71 percent of senior-year students in Inhambane were mobile phone owners in 2007.

In Inhambane, when youth manage to get some money, they tend to spend it rather quickly. "I have so many unmet needs," explained my field assistant, "that for me to even think about saving up money would be an absurdity." Communication needs are also experienced as largely unfulfilled, and, like money, phone credit rarely lasts very long. When youth top up their phones, it is usually either for a specific purpose or because they just got money and want to buy credit before spending it on other things. One young man succinctly explained the process of prioritization: "Before when I got 100 MTn, I would spend it all on beer. Now I put 50 in my phone and I buy beer with the rest!" I must have looked amazed because he added, "Julie, you grew up with a telephone, you had a landline in your house, and you grew up playing [*brincando*] with telephones. For us here, it's different; we just started to have the chance to play with phones. And that is why as soon as we get money, we buy [phone] credit."

Unlike men, however, women often find it difficult to estimate how much they spend on phone top ups. This uncertainty is mainly owing to the ways in which patterns of use mirror broader social relations and tend to reproduce socioeconomic hierarchies, many of which go beyond the scope of this chapter. Telecommunication establishes an asymmetrical relationship between a sender and a receiver, if only because only one of the parties involved incurs costs. In Inhambane, phone etiquette between men and women is guided by the ideal of the man as provider and of the woman as dependent. Men are therefore expected to cover most of the costs of communicating with women who, for their part, can attempt to reverse the charges by sending a *bip* and waiting to be called back, that is, either by phoning a number and hanging up before the other person answers or by sending a "Please call me" message, a free message asking to be called back. Customers of both mCel and Vodacom, Mozambique's two mobile phone operators, get ten free "Please call me" messages per day. Unlike with a "Please call me," one needs to have a minimum of credit in order to send a *bip*, and there is always the risk that the person receiving the *bip* will answer his or her phone, thus "eating" the credit of the *bip* sender.

Calling units can also be transferred between users, free of charge, and are a popular gift men give to women. Most of the young women I knew in Inhambane made extensive use of *bips*, and some regularly exceeded their daily allowance of ten free "Please call me" messages. In fact, I was often asked by young women if they could use my phone to send *bips*, and, more often than not, they would be called back. Men admitted usually phoning back when they received a *bip* and feeling uneasy when they were unable to reply. Some explained that it was particularly stressful when the "Please call me" came from an unknown number (such as my own), as it kept them thinking and, because of the gendered use of this kind of message, often dreaming about the lost opportunity to answer the request of a beautiful girl. It was in fact striking how young men described their experiences with mobile phones as stressful.

What is more, men are expected not only to bear the costs of telecommunication, but also, in many cases, to fulfill requests placed via the phone for things like transport money, photocopy money, sanitary pads, food, phone credit, and various other daily necessities. This practice has to be understood with relation to gendered livelihood strategies mentioned earlier and the informal sexual economy (Archambault forthcoming; see also Cole 2004). To convince me of how easy it was to get things "with her phone," Mimi, a twenty-five-year-old student, sent a *bip* to one of her suitors, whom she asked for bread. Within an hour, the man was at the door with a bag of bread. Not only had he paid for the bread, but he had also disbursed for the phone call that allowed Mimi to place her request.

In short, young women manage to use mobile phones to benefit by trading on their subordinate status. In fact, I have yet to come across a woman who had given up her phone owing to economic constraints, whereas men who "take a break" from phone use are not uncommon. Of course, responses are ultimately interpreted contextually, and actual phone practices are likely to vary according to the specificities of the situation (see Hahn and Kibora 2008; Slater and Kwami 2005). For instance, *bips* can also be used as signals that require a response other than a phone call, in which case they are not subject to the same gender rules. A *bip* often means "I've arrived," while in some cases, it can have a slightly more complex meaning. Antonio and two friends of his have established that, among them, a *bip* would act as a rallying call to meet at the nearby palm-wine bar. Or, to give another example, Betinho and his former classmate Isabella regularly send each other *bips*, as a sign of life (*sinal de vida*), like a heartbeat. In this case, the one who receives a *bip* is expected to reply with a *bip*. Equals like friends of the same sex or brothers in similar economic situations are supposed to cover the cost of their calls themselves, and a man who sends a *bip*, in the hope of being called back, is likely to be ridiculed. As the following shows, however, phone etiquette acts as an idiom to express ideas about masculinity.

Debating Mobile Phone Etiquette

Phone etiquette is a subject of great interest among youth in Inhambane, and it generates interesting debates that reveal their understandings of gender relations. Extracts of an extended conversation among a group of youth on a rainy Sunday afternoon will help illustrate how the etiquette of *biping* acts as an idiom of masculinity and how this seemingly simple topic of discussion is used to debate broader ideas about gender relations and the expression of gendered identities.

Gina, João, Tereza, and Antonio are four youths in their early twenties who live with their parents in Liberdade, the neighborhood where most of my research was set and where I also resided. At the time, Gina, twenty-four, had recently started working in a bar. She had dropped out of school after getting pregnant a few years earlier, and although they did not live together, she was still involved with her son's father. João, twenty-five, was working as a day laborer on an occasional basis. He had never been interested in going to school and preferred to work in order to support his wife and two children. A couple of weeks earlier, he had sold his phone as a source of fast cash to address a medical emergency. Tereza, twenty-two, was completing high school and had no children, just like Antonio, twenty-two, who had recently completed secondary school and was "not doing anything." Antonio was a self-proclaimed womanizer, and Tereza was the girlfriend of a wealthy older man.

Tereza was on the phone, apparently discussing a job opportunity. "Something extraordinary!" she told her curious friends after hanging up. From there, the conversation turned to a discussion of gendered experiences with mobile phones. Using Tereza's phone call as a case in point, Antonio argued that "for women there [are] always more gains." Addressing Tereza specifically, he added, "You see, you didn't even pay for that phone call, and it sounds like you're going to get a job!" He further developed his views by highlighting his own girlfriend's phone manners:

> My girlfriend gets money on a daily basis [from her parents], but I only get money maybe once a month, and I spend it straightaway. Within a week I have no more; I'm done [*tchunado*]. Even sometimes, she lends me money and then says that I'll have to give her back double, as a joke, you know. So she has money but in terms of communications, she only sends *bips*! And then I phone her. With the money she lent me yesterday, I bought credit, but she sends me a *bip*, you see, so I phone, you see.

In other words, the gender divide in terms of phone etiquette was, according to Antonio, so forceful that it even defied common sense.

Determined to get his point across, he added, "Or you meet a girl today, and you give her your number. Then, the next day . . . she'll send you a *bip,* and you have to respond. And to feel that you're a man . . . you have to respond." As a married and uneducated man, João's intimate experiences were somewhat different from the educated charmer Antonio. João concurred with Antonio, but his resigned attitude contrasted with the latter's cynicism. For example, he said, "Sometimes a girl will ask you to send her 5 MTn [credit]. Now you, as a man, you won't say no." Both young men were self conscious of expending their hard-earned airtime on women: they were, however, willing to play the game, since they saw bearing these costs as an expression of maleness and as necessary to seducing women (see also Batson-Savage 2007, 250). By testifying to a man's economic situation and owing to its role in the consolidation and management of intimate relationships, answering *bips* potently encapsulates mainstream ideas about youth masculinity.

Replying to *bips* is perhaps a small price to pay for these young men to regain some lost ground, given the slippery material base on which their dominance rests. In her study of masculinity in Tanzania, Silberschmidt shows how economic hardship challenges "the normative order of patriarchy" and argues that "the irony of the patriarchal system resides precisely in the fact that male authority has a material base while male responsibility is normatively constituted" (2005, 195). Paradoxically, it is an irony that can conversely be exacerbated through gendered patterns of phone use. For young men like João and Antonio who get money only sporadically, even the small gesture of replying to a *bip* may, at times, be beyond their reach. *Biping* not only puts added pressure on young men, but it also makes their hardship more apparent. As João pointed out, "A girl will think, 'What can this man offer me if he cannot even call me back?'" As such, some young men are always on the alert, as they never know when their masculinity will be probed next. It is little wonder then that young men often described their experiences with mobile phones as stressful. It is also in this sense that maleness goes from being perceived in terms of social process to being understood as volatile and hypersensitive to the vagaries of everyday life. Economic hardship does not translate in abstinence but rather produces a more "vulnerable masculinity" (see Mills and Ssewakiryanga 2005, 91). And by rendering these young men's economic problems more visible, it ultimately brings young women to question the traditional pattern of male dominance and female dependence.

In response to the men's comments, Gina and Tereza agreed that mobile phone use was often to their advantage. For example, Gina said, "With my phone I can send a *bip* to someone, and then I can get even more because then all of a sudden that person can tell me, 'Come get this thing,' a thing that I might have never even hoped for." They considered, however, that in reality, things were much more complex and that their experiences did not necessarily gel with the neat gender divide depicted by men. To start, both argued that women could also end up, like men, "wasting" money on phone calls, thus nullifying the gains they might have made. "Sometimes I top up to talk to someone about something very important," Gina explained, "but then I deviate [*desvio*], and I end up talking with other people. . . . Sometimes I regret it . . . [thinking to myself], 'Shit, why didn't I call that person with whom I had something important to resolve?'" Gina and Tereza also argued that phone etiquette was often neglected by pointing out that there were men who sent *bips* to women. "You know there are men who are conquered [*conquistado*][2] by women," Tereza explained, "and if the man finds out that a woman has a lot of money and that she is really fond of him, she'll say, 'Okay! Here you go.' Then he'll buy credit, but he'll still send you a *bip*, HIM as a man." The two women agreed that these practices were considered "ugly" (Portuguese *feio,* used in this context to mean "socially reprehensible") and that it would probably be difficult for the others present to believe that men could go so low as to send *bips* to women.

At this point, Antonio interjected by saying that he "recognize[d] that there [were] men who sen[t] *bips* to women" but that these instances were only exceptional cases that detracted attention from the broader picture.

2. *Conquistar* (to conquer) is the Portuguese word commonly used to describe the act of convincing someone to become an intimate partner. It underscores the perceived asymmetry in courtship by portraying one of the individuals involved as the active conqueror and the other as the passive conquered. Young men might also use the expression *latar uma dama* (put a young woman in a bottle [with conversation]). What is interesting about this expression is that it compares the powers of words with the forces of witchcraft, which is popularized as putting people's souls into cans to transform them into compliant individuals.

For the women, however, these exceptions were significant. In their eyes, they were reflective of an increasingly fragile masculinity. Indeed, they insisted that it was men "nowadays" that contravened core social values, thus highlighting their understanding that gender relations were undergoing notable transformations. By challenging the idea that patterns of phone use were gender specific, they were also questioning ideas about female dependence and male autonomy. Like women, men also did send *bips*, and, like men, women also did end up "deviating" and wasting credit on mundane conversations.

In defense of his earlier argument, Antonio said, "Well, there has to be a lot of trust and many days that they are together because, it's like this: I know a girl today, you see, and she gives me her number, and then we start seeing each other. In the early days, I'll never have the courage to send her a *bip*, or else that girl is going to think that I am a loser [*matreco*]. But then once we are used to one another, then . . ." Despite his unwillingness to complete his sentence, Antonio was ironically admitting to sending *bips* himself. At the same time, his comment further accentuated the relationship between picking up the tab and masculinity.

When Antonio pointed out that relationships were commercialized, he was highlighting the way phone etiquette served to gauge a man's worthiness. Since the entry of mobile phones, one's commitment to a relationship has in fact become easily demonstrable and quantifiable by the money spent on phone calls (see also Horst and Miller 2006). Antonio was also hinting at the way some women have shrewdly started playing a more selective role in courtship. Phone etiquette makes the selection process appear mechanical, or commercialized, and sometimes beyond the man's control. Ultimately, failing to reply to a *bip* translates into the dissolution of a man's claim to exclusivity, as it stands as a symbolic justification for women to turn to other men in order to answer their unmet needs.

In their research on mobile phone use among low-income Jamaicans, Horst and Miller (2006) also show how men use mobile phones to affirm their masculinity and to facilitate the accumulation of sexual partners, as well as how women use the Jamaican version of *bips* to gain favors from men. Regarding the role of mobile phones in the "performance of sexualities" in Jamaica, Batson-Savage similarly argues that the mobile phone "has not changed the way in which gender is constructed, but [that] it has been integrated into its construction. In many ways the cellular phone has been used to reaffirm the patriarchal thrust of gender constructions, and has become a part of the physical symbolic construction of gender playing into the use of materialism to achieve selfhood" (2007, 250).

Like Batson-Savage, I have also approached mobile phone use as participating in the construction of gender relations. I hope to have shown, however, that in Inhambane, mobile phones are not exactly "reaffirm[ing] the patriarchal thrust of gender construction." Instead, owing to the ways in which mobile phone etiquette reflects gender hierarchies, mobile phone practices participate in the redrawing of gender relations already under way in the postsocialist, postwar context. It is in this sense that the phone can be understood as both a practical and a discursive tool used to navigate the uncertainties of everyday life.

In ways reminiscent of the educational role older technologies were expected to play (Larkin 2008; West and Fair 1993), mobile phones have themselves been invested with the potential to contribute to socioeconomic development (Donner 2008; Nielinger 2006). However, as ethnographically grounded research on mobile phone practices indicates (Hahn 2009; Horst and Miller 2006; Molony 2008; Osborn 2008; Slater and Kwami 2005), the outcomes of the dialectical relationship between users and technologies evade broad generalizations and often challenge expectations. Indeed, as the material I presented in this chapter illustrates, the ways in which technologies are integrated into everyday life are locally constructed and influenced by the specificities of the sociohistorical context (Do Nascimento 2005; Hahn and Kibora 2008; Larkin 2008; Silverstone and Hirsch 1992). By the same token, I hope to have shown that by examining how technologies are used, along with the debates these practices generate, we can gain invaluable insight into what it means to be a young adult living in an uncertain socioeconomic environment (see Larkin 2008, 3). There is in fact more to men's experiences with mobile phones than a test of masculinity. Throughout the time I spent in Inhambane, I heard youth explain that when they talked on the phone, they were swept over by emotion, not to say euphoria, and that this newfound ability to communicate easily was almost overwhelming. Mobile phone ownership makes economic marginalization more tolerable for what it represents on an expressive level. Beyond symbolic capital, mobile phones also provide youth with a certain degree of freedom and control over their lives, albeit in gender-specific and contested ways. When men answer *bips*, they also do so because they can. In the Inhambane context, where opportunities are so very limited, where desires, aspirations, and dreams are so easily thwarted, being able to do something is, well, quite something. Answering *bips* is about demonstrating maleness, but it is also about feeling like a man and, ultimately, about feeling alive,[3] at least every now and then.

3. In Inhambane, the lifestyle many youth aspire to is best characterized by the Portuguese term *curtir*, which means "to enjoy" (it can somewhat ironically also mean "to suffer, to endure"). I once asked a young man to define *curtir*, and he replied, "Curtir e viver" (*Curtir* is living).

2

Claiming Youth, the Modern Feminine Self, and Womanhood in Northern Namibia

SAYUMI YAMAKAWA

Linda, a thirteen-year-old girl, pointing out one picture in her small photo album, told me, "This is me. I was the Miss XXX Primary School last year." In the picture, she had a shy smile on her face, as she stood wearing a long white dress, a sash with the title "Miss XXX Primary School" over her shoulder, and a cute little tiara on her head. Indeed, one of the most striking phenomena I encountered while conducting my fieldwork in northern Namibia was the overwhelming interest in, and frequency of, beauty pageants. Following the model of Miss Universe, Miss Africa, Miss Malaika, and Miss Namibia, "Miss *Something*" contests were taking place in various different public spaces in towns and villages; educational institutions such as colleges, universities, and even primary schools; and bars.

This chapter focuses on the life experiences of young Owambo women of Namibia in southern Africa to consider emergent identities in relation to local and transnational ideas about femininity and youth. Ideas about "modern" Namibian beauty and femininity, targeting young unmarried women, are constantly displayed in public spaces through the images embodied in the events such as beauty pageants and in the media, including South African and American female magazines and soap operas on television. These images have a significant influence on the young Namibian women's perceptions of contemporary youth. But young Namibian women do not simply imitate Euro-American trends. Instead, they use "modern" images to reinterpret, negotiate, and reconfigure their identities and personhood in a local environment so as to increase their autonomy in ways that ultimately do not challenge the prevailing social structure.

I argue here that young Owambo women use fashion and clothing to mark a new generational status as youth, an emerging life stage involving autonomy from matrilineal and family obligations, in which they use transnational fashion, music, and so on to construct individual selves. Ultimately, however, the distinction between autonomous youth, who identify with transnational consumer culture, and traditional Owambo feminine roles is more apparent than real. Female youth can postpone marriage and have children before marriage without significantly threatening the social fabric because in matrilineal Owambo society the status of children is tied to the mother's lineage, not to the father's lineage. Furthermore, autonomous female youth who mature into women with an independent income or children (or both) can gain a certain form of social respect without marrying under the condition that they satisfy kinship and communal responsibilities. Thus, as Piot (1999) argues, modernity and tradition may be imagined as opposed states, but in fact, modernity is defined and constituted in local terms.

The Owambo are Namibia's largest ethnic group. Most Owambo live in the north-central part of the country, the area formerly called "Owamboland," which extends from the north of the Etosha Pan to the Angolan border. North-central Namibia makes up only 10 percent of the surface of the country but holds nearly half of the national population (2.08 million as of 2007). Until the late nineteenth century, north-central Namibia was divided into a series of independent kingdoms and communities, controlled by Owambo kings or chiefs. Between 1884 and 1915, Namibia, then known as South West Africa, became a German colony. The Union of South Africa invaded South West Africa at the request of the British government during World War I. Later, in 1921, Namibia was handed to South Africa under the terms of a League of Nations mandate formulated by the Allied powers. The South African regime continued until the country's independence in March 1990. Agriculture and animal herding are still the main economic activities among the majority of people, but wage labor among young people has been another major economic activity since the establishment of a migrant and contract labor system in the colonial economy.

I have discussed elsewhere how the transformation of the *ohango* ritual from a female initiation ceremony to a wedding through the Christianization of the communities significantly extended the "youth" phase for Owambo women (Yamakawa 2007). In the past, the *ohango* was only for females. Parents let their daughters participate in the *ohango* soon after they reached puberty, although timing depended on the family's economic fortunes. After the girls went through the ceremony, they were recognized as mature and marriageable. Boys, however, could attain such a status only when they had economic resources such as livestock and a homestead. Hence, prior to Christianization, the period between childhood and adulthood for Owambo women was much shorter than for men. In contrast, the *ohango* practice today, which transforms the *ohango* from a puberty ritual to a wedding and involves both sexes, has the effect of launching both young women and young men into an extended youth phase that is not defined in terms of biological age. To be a youth means to have, to a certain extent, more autonomy and freedom than children but to have fewer social responsibilities than adults. These changes have created a space for young unmarried females to experiment with lifestyle options in an extended youth phase, instead of becoming a wife and mother soon after puberty. Women now also have greater access to wage labor since the colonial system of requiring people who wished to leave the village to get a permit has ended. In the past, most such permits were granted to men involved in contract labor, and few women could attain permits.

In contemporary Namibia, increasing numbers of youth, even those youth lacking the economic resources and information to fully realize their desires, define self through consumption of cosmopolitan youth culture. Individuals use what is available to create an individual style to claim personal and social position. Individuals are required to manifest "taste" that both expresses a unique personality and is deeply intertwined with social, economic, and political spheres. Taste, therefore, produces social distinctions and plays a key role in reproducing social structure (Bourdieu 1984). For female youth in northern Namibia, for instance, wearing particular brand-name clothes, speaking "good" English in addition to one's mother tongue, watching certain television programs (especially South African soap operas or ones from South American countries), as well as having a good command of local activities such as cooking food and pounding millet can all be significant items for creating a specific youth style and identity. Young Namibians are similar to other South African youth in defining self by combining local and transnational goods to create a unique personal style. Dolby's (2000) study of urban high school youth in postapartheid South Africa demonstrates how youth employ particular "tastes" in global culture, such as music and clothes, to negotiate their racial identity in order to redefine the self and to make ethnicity meaningful for them. Similarly, Salo (2003) discusses the intergenerational tensions between consumer-driven youth cultures and local social and moral gender norms in postapartheid South Africa.

Cosmopolitan youth style encourages youth to conceptualize their identity in terms of an imagined global space and to place less importance on ethnic divisions that are very important to adults. Piot (1999) argues that despite their lack of material and economic resources, some youth decide to go beyond local norms at the cost of jeopardizing social relations and networks that have a greater impact on their destiny in local society. I found similar patterns in rural Namibia. In postapartheid Namibia, "taste" and consumption go hand in hand, constituting one of the important means for constructing young people's racial and ethnic, generational, and gender identities. Music and arts as well as fashion and clothing appear to have specific class and generational connotations among the youth as their expression of selfhood and also of generational consciousness.

Young Namibians have spent most of their lives in an independent Namibia where they are not required to fight and where they have basic human rights, receive education, and have greater exposure to foreign influences than did their parents. As a consequence, race and ethnicity, which are still important and powerful identity markers for the older Owambo, mean relatively less for youth. Youth, instead, locate themselves within both local and wider cultural flows in global contexts. For example, it is becoming common for young Owambo people to get involved in activities outside a household and community, such as a youth choir, youth dance or drama group, and volunteer work with international development agencies. These activities are consistent with the idea of "creative" and "moral" young citizens that the Namibian government has been promoting through the National Youth Policy and the policy on cultural diversity and heritage in the process of nation building. However, many adults consider such activities as "just playing," since they are removed from lineage and community obligations (Durham 2005), even if these activities contribute to the civil society of independent Namibia. When lineage elders define youth contributions to a wider civil society as "nonserious," they reinforce the hierarchical lineage dependencies that structure local society.

In agreement with Cole (2004), however, I am attempting here neither to propose any immediate interpretation, such as a youth's resistance to the older generations or against conservative ideas, nor to separate youth from a wider social context of kinship and communities by "fetishizing" them. My focus is to map young Owambo women's specific life experiences, as well as look at how they express their ideas, desires, and identities to make sense of their lives in the face of contradictory and conflicting messages.

I begin with a story of a teenage girl that illustrates a typical female youth's experience in contemporary Owambo communities. I show how the girl tries to position herself as an Owambo person, woman, and a youth in a rapidly globalizing postcolonial society. She expresses her desire to become an economically independent woman who can afford modern items such as clothes, electronic goods, and her own room in town and who can also contribute to the family. However, she faces several difficulties, including seriously limited job availability in the area she lives and opposition from her family and her boyfriend, that hinder her from realizing her desires.

Saima's Sudden Disappearance

When I first met Saima, she was eighteen years old and had just completed the twelfth grade at a senior secondary school in the north-central region. She had several siblings. Two older sisters were already married and lived in their husbands' homesteads in other villages. Other sisters were single, living in their father's homestead, sister's place, or living and working in towns in the central or coastal regions. When I met her, Saima had no job and had only enough money to buy a few pieces of candy from small local shops. She was responsible for many daily tasks such as fetching water, stamping millet, cultivating fields and planting, looking after nieces and nephews, cleaning and washing, and cooking. Saima, however, was bored and started attending a public computer class in the area to get a certificate and to get out of the house.

Saima's major concerns in her everyday life were keeping up with fashion without the benefit of disposable cash and managing her relationship with her boyfriend. She had a general interest in a marriage sometime in her future life, but not anytime soon. Being a "modern" youth, she had things that she wanted to realize other than having children, getting married, and gaining a certain sense of security for her life. Saima seemed to realize that although marriage would provide her with more rights and power, it would also bring increased responsibilities and restrictions, and so she sought to postpone that event. Saima, like most of my young female informants, admired Britney Spears, Beyoncé, and some young South African female celebrities.

For Saima, being unemployed meant being a powerless dependent who had no ability to fulfill her desire for consumption. At home, she had to follow the wishes of her parents and elder family members as long as they were feeding her and she was not contributing income to the household. One day Saima showed me a list of things that she wanted to buy when she got a job and had money, which was numbered from 0 to 6 in order of desirability and importance: sweets, cell (and jeans, shirt), room, bed, radio, and stove and fridge. Her desire for an independent life in a town with an electrical supply is clearly expressed in this list. She explained that the room, bed, radio, cooking stove, and fridge must be her own and not shared with anyone. She also wanted her own kitchen where she would cook food for her future husband, a desire that also showed her focus on the technologies of urban life and on autonomy. Likewise, having a mobile phone enhanced autonomy since mobile phones enabled youth to develop their own networks without adult interference and to create new forms of communication among friends within and beyond local boundaries (see Horst and Miller 2006 on Jamaica).

The life of Saima began changing after September 2004 when she started working at a restaurant in a nearby town. She moved into the restaurant and was given a bed in a room shared with the owner's teenage stepdaughter, who also worked in the restaurant. Her initial salary was N$250 per month (US$35), including the room and board. She was not satisfied with the salary but decided to take the job anyway. She wanted a job and her own money to help change her status to an economically independent young woman who had such things as a free nightlife and ability to go to clubs and visit friends at any time.

Saima's parents and older siblings were concerned that she might become pregnant, but Saima expressed her frustration to me by portraying her older sisters as hypocrites: "How can they tell me not to have a boy-friend or sex? Look at them—they all have kids. Emma dropped school at grade 10 because she fell pregnant, Sarah got the second baby last year, and she's sick and got no job. Loide is okay now [because] she's got a job so she can support her child, but she couldn't [sometime before]; she became pregnant when she was nineteen, my age! They do the things and tell me don't. It's not fair." Perhaps to escape from her family's interference or possibly because her boyfriend was rumored to be seeing another woman, Saima disappeared in early January 2005.

A month and a half later, Saima was discovered working as well as liv-ing in the small bar building that was owned by one of the most success-ful local businessmen. She proudly took her sisters and me to her room to show us that now she had not only monthly income but also her own bed, small low table, television, radio, small and large mirrors, a series of hair- and skin-care products, some posters of South African or African American celebrities from South African magazines on the wall, and a lot of clothes. She had known that, sooner or later, she would be discovered, and in fact, she was not disappointed by the fact that it happened on that day since she had been feeling guilty about the fact that her family was probably worried about her. Two months after the discovery, Saima moved back to her village.

My next encounter with Saima was during a brief visit to Namibia a year and half later when I happened upon her living with her four-month-old baby at one of her sister's homes. The baby had been named by his father, suggesting the father's acknowledgment of paternity. Although the naming may not always be done by the father of a child in contempo-rary Owambo society, in general it is still the case. Otherwise, sometimes grandmothers may name a newborn baby. Saima's baby was accepted by her matrilineage and family, and she was concerned about being a good mother. At the same time, she still wanted youthful autonomy and did not choose to stay in the village. In 2007, Saima got a job at a tourist lodge in another region, leaving the baby with her parents and some maternal female cousins and sisters. She was receiving some financial and emotional support from the father of her baby son, but she did not seem to consider him essential for her and the baby. Later that year, the relationship came to an end. In 2008, she moved to Windhoek, the capital of Namibia, and sent money back to her parents to help with her child whenever she could.

Now she is a mother, but she is still a youth and will remain in that status until she gets married.

The New Female Youth

Saima's story illustrates well the attempts by many young Owambo women to define a "youth" identity for themselves that frees them from full family obligations and gives them a space to participate in a transnational youth culture based on consumption. Owambo discourse emphasizes that a marriageable woman is a food producer with the physical strength and knowledge to cultivate, process, and prepare food. That is why, traditionally, "You are fat!" is a compliment. One elder told me that the word *omugundjuka* (youth) refers to "those who know how to cook" (*aagundjuka ombaka siku teleka*). A young person without the knowledge of how to prepare food would just be called a "useless person," although the cooking skill is optional for boys. These skills are exactly what Saima demonstrated in her daily life before she disappeared and are also reflected in the items she wrote down on her wish list, which included a stove and a fridge. But the example of Saima also shows a shift in local notions of femininity moving from "usefulness" as expressed through being fat and able to cook and cultivate to being beautiful and able to consume fashion. The traditional emphasis on strength conflicts with perceived modern expectations of the slim body, beautifully maintained hairstyle, and ability to look good in the latest fashion items needed to win beauty contests.

Similarly, young men face a dilemma between a traditional gendered task of looking after cattle and the image of "cool" urban young man that they want to add to their modern masculine identity. Unlike women's skills, men's conventional tasks, especially herding, although valued, tended to have negative connotations, such as "rurality" and "backwardness," they believed. My male youth informants told me that they would not want to be seen by people from town looking after cattle, and thus they would go deep into the village so they would not be seen. It was not that they thought of the task as unimportant, but they rejected the image of "rurality" and "backwardness," which they associate with the activity. Looking after cattle does not fit their identity as youth or contemporary *omugundjuka*, who want to wear Levi's jeans, Converse sneakers, and

Adidas and Nike T-shirts. Both young women and men seem to be standing on common ground in that they have a personal conflict between two apparently separate domains in their lives.

Saima's list also marked the importance of clothes to youth identity. Martin (1994) discusses the symbolic significance of clothing in mediating social relations in Brazzaville in French Equatorial Africa where clothing choice marks class, gender, and generation. Just as the wealthy and the chiefs could show who they were by distinguishing their personal appearance with clothes, jewelry, hairstyles, and so on, youth could promote their youthfulness through clothing choices. Opposed to youth fashion is "Owambo dress," the mark of a mature woman. Owambo dress styles distinguish older from younger women, but both wear loose clothing that conceals the body line. Contemporary youth depart from this aesthetic in wearing "Western" or "American" clothes such as low-waist jeans and small sleeveless tops. Young women say that it is all right for youth to wear Western fashions but that older women should dress in culturally and traditionally appropriate clothes. This distinction marks youth as a liminal phase where people can experiment with cosmopolitan identities without threatening local cultural identity since older people are doing the work of maintaining that culture.

Sexual Relationships and Sexual Economies

Attitudes toward marriage and toward children born before marriage have also changed in ways that have increased the autonomy of young women. In Owambo society, only men can "officially" propose marriage, but women can influence them by encouraging or discouraging their interest. Young women may seek to prolong the youth phase by postponing marriage and then by choosing men who ideally live outside their family homestead (to maximize autonomy) when they do marry. Some young women also try to avoid meeting their boyfriend's family in order to lobby for a residence away from the family compound and near town. In this sense, young women seek to manage their transition to full adult status. They postpone marriage and try to define marriage as a union between two individuals not necessarily involving their lineages, although they recognize and understand that marriage is possibly the most important family event. Young women, such as Saima, who wanted her own kitchen to cook for her boyfriend, then, probably have an image of a married life based more on a nuclear family than an extended family.

Young women's desire to prolong the youth phase and to preserve autonomy from communal obligations is also reflected in, and helped by, a change in attitudes toward women bearing children before marriage. Many women have children and leave them with their matrilineal family without marrying the father(s) of the children. The traditional authorities in the area have made premarital pregnancies both more acceptable and easier to support in practical terms with some modifications in a couple of tribal laws. One relatively new law requires men to pay compensation to girls whom they impregnate. But this money covers only a fraction of the cost of raising children, a burden that is generally borne by the mother's matrilineage. The discourse on romance among both young males and females both justifies this situation (by blaming it on the opposite sex) and points to how common it has become. Young women claim that Namibian males are irresponsible and leave pregnant girlfriends, while young men claim that girls purposely get pregnant to extract compensation from the men and their families. Yet at the national level, the penalties for pregnancy fall much more heavily on the female side: the government policy says that a schoolgirl who gets pregnant must leave school for a year but then can return. The one-year-absence rule also applies to a boy who impregnated the girl if he is also a student at a public school. The policy on pregnant schoolgirls was even stricter until recently in that most of these girls were not allowed to return to school. However, in spite of changes in the government policy, teenage pregnancy is still likely to close the opportunity for girls to continue their education, thereby limiting their life options.

These changes have improved the position of unwed mothers and made it possible for young women to prolong youth by postponing marriage. In the distant past, premarital pregnancy was considered a disgrace for a girl's entire family (and sometimes for the king as well), and she, and probably her mother too, received severe social sanctions, the most extreme of which caused death. In contrast, despite the persistent negative perception of premarital pregnancy, girls in contemporary Owambo communities not only are able to give birth and continue to stay in their communities, but can also receive some compensation from the father of the child. This change is a crucial difference, which, to some extent, understandably evokes jealousy from men, many of whom are having to look after sisters' children in their matrilineage. In addition, it is actually common for Owambo women to have their children before they get married. It is surely not seen as desirable and has never been given official acknowledgment, but informally and depending on the circumstances, this phenomenon seems to be accepted in the communities. My female informants even said, "If you and your child have been forgiven [by attending a session at the church], it's okay," meaning that there will not be any restrictions on their social activities. Thus, these changes and trends in the attitudes and understanding of premarital pregnancy enforce the young women's social status as youth within the communities.

Limits to the Agency of Young Women

While young women have achieved some success in defining an autonomous youth phase, as Saima's case illustrates, there are limits to their ability to control their lives, and they often find themselves stuck between demanding boyfriends and older women. Many women continue to struggle with sexual relationships, since an unmarried woman who is pregnant or has a child is put in an undefined social status that is neither a proper youth nor a proper mature woman. Particularly, people's attitude is almost completely negative toward a woman who has become pregnant while still schooling. Some informants have no problem managing reproductive issues, but others find themselves torn between their boyfriends and older women: the boyfriends want to have sexual relations and children, while older women maintain ideal cultural norms of marriage before reproduction, which is juxtaposed to a compulsory reproductive ability after marriage. Young women feel that these two opposing forces are controlling their sexuality.

Loide, who is in her early twenties with a three-year-old daughter, told me that she had "a problem" with her boyfriend. When I asked her what the problem was, she said, "I asked him, 'I want to use condoms,' and he said he didn't want to. But I don't want a child anymore." She said she was going to have a contraceptive injection to solve the problem. A few days later, she told me that she had gone to the hospital for a three-month injection, but the nurses (who were older than herself) would give her only a two-month injection. This example shows the weaker position of young women relative to young men and older women. She would have been in a stronger position had she had an income, but without a job, she was dependent on her boyfriend and could do little to resist his demands. After a while, Loide decided to end her relationship with her child's father because she felt that the risks of getting pregnant again were greater than the chances that he would support her.

Receiving money in exchange for sexual favors is said to be common. I frequently heard rumors about teenage girls waiting for older men in a local hotel room, or about high school girls near the Namibia-Angola border sneaking out of the school hostel at night wearing makeup and fancy clothes to "earn" some money, all of which were talked about in daily conversation. Loide represents what young women consider an insecure social position because she is young and female and has a child to support. Women in Owambo society can receive support from their matrilineal kin, as indicated earlier, but the support may be only partial, depending on the family's economic condition. If there is not enough financial help available for a woman with a child (or children), she has to find other means of getting support. There are many young Owambo women who are in the same situation as Loide who must have a relationship with a man just to support themselves, a situation that they consider undesirable.

Note that marriage is always the only way for young people to become culturally proper adults. Young unmarried women's agency is limited in terms of their power to authorize their own activities, yet having economic power seems to confer a measure of social adulthood. If women support themselves and their children, as well as contributing to their other family members' lives, they are likely to earn a certain form of social respect.

Youth Style, Feminine Identity, and Respectable Social Maturity

Returning to the story of Saima, the dilemmas she faced derived from family pressures regarding her daily life and sexuality, unemployed status and its related economic condition, romantic relationships, and the gap between her own ideal image of herself and future and her real life. She is one of many young Owambo women who attempt to realize their own desire for modernity by consuming foreign goods, styles, and images in the process of searching for a life path beyond local boundaries. These female Owambo youths might appear similar to a group of urban youth in Madagascar called *jeunes*, a newly emerging youth category made up of youths who emphasize the role of consumption of new foreign things as a means of self-realization (Cole 2004, 579; see also Carrier 1990; and Friedman 1994). But a clear difference between Owambo youth and Madagascar *jeunes* is that the former are engaged in both familial obligations and traditional activities as well as youthful and modern activities, whereas the latter participate in sophisticated urban consumer activities. Ideally, young Owambo women seek both to express their individual identity and to become socially mature through contributing to the community.

A few women are able to realize the new form of social maturity through earning money, although it is an ideal that remains out of reach for most. It is, however, not simply about earning money but also about how the money is used. Women who use money only for personal needs and desires are never granted social maturity. The ideal for many young women, though few can realize this goal in practice, is to have a good job and children, to contribute to their matrilineage, and thus to attain some social maturity without getting married.

There are, however, numerous obstacles to achieving this ideal. It is difficult for anyone to gain the kind of income necessary to meet the ideal. Young Owambo can, for a time, free themselves from village obligations by going to school. In twenty-first-century Namibia, young people who fail to complete a high school education tend to be seen as failures because one's future economic status is believed to require finishing high school. Because of this belief, many parents and communities are willing to release young people from traditional obligations while they are still in school.

It is difficult, however, to achieve the kind of educational success necessary to get a good job. But further problems await those few women who are able to do well enough in school to go on to a college or university degree. Young female informants, who all graduated from the University or Polytechnic of Namibia and all have positions in the ministries, government institutions, and major private companies, told me that they would not hurry to get married and have a child until they met the right person. They knew that it was not an easy job to find a person who meets their expectations and ideal image of a good partner and breadwinner. Here is the dilemma they face. Despite the high educational achievement and economic capacity, these successful young women have to sacrifice their womanhood and social status of a "proper" mature woman. Their youth period is considerably longer than the generations before, but until they marry they are youth and girls as part of what they consider their Owambo tradition.

These women do receive respect and a measure of adult status through their economic achievements, although this falls short of full social adulthood. This situation is reminiscent of the effects of the migrant labor system, along with the creation of new leaders such as teachers and pastors, that eventuated in weakening the power of the Owambo traditional elites (for the latter point, see McKittrick 2002; and Miettinen 2005). Although it is still an occasional event, there is a trend among the local people that recognizes a young unmarried woman being a main income source for her family as respectable. On the other hand, young women who grew up in a society that has been changing rapidly under the influence of global capitalism and consumerism tend to be frustrated with a reality where they can barely obtain cash income.

Saima, as an unemployed high school graduate, represents both the potential and the frustrations involved in new female imagined identities. Saima, like many young women, wanted to be a youth who defined her identity through consumption. For her, to establish an economically independent condition and to be recognized as an individual person by others were more critical than to be integrated into her family network and local community at that time. But she was not fully satisfied with her autonomous condition and, in fact, showed a desire to be part of her family. Discussing the significance of social relationships for identifying personhood, Piot (1999, 18) states, "Persons here do not 'have' relations; they 'are' relations." Even those persons who think they are autonomous individuals are in fact in many ways defined by webs of relationships. This point explains why Saima was not satisfied with the life she desired when she actually experienced it. Saima in a way managed to succeed in nurturing her identity in the world of global capitalism and modernity, embodied by the lifestyle of freedom, financial resources, and her own room full of consumer goods. However, she had a sense of being an incomplete self and woman. Without social relationships, especially kinship relationships, and a local network, one cannot be recognized in the society because these relationships are vital to one's locality and identity and within which their social identity is embedded.

In a similar manner, young women who find a way, whether through short- or long-term sexual relationships, to access money and commodities may be perceived differently depending on how the wealth they gained is distributed in their kinship network. In the local view, there is an ambiguous but recognizable dividing line separating an independent woman and a prostitute, where the latter is considered as engaging in sexual transactions solely for selfish purposes. The independent woman, therefore, should also be a good daughter (for her parents and elders) and mother (for her children and younger kin members). The more women contribute to their family, the more they accumulate a sense of social maturity and power to make decisions for their lives. Nonetheless, as I have shown, this kind of social maturity alone does not lead women to gain a full and proper adult status.

Moreover, whether families and kin are an obstacle or a source of wealth, in Owambo communities kinship relationships and networks still convey a considerable moral weight upon which one has to rely when she or he attains full adult status. On the other hand, people in the area are able to find more opportunities than people in more remote areas to be involved in the "modern" lifestyle. For young women following the "modern" youth style, marriage can nonetheless be delayed until they find an advantage to, or a necessity of, becoming an adult. Despite the separation from their locality, marriage, or anything else, does not affect women's matrilineal lineage connections, in which the core of their selfhood lies.

Conclusion

In this chapter, I have focused on young Owambo women and their understandings, as well as their practice, of womanhood and identity in a changing socioeconomic environment. Saima's transition from the completion of secondary school, through the pending period of unemployed youth, her first job in town, a growing desire for consumer goods, her boyfriend's betrayal, her disappearance, and finally to motherhood represents the experience of many young women in the area. Although family members were negative about Saima's becoming pregnant, they accepted her baby when it was born, just as it was the case with her unmarried sisters and cousins. Eventually, Saima's various life transitions have resulted in enforcing her kinship connections and still enabled her to find a way to integrate her idea of modern life into a culturally correct Owambo lifestyle. I also suggest that there is a significant effect of the matrilineal descent system on the life experiences, relatedness, and self-hood of Owambo women.

On the other hand, some increasing opportunities for women to be involved in income-generating activities have produced important implications for women's social position and life plan engendered through the economic power they gain. Although the social status of adults is not attainable through work experiences or an ability to gain income, the ability to gain the access to commodities and to distribute wealth among families that some young women demonstrate seems to have a potential to alter the notion of maturity. Therefore, the various social, sexual, and economic consumption practices that young females are involved in should be analyzed not only in relation to their individual or youthful desires, but also, and perhaps more important, in connection to the dynamics through which intergenerational as well as gender relationships are reconfigured.

In short, young Owambo women may seem as if they are trying to emulate Euro-American youth. However, I have argued that young women's feminine identity is not formed only through mimicry of Western or "modern" styles. On the contrary, I have found that young women seek to display the necessary qualities for Owambo womanhood. They intentionally maintain certain traditional constructions of female identity by deploying a contradictory understanding of "tradition" with respect to social statuses and clothes in order to separate their youthful position from the position of adults, claiming youth and creating space for the individual self in ways that ultimately do not contradict Owambo ideals for embedded social personhood.

3

Still a Child?

Liminality and the Construction
of Youthful Masculinities in Japan

EMMA E. COOK

"I'm still a child," twenty-two-year-old Kazuyuki noted by way of explanation for his refusal to work full-time, as a *seishain,* in favor of pursuing
his professional break-dancing dreams. Kazuyuki is one of many young
men known as "freeters" (a category of part-time workers) in Japan, and
their reluctance to fit into normative masculine roles has provoked profound controversy. In this chapter I explore how the concepts of youth
and childhood are utilized by young men who work as freeters. While
some authors, such as Liechty (2002) in his work on Kathmandu, have discussed how youth is essentially a new social category, in Japan it is a social
category that has some history under its belt. As Alisa Freedman notes,
"The discourse on urban youth has been a perennial favorite among writers since the early days of modernization and urbanization in the Meiji
era [1868–1912], though in the past decade it has acquired a new sense of
urgency with the rapid transformation of the cityscape and the increased
instances of juvenile delinquency" (2006, 383).

Yet this most recent urgency on discourses of youth in Japan is also
linked to the rapid changes that the nation has undergone since the
bursting of the economic bubble at the beginning of the 1990s and the
increasing neoliberalization of the economy that has subsequently taken
place. With the popping of the bubble economy and Japan's decline into a
near two-decade recession, large-scale changes have been wrought in the
employment sphere. As companies struggled to stay afloat and competitive in the global market, they restructured their workforce. Hiring of new
permanent graduates was frozen, older workers were encouraged to retire,

58

bonuses were curtailed, and, perhaps most important, the hiring of flexible temporary staff became widespread. Indeed, just over a third of the workforce is now employed on irregular contracts. This figure is up from 16.4 percent in 1985 (Chatani 2008; Weathers 2009). Increasing numbers of youth entering such employment have significantly contributed to this rise. For example, in 1989, 20.4 percent of fifteen- to twenty-four-year-old males were in nonregular employment. By 2007 this number had risen to 45.6 percent (Chatani 2008).

Alongside economic restructuring, new social attitudes regarding work and the life course can slowly be seen to be emerging as young people seek to adapt to the demands of a newly flexible labor market. A clear generation gap thus exists between the expectations and life courses of men and women currently in their forties, fifties, and sixties and the ability of the younger generation in their late teens and twenties to be able to live up to these expectations and follow a similar life course (cf. Mathews and White 2004). However, as I show in this chapter, many youth clearly do not want to follow their parents' examples in work and lifestyles.

The university years (roughly between the ages of eighteen and twenty-two) are a time for youth to relax a little after the rigors of high school education and before the demands of adult working life. Ando notes that "leaving home used to synchronize well with the first job among those who grew up in Japan's economic booming era in the 1960s. Today, however, it synchronizes more with the first marriage among the younger cohorts" (2004, 227). Thus, younger people remain at home and dependent on parents for longer than before. This trend has also been well documented in the UK and other countries (Furlong and Cartmel 1997). Transitions from school to work have also changed greatly, as links between schools and the workplace become more tenuous owing to companies' decreased hiring of new graduates (see Honda 2004; Kosugi 2005). Well aware of the possibilities and constraints of the labor market, and supported by their parents at home, young freeters made conscious decisions to enter the irregular employment sphere, for a time at least. They believed they had time (and youth) on their side to try out alternative jobs and realities to help them decide the path they wanted to take into the future.

Through thirteen months of ethnographic fieldwork in the city of Hamamatsu in 2006–7 and numerous discussions with informants, it is clear that the period of the early twenties operates as a liminal space where youth are not yet expected to be adults, nor do many of them expect themselves to be. I will show in this chapter how, through their self-positioning as children, two young men—Kazuyuki and Shiro—seek to postpone adulthood in order to explore alternative lifestyles and stave off conforming to contemporary hegemonic masculine ideals.

Freeters, Ambivalence, and Popular Culture

Kazuyuki was working at the local nine-screen cinema when we met. He was a quiet young man with shoulder-length black hair, large almond-shaped eyes, clear skin, and high cheekbones. He dressed simply though accessorized boldly. On one sunny Saturday afternoon, we met up at a local coffee shop for an informal interview. When I arrived he was lounging on a chair outside, iPod earbuds snugly sitting in his ears, watching the world go by. When I was almost at the table he noticed me, grinned, and removed his earbuds slowly, giving me a casual nod and a slow *"Uiissu,"* an informal greeting common among young co-workers. He wore black jeans turned up to three-quarter length, Converse tennis shoes, oversized eighties-style sunglasses (all the rage in 2007), a flat cap (again eighties style, with a square pink-and-blue pattern adorning the visor), and a lot of jewelry. He regularly wore two necklaces, one with a blue opal, the other featuring a gold sneaker; a gold signet ring on the first finger of his right hand; a large watch on the left wrist; and three earrings—a big silver-dollar sign in his right ear and a small stud and large gold hoop in his left. Finishing the look was an iPod shuffle hanging around his neck.

After completing a two-year English course at a vocational college in the nearby city of Nagoya, he returned home and began working at the cinema part-time.[1] His main hobby and aspiration was to be a professional break-dancer, and to that end he spent most evenings, when not working at the cinema, training with friends. This practice was either

1. Tertiary education comprises vocational schools and junior colleges where students can take a two-year course, often involving learning a skill, and universities that offer four-year degrees, leading to a bachelor's degree qualification. People hoping to gain a "good" job in a large company have less chance of succeeding without a degree from a four-year university course. See McVeigh (2002) for a critical look at the Japanese higher-education system.

out on the street with a small boom box or in a dance studio that they were able to hire cheaply because one of his friends was friends with the manager of the school. Kazuyuki was definitely not alone in his interest: street dance, including break dancing, is increasingly popular in Hama-matsu, with different groups of young people often out dancing on the street in front of large floor-to-ceiling shop windows in the evening (see also Condry 2001).

Shiro, the other main character in this chapter, was also twenty-two years old. He was a shy and quiet young man. We initially met in 2006 at a lecture held in a local community center on the topic of NEETs (people who are Not in Education, Employment, or Training), originally a Brit-ish term describing youth between the ages of sixteen and eighteen. The Japanese government appropriated the term, but extended the age range from fifteen to thirty-four. This age extension is significant, as it reflects the Japanese government's general view that between those ages people are not yet fully adults, but are in fact still youth.

After the lecture, I struck up a short conversation with Shiro and his friend, who I assumed to be students as they were conspicuously the youngest listeners in the room. After saying good-bye and while I was waiting for the bus, Shiro ran out, introduced himself properly, asked why I had been there, and on hearing that I was doing research on freeters pro-claimed himself to be one. At that moment my bus arrived, and he urged me aboard. I thrust my business card in his hand and at his insistence got on the bus.

A week later a letter arrived, written on Mickey Mouse paper and enclosed in a Mickey Mouse envelope. Shortly thereafter, we arranged to meet up and have a picnic lunch in the park. Just after the appointed meeting time he came rushing up to our meeting place on his bicycle, shyly apologizing for being late (he had bicycled forty-five minutes from his house, which was in the more rural outskirts of the city). Shiro sported a shaved head and a distinct lack of fashion consciousness compared to many of the überfashionable youth I worked with. He often wore jeans that were slightly too short, old black sneakers, and a camouflage-style T-shirt. He was uninterested in fashion and generally uninterested in many of the must-haves of today's contemporary Japanese youth. For example, he owned neither a cell phone nor a computer, though after starting a new job (halfway through my research year), he purchased a refurbished laptop with his first paycheck. On the whole, he held to a simpler and more rural way of life, quite a contrast to the more consumer-conscious and hip street dancer Kazuyuki.

Shiro graduated from an agricultural high school (*nôgyô koko*).[2] Rather than go to a more academically focused school, he wanted to go somewhere where he could learn about plants and growing vegetables. However, at the time his dream was to become a voice actor for Japanese animated films (anime). Consequently, after graduating from high school he went to a vocational college in Tokyo that specialized in training voice actors. However, after completing the first year of the course, he dropped out and moved back home: "I was very lonely living in Tokyo on my own, and I did not want to continue living there." At the time he had purchased a cell phone because he thought it would be necessary when living alone, but "for most of the time I kept it turned off. . . . I didn't like to be contactable all the time and at any time." Partly as a consequence of his inaccessibility he had made no friends and thus spent his days alone in the urban jungle of Tokyo—a drastic lifestyle change from the quiet rural paddy fields of home. After returning home, he decided to revisit his interest in agriculture and set his sights on becoming a small-scale horticulturalist while also working part-time.

Both these young men were considered, and considered themselves, freeters, a term that has come to embody competing discourses surrounding youth, and young men in particular. Created in the late 1980s by the head of a part-time employment magazine called *From A,* the term *freeter* was created to denote a "free" part-time worker. Significantly, part-time work in Japan is defined not by hours worked but by receiving an hourly as opposed to monthly wage and by receiving none of the benefits that regular (*seishain*) workers receive: no bonus, no sick pay, no paid holidays.

Initially, the spin on the term *freeter* was positive; it was the height of the Japanese bubble economy when jobs were plentiful, thus taking time out to work in different jobs and exploring alternative lifestyles were

---

2. There are various types of high school in Japan: academic high schools that teach general courses and also more technical high schools that specialize in, for example, agriculture or manufacturing. See Rohlen 1983 as a good starting point for exploring Japanese high schools.

not deemed particularly problematic. This perception, however, changed drastically after the economic bubble burst and the recession wore on through the nineties (now dubbed the "lost decade") and into the early 2000s. The term *freeter* is now far more ambiguous. For some, such as the Japanese government and labor economists (see Genda 2005, 2007; Kosugi 2003, 2008), the definition of a freeter now appears somewhat clear-cut, although they have also had their difficulties pinning down just what they mean by the category. This point can be clearly seen by the fact that the Japanese government has had three definitions since 2003. Understanding the number of freeters working in Japan today is therefore quite complicated. Initially, in 2003, there were estimated to be 4.17 million. This number was drawn from the first definition, which stated that freeters were those people aged fifteen to thirty-four who were not housewives or in education and worked as temporary, dispatched (*haken*), or part-time workers. It included people who wanted to work in any capacity (Ministry of Health, Labour, and Welfare 2003). The 2004 definition was essentially the same, but was amended to include people who specifically wanted to work as temporary, dispatched, or part-time workers (Ministry of Health, Labour, and Welfare 2004). The estimated number of freeters consequently declined to 2.17 million people. The most current (2007) definition is as follows: "Freeters [are] . . . those aged between 15 and 34, graduate in the case of male, graduate and single [unmarried] in the case of female and, (1) for those currently employed, who are treated as part-time or *arbeit* worker by their employers, (2) for those currently unemployed, who seek the part-time or *arbeit* jobs and (3) for those not currently employed, who are neither engaged in household duties, attending educational institutions nor waiting to start a new job, and wish to find part-time or *arbeit* jobs" (Ministry of Health, Labour, and Welfare 2007b, 26; Ministry of Internal Affairs and Communications n.d.).[3] There are now considered to be 1.8 million freeters, with numbers being split almost equally between men and women (920,000 and 950,000, respectively).[4]

---

3. With the rise in the use of the term *freeter, arbeit* (or *arubaito,* as it is commonly pronounced) is now used more, in popular parlance, to signify students working part-time. However, generally the word *arubaito* denotes part-time work.

4. Previously, numbers of female freeters consistently outstripped their male counterparts. In 1997, for example, there were just over 1 million female freeters and 490,000

While the term *freeter* is now recognized as a distinct way of working in Japan, with free job magazines routinely advertising for freeters and with definitions appearing, on the surface at least, to be relatively clear-cut, the reality is more complex. Talking to freeters, temporary workers (*haken*), and regular employees (*seishain*), the term becomes more fluid, more nebulous, and far more dependent on who these workers are talking to, their purpose, and their feelings about their lives at the time regarding how they relate to the label of freeter. Part of this ambiguity stems from the way freeters are viewed in wider society. They have, in recent years, been debated about vociferously in the mass media: illustrated as lazy, irresponsible youth (see "'Freeters' Shun" 2003; Kitazume 2005) or portrayed as victims of the recession and the subsequent corporate restructuring that began in the 1990s (cf. Genda 2005; Hirano 2005; Pilling 2005). Both positions (and variations thereof) remain active in the public sphere, at regular intervals being debated in newspapers and on popular television shows.

The emergence of increasing numbers of male freeters, many of whom are now entering their late twenties and early thirties, and the widespread concern and moral panic that have followed regarding freeters and other youth in general have had a large effect on popular opinion in Japan. Indeed, moral panics have erupted around NEETs, *hikikomori* (youth who "shut themselves in" their rooms and rarely venture outside) (cf. Furlong 2008; Horiguchi 2011), and young people engaged in *enjo kôsai* (compensated dating), among others (cf. Ching 2008). Although freeters are often romanticized in popular culture, there has been a great deal of angst and negativity about them—making youth today seem somehow more deviant than the youth of bygone days. In addition, the Japanese government has instituted various policies such as the Wakamono Jiritsu Chôsen Puran (Plan to foster a spirit of challenge and independence in youth), to try to improve youth's (bad) attitudes toward work and encourage more young men to find work in the regular full-time employment market (cf. Inui 2005; Matsumiya 2006; Toivonen 2008, 40). Yet given that companies *want* to utilize this growing flexible labor market, and the fact that it was the government's actions

---

male. In 2003, there were 1.19 million of the former, and 980,000 of the latter. Numbers of male freeters are increasing steadily year to year (Ministry of Health, Labour, and Welfare 2007a).

itself, through the relaxation of protective labor laws and the deregulation of recruitment practices in 1998, that allowed companies to employ larger numbers of flexible workers for longer periods of time (Lukács 2010), the government's actions seem both contradictory and shortsighted.

During fieldwork, it became clear that the majority of people I knew often held their personal views of freeters somewhere in between the two main positions outlined above. It was apparent that when people talked of freeters, particularly when discussing negative views, they were talking of male freeters, not female. This attitude can be attributed to the fact that part-time work has often been associated with women in the postwar period (cf. Broadbent 2001). However, as already mentioned, increasing numbers of young men have in the past ten years been encroaching into this previously female domain (Weathers 2009). Age, gender, and social standing all played into how freeters were viewed. Many men (of varying ages) saw them as idle, irresponsible good-for-nothings who shirked their responsibilities. Many others, however, made the distinction between those freeters who had dreams (*yumei ga aru*) and those without. For example, Tatsu, a man in his late twenties who had recently quit his full-time job, stated, "I don't know any freeters, but I think that those freeters with a dream are okay. However, those without are not. I wonder, 'Why don't they want to work if they don't have a dream?' I want to know what they are doing." Meanwhile, Tani-san, a twenty-four-year-old man, said:

> Many people become freeters—those with a purpose and people who don't want to work much. Also people who find it difficult to become a regular worker might become a freeter. It's difficult to give one image of them. I think that if a freeter has a purpose, it is probably okay [*tabun daijôbu*]. However, it is hard for freeters to get married because their income is low and they get no bonuses. I think that if a freeter gets married, he is not responsible [*sekinin motteinai to omoimasu*] because they cannot offer stability.

Sato-san, a fifty-eight-year-old owner of a small computer school, reflected the changing views on freeters when he said, "Before, when the recession was bad the image of freeters was very negative. Now though, this has been changing. Now there are many views . . . and there are a growing number of people who think that freeters are okay." These ideas and images are also transmitted through popular culture that tends, however, to take a more romantic view of the freeter, as shall now be briefly discussed.

Popular Culture

In the late 1980s, Michishita Hiroshi, the head of the job magazine *From A,* set about creating a new image of part-time work aimed at young people, and he did this via a campaign that utilized popular culture. Numerous stories about freeters and their lifestyles were published, most of which featured people working in part time jobs by day and then pursuing creative or artistic endeavors by night. The job magazine also published a book about celebrities who had been freeters before making it big in their chosen professions. Furthermore, in 1988, the magazine produced a feature-length film titled *Furiitaa* (Freeter), the hero of which lived in Tokyo, played in a rock band by night, and did various one-day jobs while working for an agency named the Freeter Network. Part-time work was thus a way of enabling freeters to do the kind of work that they really wanted to do (C. Smith 2006, 95–97). The freeters depicted were confident, full of ambition and energy, and living lifestyles that they wanted, as opposed to regular workers, who were depicted as being slaves to their companies. Michishita and his team were thus creating, through the medium of popular culture, "a new way of relating self to work and company" (ibid., 96).

Aside from these carefully crafted and popularizing images, popular culture (films, television dramas, literature, and so on) tend to overwhelmingly focus on female freeters. They often romanticize the freedom thought to exist in working part-time: freedom to choose when and where to work, but also a freedom from being outside of mainstream rules and expectations. This view thereby gives not just a sense of labor freedom (to move from one job to another), but also the idea that it is possible to move outside of social constraints if working in a part-time capacity. Lukács gives a very interesting exploration of a workplace drama in the late 1990s called *Shomuni* that centered on the lives of female office workers. The show was so popular that its stellar ratings of more than 28 percent ensured the commissioning of three additional seasons and two feature specials. Although the show did not explicitly deal with the lives of freeters, Lukács discusses how many male freeters could relate to the show's main character, Chinatsu, who stridently claimed that no career was "worth losing oneself for." She continues:

> By introducing a freeter attitude into the corporate world, Chinatsu became a reminder that a symbiotic dependence between corporations and employees was at odds with the demands of the new economy for entrepreneurial spirit, mobility, and flexibly reconfigurable work skills. By representing these values, Chinatsu epitomized a new worker subjectivity. Yet the answer she offered was nothing more than a labor fantasy: an uncritical celebration of freedom that obliterated the fact that neoliberal economies thrive on the liberal rhetoric that recognizes freedom as an inalienable property of individuals. (2010, 170)

Workplace television dramas problematically celebrate, Lukács states, "freedom as courage on the part of young people to steer clear of secure employment that would require them to sacrifice their individuality by becoming part of a homogenous and highly disciplined workforce" (forthcoming, 15).

Male freeters, however, are conspicuously absent as main characters in much of the popular culture representations.[5] Whereas it is acceptable to be a freeter if female, for male freeters the issue is far more complex. Thus, references to male freeters have tended to be more implicit rather than explicit, as in the case of Yū Yoshizawa's character in the 2005 horror film *Chakushin ari 2* (One missed call 2). Yoshizawa's character is a part-time restaurant worker who dreams of becoming a photographer. His role is rather romanticized compared to the other adult men in the film, who are depicted as working full-time and supporting families. It is Yoshizawa's character that can travel to Taiwan with a friend and journalist to try to unravel the mystery, thus again suggesting that part-time workers have the freedom to leave work and travel whenever they wish. Depictions of

5. Since the writing and submission of this chapter, a television drama titled *Furiita ie o kao* (Freeter buys a house) was broadcast by Fuji TV in the fall of 2010. It focuses on a young man who quits his job soon after starting largely because of an inability to fit in with the politics and demands of salaried life at a large company. The drama then follows his job search, subsequent jobs, and his resolve to buy a house for his mother, who has a breakdown and falls into severe depression early in the series.

male freeters tend therefore both to be implicit (not naming the character as a freeter per se but focusing on the aspiration they are attempting to achieve) and to romanticize the freedom they are supposed to possess. Yet this presumed ability to do what they want when they want is a far cry from the lives of most of the freeters I knew who worked long hours for little money.

Kazuyuki and Shiro, however, also chose to focus on the freedom that working as a freeter afforded them. Kazuyuki mused, "I'm a freeter because I work part-time, but I can choose my working times and I can easily quit. I want to experience many different things while I am young. I want to try many different jobs to see what makes me happy before I make any decisions about the future." For him, being a freeter was something that he considered transitory. Shiro felt similarly: "I'm a freeter because I can choose what I do and when I do it. . . . I am free to choose." The debates that rage over these workers, however, remains relevant, as older freeters I knew came to gradually have contradictory feelings about "freeterhood" as they aged and found themselves slowly losing the ability to find full-time work because they had worked so long in the irregular employment sphere. Kosugi (2005) notes that since Japan continues to have rigid age norms in the regular employment sectors, it becomes increasingly difficult for freeters to find regular employment after they reach their late twenties and thirties. Kazuyuki and Shiro were also not immune to this worry and did express mild concern over their futures. Yet, as Kazuyuki said, "That's years away. . . . I cannot think about that now. I don't know where I will be or what I will be doing in even three years' time." The here and now remained for the most part their focus.

Youth, Work, and Masculinity

For Kazuyuki, work was a means to an end, a way of supporting himself while dancing. He planned to move back to Nagoya, a city about an hour by train from Hamamatsu, to live with friends, work in a café, and pursue his dream of being a dancer. He wanted, ultimately, a job that "was more like a hobby than work," and he was vehemently against working as a regular worker, stating, "I couldn't imagine it. There is no room for self-expression working as a *seishain* [full-time regular worker], and therefore I absolutely cannot think about it [*zettai kangaerarenai*]." Throughout the course of my fieldwork, he remained working at the cinema effectively full-time, with five or six shifts a week, noting that "generally I like working here. The only thing that is not so good is that often my shifts end late, and then I miss the dance practices that my friends do, but still . . . I feel supported here. The manager often listens about what I want to do and gives me advice." Thus, although his shift times were often not ideal, feeling supported and comfortable in his work environment made him want to stay with the cinema until he moved back to Nagoya.

Shiro's work life over the course of the year was patchier and followed more closely the stereotype of the job-hopping freeter. After arriving home from Tokyo, he began to work part-time planting and harvesting organic vegetables at two local family-run farms. They were flexible on work hours but paid little; however, he felt that the learning experience made up for this fact. Complementing this work, he also planted some of his family's land on the outskirts of Hamamatsu, using a plot 33 feet by 230 feet. He said, "I could never be a salaryman [a full-time regular worker]. I think that it is better for people to do jobs they like." Salarymen, Shiro thought, had to endure difficult working conditions for good wages, something that he was not prepared or willing to do.

As my fieldwork progressed, changes were, however, afoot in Shiro's work life. Initially, he took two months off to do an 870-mile trek-cum-pilgrimage around the eighty-eight temples situated on Shikoku, one of the four main islands of Japan located off the southeastern coast of the main island. This trip he undertook to try to challenge himself and to increase his confidence. Yet, he said, "While walking I realized that if I want to make a living from growing vegetables, I will need to sell them, but I am not confident I can." As a result, when he returned home he signed up with a local job agency and shortly thereafter began working at a bread factory part-time during the day and cultivated the family field in the evenings.

A few months later Shiro quit this job and decided to work with a temporary agency, citing the fact that he wanted a more varied work experience. Yet at the same time, he wanted a job that did not require much communication with co-workers. After a few days working at a new assignment sorting newly delivered stock in a storeroom, he quit, stating, "Everyone was very quick and very good at their jobs, and I was not. The men were not unfriendly but were not particularly friendly. Sometimes I thought they were angry. Anyway, I felt they were not approachable, and

I didn't want to continue." This experience left Shiro deflated, concerned about his ability to communicate with people and feeling like a quitter. The absence of a supportive environment, something that Kazuyuki felt he had at the cinema, was a crucial factor in Shiro's decision to quit. He wanted to have increased confidence and independence, yet felt unable to achieve these aims in an environment that undermined the very things he was attempting to develop. After this Shiro returned to his previous agricultural employers. However, just before I left the field, he began working at another factory, this time putting together pistons for car engines; it was a job requiring little communication with co-workers, but he hoped to gain experiences that would help him develop himself.

Neither of these young men was unusual. I met many freeters who worked for a long time in one place of work as a freeter, renewing their contracts every six months or so, and I also met many young men who job-hopped in the search for meaningful work where they felt comfortable. Feeling comfortable and happy at work was a key component of most freeters' narratives. This desire contrasts significantly with older full-time male workers' narratives, who described working loyally for their company, irrespective of personal happiness. These differences can be attributed to the different economic climates and opportunities that were prevalent throughout much of their working lives, compared to the situation in which youth today find themselves.

Being a salaryman or "corporate warrior" was both an ideal and an idealized position during the period of economic growth from the 1960s onward. Linked to rapid expansion, the rebuilding of the nation, and a growing economy, salarymen were said to embody "the samurai spirit." The values most respected in men today—for example, respect for order, discipline, self-control, endurance, loyalty, and activeness—are those traits attributed to the samurai, and it was this spirit that was said to be evoked by the new middle class that arose in the 1960s and paralleled the economic recovery of Japan (Sugimoto 2003).

Dasgupta (2004, 83) notes that it was in the 1960s when the salaryman "became the overarching embodiment of hegemonic masculinity, as alternative/competing masculinities such as the soldier and farmer became neutralized as a consequence of Japan's defeat and subsequent social and economic transformations." In its narrowest sense, the salaryman usually refers to university-educated white-collar male employees who work full-time in large private-sector companies and institutions. Within work they are expected to be loyal to their employers, diligent, dedicated, and self-sacrificing. Outside of work the salaryman is expected to marry at a suitable age and once married perform his role of husband, provider, and father appropriately by providing for the family (Dasgupta 2003). Until relatively recently, the idea that a "real man" should sacrifice his family life for his life in the company was a given (Henshall 1999), in the middle classes at least.

While the salaryman may appear to be symbolic of a post–World War II generation of Japanese men, it is also important to note that it is a firmly middle-class ideal, and in recent years the idea that "one should 'live for one's company'" (Mathews 2003, 113) has lost ground. Mathews states, "Walk into any bookstore [in Japan] and one will find dozens of titles . . . [stating]: 'Live as you yourself want! Don't be chained to working for your company!' as the cover blurb for one recent bestseller proclaims (Ôhashi 2000)." Many other books urge people to take alternative paths, and Mathews notes that "the ideal for many aspiring young people today is to be not a salaryman but an entrepreneur" (ibid.), with the focus being on individual self-fulfillment rather than on self-sacrificing loyalty to a company. While this situation may well be the case and is the dream of many, including many of the freeters I knew, people are also aware of the difficulties of achieving this goal: being a successful entrepreneur is a risky business. Furthermore, it was this discourse of masculinity, this *ideal* of the salaryman, or of the humdrum job and regular full-time (*seishain*) contract that he represented, that was invoked by all my male (and female) informants in various ways, even by those individuals who wanted to be entrepreneurs. For Kazuyuki and Shiro, it was something they definitely wanted to avoid.

For older freeters I knew with limited educational backgrounds, whose interactions with the employment market were more diverse and more complex, becoming a full-time employee often became their aspiration. However, for tertiary-educated graduates with dreams of becoming an entrepreneur, musician, or artist, the stability of a full-time position was often something to consider when thinking about marriage prospects and deciding whether they should continue to pursue their dreams. Thus, all the freeters engaged with the idea that adult men should be engaged in full-time permanent employment, and as they aged they often considered the repercussions of remaining outside what they perceived to be the mainstream.

What is interesting here is the strength of this discourse of masculinity that links productive adult men to full-time positions, especially given that although the salaryman has become the dominant masculine discourse in contemporary Japan, the vast majority of Japanese men are not now and never have been one (Dasgupta 2003; Roberson and Suzuki 2003). Indeed, a growing number of people, approximately one in three, are currently working in the irregular employment sector (Ministry of Health, Labour, and Welfare 2007c) with limited chances of gaining regular employment status. I would suggest that partly it is the irregularity, the fear of instability, and a heightened sense of risk (cf. Beck 1992; Furlong and Cartmel 1997), especially in an increasingly flexible, neoliberal labor market that allows this ideal to remain a potent, albeit ambivalent one, force for so many.

Younger freeters in particular, the ones who position themselves as children, are specifically trying to avoid these ideals of what men *should* do and be. This particular life course, so clearly enacted in various ways in their own families by their fathers, is one that they ultimately do not want to embody. Typically, fathers in Japan, though extolled by media and government policies to be more active in their family lives, remain rather in the background (cf. Mathews 2003). Women are generally expected to be the main child rearers, with men participating in family activities on the weekends (cf. Ishii-Kuntz 2003). This situation, of course, is also dependent on other factors such as class and occupations, but for a large part of both Kazuyuki's and Shiro's lives, their fathers were in the background, though in differing ways. Kazuyuki stated, "When I was young my father was typical. Always at work [he was a white-collar worker in an office job] and not around much." However, as Kazuyuki described it, that situation changed when his mother ran away (*nigeta*) when he was thirteen. This had altered his relationship with his father, a man who had previously been quite distant, mostly because of the demands of his work. Watching how his father coped with adjusting to the demands of bringing up two children elicited a newfound respect for him, and Kazuyuki talked warmly about him, describing him as "really cool" (*hontô ni kakkoi*). He said, "I feel my family really support me; my father has implied that he does. Although he has never said it to me, I feel that he wants me to do something that will make me happy." His disdain at the thought of working as a salary-man was largely derived from watching his father working long hours each day, unhappy in his work, but having to keep at it to make ends meet and provide for his family. For Kazuyuki, control over the direction of his life was of great importance. He did not want to follow the crowd or follow his father's footsteps into unrewarding work. He felt that there was more to life than work. Kazuyuki's father implicitly agreed and was keen for his son to carve out a productive but enjoyable life for himself.

Shiro's father(s) had also been distant. His mother and father divorced when he was very young, and although Shiro saw his father occasionally as a child, all contact ceased when his father died when Shiro was seven. His mother had remarried when Shiro was still very small (he thought it was when he was three or four), and while his stepfather is a good man, Shiro does not feel close to him, though he felt well understood, particularly by his mother. Although he talked of his family relationships during his early years as being difficult, he now felt very differently, "I feel very lucky and blessed. I feel most parents tell their sons that they must work properly, but my parents want me to do something that I enjoy and like. I think they are really kind, and I feel safe and secure with them."

These two young men were not, however, unusual. Many freeters and nonfreeters talked similarly of watching their fathers from a distance, and desiring an alternative, closer relationship with their future families. Furthermore, many people discussed how their parents wanted them to find work they enjoyed. However, the difference between many freeter and nonfreeters was that many male freeters, especially those from middle-class backgrounds, were vehement in their desire to not work like their fathers. Mathews also makes this point when discussing one of the main reasons (male) youth become freeters. He concludes, "Some young people may fully understand the economic odds against them, but may feel such repugnance at the lives their fathers have led that they are willing to abandon the pursuit of regular employment in order not to have to live such a life themselves" (2004, 129).

For Kazuyuki, the changes wrought by his mother's departure led him to see his father in a new light. Rather than being a distant figure, his father moved more to the foreground of his life, and he was then able to see what the demands are on a man who embodies the hegemonic discourses of adult manhood: working hard in a full-time white-collar salaryman job, doing mandatory overtime, and having very little time left over to spend time on himself. Kazuyuki was adamant he did not want to emulate this life and was thus actively seeking to resist normative expectations of what he should do and be by devising alternative lifestyle strategies that would enable him to make a living in a different and more meaningful way. The problem with this plan was that his strategies (to become a professional street dancer and café owner) looked to remain a dream—he did not believe that he was good enough to be a professional street dancer, and he had no financial capital nor a family with spare money to open such a café.

I have shown in this section how work expectations are intricately tied up with hegemonic masculine discourses of what an adult man should do and be in Japan. Many young male freeters struggled with this ideal, and the younger men in particular tended to retreat into a liminal space of childhood in order to postpone the realities of adult manhood.

Youth, Liminality, and the Expectations of "Full" Adulthood in Japan

The dominant masculine (adult) ideals of responsibility, stoicism, bread-winning, and fatherhood are all far away from the current realities of these young men. Yet the early twenties is just such a time when people are almost *expected* to resist, reject, and consequently learn to negotiate adult norms as they move *into* adulthood. Wider Japanese society considers the early twenties to be a time when young people are learning the social skills necessary to fit into adult society, while also operating somewhat outside of the constraints of it. Youth are not yet expected to conform to adult norms. For example, Takehiko, a thirty-eight-year-old man, commented, "I think it is good for young people to take time to think about what they want to do, to try new things, while they are young, before marriage and regular life." Youth is thus not only a transitional space but also one of liminality.

As Dewey and Brison state in the introduction of this volume, the very notion of youth as a liminal period of exploration that gives license for innovation defines youth as immature, insignificant, and not to be taken seriously (Caputo 1995; Wulff 1995b), thus limiting their impact on adult worlds. Kazuyuki and Shiro positioned themselves firmly within this liminal space of youth. Yet simultaneously, many young freeters felt stuck: stuck between the kinds of lives they felt they wanted to construct for themselves, the kind they felt they were able to construct, and the wider social expectations of the types of lives they should attempt to achieve. Or as Liechty puts it, they are stuck "in the 'in-between' space: between expectations and reality; between past and future; . . . between child- and adulthood; . . . between education and meaningful employment" that is the lived experience of modernity (1995, 191).

Garsten, in her article on temporary workers and agencies, notes that in at least a metaphorical sense, temp workers are also liminal: they are transitory and exist outside of the structures and social relationships of the organization for which they work. She states, "The attributes of liminality or of liminal *personae* ('threshold people') are necessarily ambiguous, since this condition and these persons elude or slip through the network of classifications that normally locate states and positions in cultural space as Turner (1977, 95) puts it" (1999, 606–7).

Young male freeters, by dint of their youth, are in a liminal space—not children, yet not adults, somewhere, as Liechty (2002) puts it, "in-between." Yet as freeters they are also liminal—temporary or irregular workers whose contracts are up for renewal usually every six months: crucial to the company as cheap labor, yet easily dispensable. If we consider mainstream expectations, freeters are at the margins of society and work, yet they are also part of an irregular workforce that is increasingly part of the employment norm. Thus, young male freeters exist in a dual liminality. As work is deeply implicated in male transitions to adulthood in Japan, young male freeters are betwixt and between in two interrelated senses.

I have already noted that becoming an adult man in Japan has been linked, in the postwar period, to successfully completing the school-to-work transition. Roberson elaborates, "In Japan, the transition from school into the working world marks one's transformation from student (*gakusei*) to social person (*shakaijin*). This transition is particularly important for men, for whom work remains a more permanent source of social identification than it typically does for Japanese women" (1995, 294). Socialization into a company as a salaryman is considered one of the core parts in the process of becoming a *shakaijin*, but becoming an adult is far more complex than just becoming a full-time worker.

Becoming a full adult (*ichininmae*) is more than job status. Self-awareness, responsibility, self-discipline, and internalization of social norms are all part of being a full adult. It is a long process of social *becoming* (cf. Christiansen, Utas, and Vigh 2006) that does not end at the acquisition of a full-time job or marriage, though these events are important markers. Kazuyuki and Shiro were just at the beginning of this journey but taking advantage of a window of opportunity, seeking to postpone all thoughts of adulthood.

Postponing Work and Marriage

As already noted, work and marriage are two of the main signifiers of adulthood, and they play key roles in normative ideals of Japanese masculinity. They are consequently important concepts to analyze in a discussion of the postponement of adulthood. Taga (2003) states that young men in Japan continue to embrace the ideals of men being main breadwinners and good responsible husbands and fathers, while also negotiating and resisting this notion in various ways. Although both Kazuyuki and Shiro rejected the idea of becoming a full-time worker by clearly stating that they would never want to get such a job, this attitude can be seen as part and parcel of being young and being expected, at an age when it is socially acceptable to resist normative notions of work, rather than being an outright rejection of hegemonic masculine ideals.

Their engagement with the model of "being a good, responsible husband and father" is, however, more ambiguous. In general, it is possible to see that as marriage is increasingly coming later and education longer as the transitional stage of youth and adulthood is increasing for many, with the mean age of first marriage in 2007 at 30 for men and 28.2 for women (Ministry of Internal Affairs and Communications 2008). Postponement of marriage is happening in many places, not just Japan (cf. Fornäs 1995; Furlong and Cartmel 1997; Hogan and Astone 1986; Hogan and Mochizuki 1988). However, while the majority of young people I worked with did want to marry in the future, both Kazuyuki and Shiro were unsure as to whether they wanted to marry at all, or even if they could, citing financial barriers. Shiro noted, "If I remain a freeter, I think it will be impossible to get married. If I can make good money, then it might be possible, but really I would prefer for my wife to work and for me to be a househusband at home. I don't want to be the breadwinner."

Financial barriers to marriage are, of course, not something unique to Japan. Mains, in his article on the lives of Ethiopian youth, states, "Many young men believed that nearly insurmountable financial barriers prevented them from dating, marrying and having children. They claimed that they would not marry before the age of 30 or 35 and then only if they had become wealthy" (2007, 665). Shiro was not wrong, however, in his assertion that being a freeter would prove problematic for marriage. Awano, a married woman aged thirty, said, "Freeters who have a dream are 'okay,' but those without are no good. However, I would probably never have married one, even if I loved him." Younger women were more forceful in their views. For example, twenty year old Kawai-san mentioned that she would never marry a freeter. "I would always be worried about money. I want to marry someone who has a good job, can offer a stable path [*antei michi*]." Many other unmarried women echoed this concern about financial stability in the future. They all wanted to marry a man with a stable job.

If Kazuyuki and Shiro choose not to, or are unable to, marry in the future, this decision will have potential repercussions not just on how they are viewed in wider society, but also on their work possibilities. Indeed, marriage is often thought of as proof of responsibility and of adulthood in Japan. Moreover, larger companies effectively reward men for being married by providing them with special allowances (Iwao 1993, 236; Mackie 1995, 237}, and marriage may also be a prerequisite for transfers aboard in some companies.

In the case of Kazuyuki and Shiro, their general resistance to marriage is linked to their immersion in the social space of being a youth, and both men mentioned their age when talking about it. They felt that thinking seriously about marriage and relationships was not something to be done then, in their early twenties, but more appropriate for the late twenties or early thirties. Thus, not being ready to marry or wanting to be a breadwinner can be seen as a product of youth rather than a desire to actively resist hegemonic ideals of masculinity. Both men sought to delay the onset of adulthood and adult masculinity and thus postponed thinking about adult things such as marriage and breadwinning responsibilities.

Although they are not expected to conform fully, just yet, to dominant adult and masculine ideals, the pressure to do so in the near future exists. What differentiated Kazuyuki and Shiro (and other young freeters) from students of the same age, however, was a reluctance to accept these norms as an inevitable part of their lives. Whereas most of the students

I worked with felt it was unavoidable that they would soon graduate and find socially approved jobs, effectively ending the liminal time of studenthood and entering the adult social order, many young male freeters sought to evade this outcome and prolong their time in the liminal space that being a youth afforded them. Peers were an essential part of this resistance.

Youth and Their Peers

While Kazuyuki tended to take his time before speaking and listened to others' opinions before vocalizing his own, he was also outgoing and social with his peers. He spent the majority of his free time with friends who also engaged in break dancing. Shiro, meanwhile, was shy and had only two close friends, whom he saw roughly once or twice a month. Both were working part-time in agriculture. One was an avid train spotter who had failed twice to get regular employment with Japan Rail; the other was interested in agriculture and was a keen fan of anime. Shiro attributed his small number of friends to a lack of confidence in himself and in his ability to communicate with others. Shiro's peer group, though very different from Kazuyuki's, effectively did the same things: they reinforced each other's lifestyle choices, provided mutual understanding, and gave them a sense of belonging.

Kazuyuki had a strong desire to make his own way in life, and he spent his free time with peers who had similar aspirations, "I want to do the things that I want to do, whatever other people say. I want to be that way. I want to make my own path. . . . My friends are the same. None of us wants to be company men. We all want to live differently." One of his friends was, however, about to get married, and he described feeling sad at this prospect, "Once he is married, he will not be able to come out with us much. Family becomes the most important thing, not your friends." Kazuyuki lamented the change that this marriage was to bring to the dynamics of the peer group. Furthermore, it brought home to him the realization that his peer group would not always be as close as they were now. In some ways, Kazuyuki found this thought threatening: it would impose limits on his own choices by being a reminder that friends were growing up and moving in different directions. Although he did not explicitly express this point, some other young freeters did. Hiro, a twenty-five-year-old freeter, said: "Lately I look at my friends, and most are working full-time now. They work hard, but they get bonuses each year; they don't have to worry too much about money, and they can live independently. Some are in relationships and are beginning to think about marriage. But I cannot think of those things. Lately I wonder if trying to achieve my dream is good or not."

Peers, as reference groups, give space within which it is possible to remain a "youth." They also indicate when it is time to move on from the edges of youth into adulthood. Kazuyuki created facets of his masculine identity through the peer group that he identified most with—his fellow break-dancers. Being part of this group was one such way that Kazuyuki got his sense of belonging, as well as mutual support, understanding, and acceptance of his views about life, work, and manhood (cf. McDowell 2003; Swain 2005).

All of Kazuyuki's friends believed that it is important to do enjoyable jobs. Although it could be expected that most youth thought the same thing, the majority of young students I knew braced themselves when looking for jobs. Many accepted jobs that they had not envisioned themselves doing and did not particularly enjoy, but felt that they had to endure (*gaman*) and try their best (*ganbaru*). Kazuyuki and the majority of his friends, meanwhile, were not doing that and not willing to. They reinforced each other's lifestyles and aspirations through tacit approval and thus were able to remain within a transitional space of youth. While all members were doing the same, it remained a valid, uncontested option, and being in such a liminal space felt normal. As Liechty has stated in his work on youth in Kathmandu, "Peer groups allow young people to abandon themselves in the utter banality of a day-to-day material existence, consciously avoiding the future by living for each other in the present" (1995, 190). Here is perhaps another reason Kazuyuki was sad about his friend getting married: it was a clear sign that one of his inner circle was moving beyond "youth" and into adulthood.

Conclusion

The two freeters in this chapter rejected normative adult ideals of a "normal life" (*futsû na seikatsu*). Like many youth around the world, they did not want to be like their fathers—business owners or salarymen—whom they saw as sacrificing their own desires for their families. They wanted to find themselves, nurture their aspirations, and ultimately create a life that made them happy. Although there were mild echoes of concern about their futures—about whether they could marry if they did not find stable work—they continued to eschew normative gender ideals: Shiro wanted to turn gender norms on their head and be a househusband, and Kazuyuki wanted his future wife to work and for them to share everything fifty-fifty. These young men were not unusual. Most of the male freeters I knew were seeking to break out of the normative life course. However, the older a man gets, the harder it is for him to ignore wider social expectations of what he should do and be as an adult man. Kazuyuki and Shiro were thus in a privileged and liminal stage where they were not only allowed to seek alternatives but encouraged to do so by their families, and often implicitly by friends who were doing similar things.

Although Kazuyuki and Shiro were seeking flexible work to finance their aspirations, they were at the same time responding to changes in the economy and employment systems, which have inexorably become more neoliberal in their shape. Yet in spite of the fact that these economic and employment changes have taken place, wider social attitudes of what men are supposed to do and be remain largely rooted in postwar ideals of the salaryman, in Hamamatsu at least. Freeters are thus portrayed as either deviants or victims. However, by appropriating the space of youth, Kazuyuki and Shiro were able to gain time, space, and a certain amount of acceptance of their choice to be freeters at this time in their lives. By referring to themselves as children, they gave themselves some psychological breathing room, some space to move in, before having to decide what they were to do, and, perhaps more pertinent, before they began to receive pressure from others to conform to expected life courses and routes.

While many of the young people I knew did not share Kazuyuki's and Shiro's explicit positioning as children per se, they did speak of the early twenties as a time to try out new jobs and alternative ideas, though this discussion was often followed by resignation when they talked of the time limit they felt existed. This period of time was usually articulated as being around the age of twenty-five, which was when they felt they would have to give up irregular work to look for stable, regular employment. Other non-freeter contacts of various ages concurred and spoke, with some nostalgia for some, about the freedom of the early twenties, when exploring different jobs and identities was socially acceptable. These views were in stark contrast to the youth policies of the Japanese government, which appears to consider young people as being in need of both moral and practical guidance regarding their attitudes and ethic toward work.

Even though Kazuyuki and Shiro appeared to be rejecting core values of adulthood and masculinity, their actions were condoned and expected because of their young age, which they knew and relied upon. They acknowledged, with some trepidation, that it would not always be so easy. Neither of them had solid plans to start moving in the direction of regular employment, and both were looking to prolong the transitional stage of youth past what has previously been considered the norm. Peers with whom they worked were graduating from four-year universities (or had already graduated from the vocational colleges) and were, for the most part, starting full-time jobs or searching for such work. Both men, however, situated themselves within groups or around people who were not doing these things, who were in a similar place to them. Neither knew what he would end up doing in the future. With the changes in school-to-work transitions, the later age of marriage, and an employment system that favors hiring more nonregular staff, this transitional stage leading into adulthood seems likely to continue to be prolonged for increasing numbers of youth.

Kazuyuki and Shiro were, in Durham's words, "neither . . . autonomous liberal actors nor . . . overdetermined victims" (2000, 113). Instead, they were negotiating a largely liminal space in which to explore their dreams and make new paths for themselves, while simultaneously being constrained by their perceptions and expectations of adulthood and the new realities of an increasingly neoliberal economy. By using the liminality youth provided, they were able to give themselves time and space to explore different options before becoming (and before being expected to become) full members of adult Japanese society.

PART TWO

Mass-Mediated Modernities

4

Gendered Modernities among
Rural Indigenous Fijian Children

KAREN J. BRISON

On the day that I returned to the Fijian village of Rakiraki to spend the summer studying play, the local children decided to help me by organizing a large game of American-style baseball for me to record for "TV" with my video camera. This game resulted in two hours of raucous fun, as more and more children joined in and one very puzzled anthropologist struggled to understand the Rakiraki version of baseball. Innings continued until the "team captain" had struck out three times, regardless of the number of outs accumulated by his team in the meantime. I was intrigued by the children's choice of the game of baseball, which I never before or since have seen played in Fiji. Playing baseball signaled the children's preoccupation with presenting themselves on "TV" to the outside world as fully competent in the mass-mediated world of international sports. Even more intriguing were the rapid verbal jests. "Fuck off, Max. Fuck off, *uba*," one twelve-year-old boy called to his brother. These jests involved a puzzling combination of deep local dialect, something that usually indicated respect for local ways, forbidden English swear words that most definitely did not signal respect, and an anglicized nickname that similarly eschewed identification with the local ranked community. "Oh, look at the *kai colo!*" (literally, someone from the interior, like a hillbilly) one of the girls later remarked scornfully as her younger cousin proudly came to display her bag of Bongos, a favored snack food purchased only in flush times. Over that summer, as I recorded spontaneous play among the children of the lineage and at a local kindergarten, I noticed repeatedly a preoccupation with appearing to be "suitably modern" as indexed by an assumed disdain for consumer goods meant to suggest a deep familiarity with them,

85

casual use of colloquial and forbidden English words, frequent references to mass-media sports, and other practices. Here I explore constructions of modernity in children's play to show that children were creating distinctively gendered identities with potential to challenge the strong rank and ethnic divisions that structure contemporary Fiji.

A Fijian Modernity

Modernity and chiefliness are closely associated for many indigenous Fijians. Traditional chiefly groups and contemporary professionals imagine a local modernity strongly resembling the traditional chiefly polity. In traditional villages, indigenous Fijians, males, older people, and those born to high-ranking clans, were accorded deference and respect because they were believed to possess the spiritual power and social wisdom necessary to maintain a harmonious, prosperous community (Toren 1990). Now indigenous Fijian traditional leaders argue that they are naturally "modern," and traditional leaders were always independent and innovative just like successful modern professionals (Brison 2003). Conversely, modern professionals such as schoolteachers and Pentecostal businessmen say that they are naturally "chiefly" and have taken over the chiefs' functions of nurturing, providing guidance, and supplying spiritual efficacy to the community.

Such rhetoric naturalizes the privileged position of chiefly and male indigenous Fijian elites, by suggesting that they possess a special kind of individual potency and social insight necessary for prosperity in the contemporary world community. Fiji is a multiethnic nation where about 35 percent of the population consists of South Asian descendants of turn-of-the-century indentured servants. When indigenous Fijians equate chiefliness and modernity, it justifies a privileged place for the indigenous community in Fiji (e.g., Brison 2007b).

Ideas about modernity are changing. For instance, the ability to speak English, generally an index of modernity, is usually associated with traditional elites. But English, as in many areas of the world, is also associated with women, who tend to speak English better, perhaps because they wish to escape patriarchal traditions (Gal 1979). Besnier (2002, 2004) also shows that transgendered "fakaleiti" in neighboring Tonga speak English to show that they are both feminine and modern.

Here I follow Besnier and others in showing that modernity is imagined differently within the Fijian community. Rural indigenous Fijian children are far removed from discussions of professionalism, economic development, ethnic relations, and chiefly tradition. In Fiji, as in neighboring Tonga and Samoa (Morton 1996; Ochs 1988), low-status children are not supposed to distract higher-status adults from the important work of maintaining the community, and so children spend a lot of time away from adults supervised by older children and are excluded from many important communal activities. Consequently, their ideas about modernity come largely from television, movies, sports, church, and school. Because children's social experiences differ from adults', they see the world differently.[1] For example, religious affiliation was one of the most significant components of identity for many Rakiraki children, particularly girls, since parents often restricted girls from playing with children from other religious groups. Children construed religious identity differently from adults and often associated more with religious groups than with local landed polities.[2]

Furthermore, boys and girls were positioned differently in local society and so had different ideas about modernity. Boys were expected to develop ties with the local polity and express commitment to it through

1. Toren (1990, 1993), for instance, found that Fijian boys and girls have significantly different perceptions of ranking in the community than do adults.

2. The generation gap may be increasing in the contemporary Pacific. LiPuma (2001) argues that the encompassment of Melanesian and other Pacific societies by Euro-Americans has produced distinctive generational cultures for the first time where each generation defines itself in opposition to the previous one. This demarcation is particularly acute for young people, who experience the world differently since their lives have been shaped by churches, schools, government agencies, and other forces in ways distinctive from their parents' experience. Kulick (1992) suggests that peer socialization among children has contributed to a shift from a local language, Taiap Mer, to the national lingua franca, Tok Pisin, in the Gapun village of Papua New Guinea. Likewise, Toren (2007) found that children of Gau, Fiji, view kinship networks differently than do adults of the community. Children, who have grown up in an economy increasingly based on money, know fewer members of their extended family than did previous generations of children. From their distinctive vantage point within society, children pick up some values and beliefs more than others and form identities that draw upon adult values and beliefs selectively.

using regional dialects of Fiji. Girls, however, were expected to marry outside the community, and parents often thought it was more important for them to learn English and Bauan, the national standard version of Fijian, so they could do well in school and get a good job. Because boys and girls were treated differently, they developed different aspirations. I found, however, that few children saw themselves primarily as members of the local village, and all defined their identities as part of larger international communities.

Children and Modernity in Rakiraki

Both boys and girls were aware of a wider world of more prosperous urban and international relatives who might look down on rural villagers and had a pervasive concern with appearing "suitably modern." These preoccupations were indexed by frequent criticisms of other children as *kai colo* or for having yellow, red, or "smelly" teeth, the mark of an unsophisticated "primitive" who failed to brush regularly. In children's discourse, *kai colo* were those who showed excessive fascination with consumer goods, thereby revealing that these items were not part of their everyday lives. Ironically, it was often children whose families had come into money and had just purchased expensive items such as television sets who were accused of being *kai colo* for showing off about these new items. For instance, one day a delivery truck arrived in the village bearing a new television and some groceries from town, including Bongos, a favored snack food. As the children began to talk excitedly about their new television, one of the older girls, Kelera, remarked in Fijian, "Look eating Bongos. You are a *kai colo*." One of the older boys, Josefa, chimed in a similar vein, "You are acting like a *kai colo* with your Bongos." On another occasion, as a bunch of children crowded in front of my video camera, trying to make sure they would be on the video, one of the older boys scolded them, "You are a bunch of *kai colo*."

These remarks index a disdain for those children who lack sufficient familiarity with the world of consumer goods. But it is important to note that in these cases and others, children who were accused of acting like *kai colo* were acting in ways that violated traditional indigenous Fijian values by doing such things as showing off, refusing to share, and inconveniencing an adult (the ethnographer). In this way, the children endorse the hegemonic equation of chiefliness and modernity among adults: a suitably modern child, well versed in the world of consumer goods, would and should act according to traditional Fijian values by being humble and generous and accommodating to those persons of higher rank.

Children's preoccupation with the contrast between rural villagers and their urban and overseas relatives were also apparent in frequent jokes about having smelly, yellow, or red teeth. Once, for instance, I happened upon two boys, playing tug-of-war, each claiming to have white teeth and accusing the other of having yellow or red teeth (Brison 2009b). The equation of toothbrushing with modernity was evident in the way that the boys used the English words *white, yellow,* and *red,* while speaking primarily Ra dialect, and also called each other "boy," in the course of the insults. "White teeth on this side, boy! Yellow teeth on that side." Again, this discourse is consistent with indigenous traditional values, since frequent washing and attention to one's appearance were considered a mark of proper respect for others. This point suggests that children, like adults, saw modernity and tradition as requiring very similar behaviors and used a discourse of modernity to reinforce very traditional indigenous Fijian values.

Although all children revealed a common preoccupation with modernity as a component of the competent self, close observation revealed some rather different gendered conceptions and ones that moved away from the neat equation of tradition and modernity.

Girls: Empowered Modern Women

I was first alerted to the possibility that boys and girls conceptualized themselves as different kinds of modern subjects by their use of language. All of the children spoke Bauan, the standard variety of Fijian taught in school and used in broadcast media, and some English. Most of the children also spoke Ra dialect, a regional variety of Fijian that was the preferred language of interaction within the village for most adults. I noticed, however, that girls used Bauan and English in spontaneous conversation to a greater extent than did boys, and some girls did not speak Ra dialect at all. When I asked people about particular children, they generally suggested that Bauan-speaking children had either lived elsewhere or had a parent from another region of the country. But this clarification did not explain the fact that girls seemed to use more Bauan and English than did their brothers. For instance, people said that one girl, Sera, spoke only Bauan even though both she and her parents had grown up in Rakiraki because her grandfather was from another area of Fiji. Consequently, the whole family was not from Ra, and it was not appropriate for his children and grandchildren to speak Ra dialect. But I noticed that Sera's brother, Viliame, did speak Ra dialect.

My own observations suggested that girls' greater use of Bauan and English indexed their orientation toward nonlocal communities such as international Pentecostal churches and urban areas of Fiji. Pentecostal pastors generally mixed English in their sermons to a greater extent than pastors in the dominant Methodist church, which was closely allied with the traditional *vanua* (landed community). Pentecostals also distanced themselves from local tradition by avoiding kava drinking, central to all village ceremonies, and by preferring hair and clothing styles (such as calf-length dresses and straightened hair) considered disrespectful in indigenous Fijian village culture. There was one boy from a Pentecostal family who had also lived much of his life away from the village who spoke mostly Bauan. But generally it was Pentecostal girls who preferred Bauan and English over Ra dialect. For instance, several small girls who had spent their whole life in the village and spoke Ra dialect also spoke Bauan and English in more contexts than did their male peers.

Girls' orientation toward a larger transnational Pentecostal world, as defined in church and by urban relatives, was evident in a series of interaction I recorded involving five-year-old Meri, who spoke primarily Bauan and English and who had lived in Suva, Fiji's capital, until she was three; and her cousin, Leba, also five, who had grown up in Rakiraki and whose parents were both from the village. Leba and Meri were sometimes joined by Leba's younger sister, Alisi (three), and by Sammy (four), a boy who lived nearby and spoke only Ra dialect. All of these children attended Pentecostal churches, so it was significant that Sammy spoke less Bauan than did three-year-old Alisi, possibly signaling gender differences in the place of Pentecostalism in the children's imaginary.

The prominence of church in the girls' world was evident when Leba climbed up on a stump and spread out her arms (as if on the cross), declaring, "Karen one Lord, this." This performance prompted a friendly rivalry when Meri ignored her and continued a previous game involving pretending she was taking Alisi for a ride in a car. Most of this conversation occurred in Bauan with some English interspersed, as indicated:

LEBA: Karen one Lord, this (pretending to be Jesus on the cross, spreading her arms)
... (to Meri) me Lord.

MERI (CONTINUING LEBA, PRETENDING TO DRIVE A CAR): Kua na
dua lako mai noqu motoka. Kerea na key.
No one can ride in my car. Please the key.
...

LEBA (to Meri): Me the Lord.

MERI: Alisi!

ALISI (to Meri): Au varau kauta yani qo na key.
I am getting ready to take away the key.

MERI: Karen Karen Karen Karen Karen ... my Mum is big fast because the baby [i.e., her mother is getting really big because she is pregnant] oh just my friend Vaseva and Buna (as her sister Buna approaches). Alisi, kerea na key.
Alisi, please the key.

LEBA (stands on the stump and spreads her arms again): Au na Kalou.
I am the Lord.

MERI: Kedaru na Kalou.
We two are the Lord.

LEBA: Au na Kalou; iko na egelosi.
I am the Lord; you are an angel.

SAMMY: Kedaru na Kalou.
We two are the Lord.

LEBA: Iko na egalosi.
You are an angel.

MERI: Au na egalosi.
I am an angel.

LEBA (waving to her cousin who looks after her, calling out to her in Ra dialect): Talei Karen u qoi o hoya abaki kei'ou iko!
Talei Karen is here and she is photographing us!

MERI: Au na egelosi; au Jisu.
I am an angel; I am Jesus.

LEBA: O au vaqo tiko kemuni dabe tiko I ra.
I will be like this and you will sit down there.

MERI: Au sega ni vako; iko vako ga. O au sega ni butako; iko ga butako.
I am not on the cross; just you are on the cross. I am not a thief; just you are a thief.

LEBA: Au sega ni butako!
I am not a thief!

MERI: Vakachiga ni iko butako vakachi.
Just pretend that you are a thief.

LEBA (POINTING AT SAMMY): O koya ga na gone qo me dau butako tiko; iko qai lai vako I koya.
Just him this child here can be the thief; you can then nail him on the cross.
. . .

MERI (STARTS SINGING): Jesus loves me . . . (Leba stands up and spreads out her arms again as if on the cross).

This interaction revealed an engagement with Christian themes by Leba and Meri, as well as concern with activities like driving cars, highly unusual for village women. The two older girls first vied for control of the game, with

Leba wanting to play Crucifixion and Meri pretending she was looking for her car key so she could take Alisi for a ride. When Meri joined the Crucifixion game she first claimed that both she and Leba were Jesus and then, when Leba told her she had to be an angel instead, pointed out that Leba, on the crucifix, must be a thief (since a thief was crucified along with Jesus).

These maneuvers revealed a sophisticated knowledge of Christianity for five-year-olds. Along with Christianity came a style of behavior frowned upon in the village. Both girls showed a keen desire to be in control of the game, which violated local norms. Meri was known among the local children as one who was unduly assertive for her young age. On several occasions, I observed local boys chastising Meri for being *siosio* (acting impertinent, as if one is someone of high status) and for showing off. In one instance, one boy remarked that Meri was the leader of the "bad girls." His use of the English phrase "bad girls" indicated that he associated this behavior with a world outside of the village. Meri's mother told me proudly that Meri was *siosio vinaka* (literally, impertinent in a good way) and that in contemporary Fiji, it was good to be friendly and outgoing with people you did not know because you needed to sell yourself to get a good job. These young girls, then, adopted a new assertive style of behavior along with the Bauan and English, marking an orientation toward a world beyond the village.

The girls' interaction also showed that they saw themselves in powerful roles as Christian women. For Pentecostal adults, Jesus and God were clearly male, and women were subordinate to men in the church hierarchy. But the girls were oblivious to this gender hierarchy and saw no problem with females pretending to be Jesus. From the child's perspective, Pentecostal women, including the wife of a Pentecostal pastor who drove a car, were more powerful than local women.

The appeal of this Pentecostal-extralocal identity for the girls was indexed by their facility with both Bauan and English, the predominant language of Pentecostal gatherings but not the preferred languages of most interaction in the village. Leba switched easily from English (addressing me) to Bauan (speaking to Meri and about Christian matters) to Ra dialect, when calling out to her caretaker. Even her three-year-old sister, Alisi, had a command of Bauan unusual for village children of that age. Meri had lived in Rakiraki since she was three. Her facility with English was unusual for a child of five, suggesting a knack for acquiring languages. But she spoke no Ra dialect at all. These linguistic patterns index the attraction of an extralocal world for these three girls where people do exotic things like drive cars.

The children's association of Pentecostalism with female autonomy was evident a few days later in a game of house involving the same children. The children alternated between pretending that a bush was an airplane they were about to board and a house where the mother was getting ready to leave her children to go off to work.

LEBA: Au na qai lako yani.
I will go later.

MERI: Mai tou lako sa vuka na waqa vuka.
Come let's go to the airplane, the airplane.

LEBA: Au na qai tu sa dua e noda'ou.
I will just be by myself at ours (at home).

ALISI: Keitou cakacaka.
We are working.

LEBA: Keimudou qai lako mai au sa tu vale. Au tu e vale au sa moce tu.
When you come back home I'll be at home. I am at home sleeping.

ALISI: Au lai cakacaka.
I am going to work.

LEBA: Kemudou qai lako mai vale. Au sa moce tu. Raica kemudou qai vaqo.
You will come back to the house, and I will be sleeping—look you two will be like this.

MERI: Sobusobu, Alisi.
Get off the plane, Alisi.
. . .

MERI (high-pitched voice): "Hey, who's in the house? Eh, it's Leba. What are you doing in my house?" Au qai lako tale.
I'm going back.

ALISI: Au sa kaba mada.
I will climb a bit.

Here again, the girls spoke mostly in Bauan and English, indexing an orientation toward an extralocal community. Alisi and Leba's mother worked in town, and the girls' house fantasy involved the mother going off to work, telling her children that they would be asleep when she came home in the evening. Although their parents were both from the village and had grown up speaking Ra dialect, the girls played house in Bauan. Interwoven with the house theme was a fantasy of getting on an airplane, an activity associated for all three children with Pentecostal pastors and their wives, who frequently traveled to international Christian conferences. I spent an afternoon with Leba and Alisi's pastor and his wife, looking through their photo album documenting their international travels. Meri's mother also recounted proudly how the pastor in her church and his wife traveled all over the world. The girls, then, imagined themselves within a transnational Pentecostal community where women worked, traveled and drove cars, and spoke English to visiting guests. Older girls also spoke more Bauan and English than did their male peers.

I suggest here that girls were oriented toward a larger world because parents were less likely to encourage them to form bonds with the local community. But girls also saw women's lives outside the community as superior. When the local girls imagined themselves as Pentecostal moderns, they constructed a world with potential to undermine the adult association of chiefliness with modernity. Chiefliness is ultimately a local identity, with each individual performing his or her role in a traditional, landed polity. But girls saw themselves as part of a larger world. Furthermore, the girls' play favored very unchiefly characteristics such as assertiveness and an ability to engage with high-status outsiders like myself.

The potential of such imagined modernities to lead to a very different kind of Fijian society in the future was evident when I interviewed Ema, a teenager in the lineage. Ema showed disdain for village life, which she described as full of gossip, jealousy, and "voodoo." She said that her parents wanted her to socialize with her fellow villagers, to speak Ra dialect, and to marry a boy from Ra but that she was determined to do none of these things, since local boys were "irritating" and tried to do love magic in order to "spoil" any girl bound for success outside the village. Ema took pride in behaving in ways that were frowned upon in the village, such as staying in her own room to "get something done," instead of wasting her time on visiting and socializing.

Ema was proud of the fact that she spoke English very well, in fact so well that a boy visiting from Australia had assumed that she must also have lived overseas. She saw no point in speaking Ra dialect, since she intended to live somewhere else when she grew up and had limited interest in keeping up ties with people in the local area. Indeed, she said that she had chosen to go to an Indo-Fijian secondary school instead of the indigenous Fijian school in Rakiraki village and had chosen an Indo-Fijian boyfriend in high school. Later, when she was attending teachers college, she had had several indigenous Fijian boyfriends, but she found them all "irritating" because they tried to control her and forced her to assume the proper modest dress and traditional hairstyle of an indigenous Fijian female.

Furthermore, unlike older women who were teachers (see Brison 2003), Ema did not see teachers as having any special responsibility for looking after the children of the community. She said she preferred to be posted in an Indo-Fijian school where she would not have to follow traditional indigenous Fijian ways. Ema's modern imaginary, then, broke the connection between modernity and chiefliness evident in adult discourse. She also challenged the firm ethnic divides in Fijian society by suggesting an emerging culture of autonomous, achievement-oriented youth who formed relationships across ethnic lines and resisted the pressures to bow down to ethnic traditions.

In contrast, as will be evident below, the boys of the lineage showed much more identification with the local group through their use of local dialect and awareness of dialect differences between regions. But they, too, blended this very local identity with a larger modernity, constructing an identity quite different from the girls' identity but equally defined in dialogue with a larger imagined modernity.

A World of Young Males

The boys of the lineage appeared at first glance to be much more firmly oriented toward the local community than were the girls. Like local adults, the boys distinguished people from their own lineage and village from those individuals from nearby villages or those persons who had lived part of their lives in Suva. Following adult practice, the boys defined a local in-group by speaking Ra dialect to each other but switching to Bauan in the presence of outsiders, indexing an identity rooted in the local *vanua*. But closer inspection revealed that the boys' orientation was less to a traditional village community than to their own local peer group. They saw themselves as part of a cadre of young antiauthoritarian males, which also included international sports and movie stars. This view was consistent with patterns observed by Union College undergraduates who accompanied me first to Rakiraki and later to Suva, the capital city, who noted a bonding among young men based on common school and sports team experience. These communities of young men often served as alternatives to traditional communities, where young men felt they were subordinated to older men and chiefs in ways they disliked.

Boys' preoccupation with fine distinctions in locality was evident even among very young boys. When I visited the local kindergarten, for instance, I found Leba and Meri playing with their cousins Tima and Mila, who had both grown up in Rakiraki. The four girls generally spoke to each other in Bauan. In contrast, the kindergarten boys spoke mostly Ra dialect, except when addressing Meri, who never spoke Ra dialect. The little boys were also aware of minor differences in dialects spoken by children from different villages. For instance, on one occasion two four-year-old boys, Morgan and Jone, were climbing some pipes stacked against a tree and then sliding back down again. At one point Morgan started imitating Jone, who had recently come to Rakiraki from a nearby region of Fiji and spoke a very slightly different dialect, saying, "Oso me au liu maqa maqa" (Move so I can get in front, no no). Here Morgan spoke primarily Ra dialect but used *maqa*, the word for "no" in Jone's dialect, instead of the Ra *ikei*. Morgan followed local adults in focusing on regional variations in common words such as *yes* and *no* and using these distinctive regional words to index someone as from another community.

On another occasion, some older boys began imitating the dialect of a nearby village in the presence of two boys whose grandmother came from that village. When I asked about it, they said that these two boys sometimes spoke this other dialect. The boys also showed their preoccupation with those individuals who were not from the village by switching to Bauan in the presence of children from nearby villages or in the presence of children who had lived part of their lives in Suva. My twelve-year-old neighbor who had lived in Rakiraki since she was five complained that none of the local boys would speak Ra dialect to her and that they laughed at her if she tried to speak it to them. In these ways, the boys clearly demarcated a local in-group that closely resembled the adult focus on the local *vanua.*

The boys' construction of a strong local in-group was also marked by nicknames they used for each other that were not used by the girls. None of the girls appeared to have such nicknames. One boy was called "Mr. MG" after a mongoose character on a children's television show whom he was supposed to resemble. Other names such as "Max" and "Mets" were anglicized short forms of names. Even little Sammy was called "Matua" (mature) because he was considered to be unusually precocious. The girls were familiar with the nicknames but did not use them.

These nicknames in some ways followed on a traditional practice of calling people by comic nicknames to mark some kind of idiosyncratic behavior in order to avoid using their given name. Name avoidance was an act of respect for some prominent namesake. For instance, everyone called one boy Mandela because he had been born on the day Nelson Mandela was released from jail. This boy was named after his grandfather, so calling him by his name would have been disrespectful to his grandfather since senior males' names were not used. But the boys' nicknames for each other differed from these traditional nicknames. The nicknames were used exclusively in the boys' peer group and were anglicized, unlike traditional nicknames. Adults placed people within a hierarchical community where one must exhibit respect by avoiding the personal names of high-ranking people, but the boys used special names known only to peers to show their solidarity as a group of young males.

Furthermore, the fact that these names were anglicized and sometimes drawn from television shows showed that the boys' sense of self was linked to a wider world of young men. The centrality of a larger world of mass media and modernity to the boys' identity was also evident in the frequency with which sports and mass media showed up in their play. For example, when I began videotaping a spontaneous game of rugby in the lineage compound one day, the boys stopped playing and suggested that we move over to the school yard because the videotape would come out better that way. When we reached the school yard, however, the boys quickly realized that they would not show up well if they played across the whole field and suggested that we move to one corner, where they could do "instant replays." This suggestion indicated a fantasy world structured by watching televised rugby. The boys began to reenact slow-motion instant replays, moving slowly through a series of dramatic plays and imitating the dialogue of international rugby players. Here the boys spoke almost entirely in Ra dialect, with English words interspersed as indicated:

SAMWEL: Slow motion! (They tackle each other slowly passing the ball slowly) . . . Herau va'akei Sikeli.
Uo two with Sikeli.

PITA: Bu sota sa naka.
Oops, knocked out.

SIONE: Ooo sa naka.
Oooo knocked out.

PITA: Sa naka ga o iko fuck off and die.
It's just you who are knocked out fuck off and die.

LUKE: Na lutu lutu liu . . . in the name of Lulu!
Fall in front . . . in the name of Lulu! [this is a nickname drawn from Pita's last name, Ralulu]
. . .
(Pita runs with the ball; Sione tackles him.)

PITA (to Samwel): Hia, hia.
Here, here.

LUKE: Au pasi ga.
I will just pass.

PITA: Mai boy, loma.
Here boy, inside.
. . .

LUKE: Kua ni bisaakinia ka vo'a ca!
Don't throw it to Bad head!

SAMWEL: Max, mai qi'o!
Max, come and play!

. . .

LUKE: Max!

MAX: Pasi, pasi. Solia!
Pass it, pass it. Give it!
(Everyone laughs): Out ball.

. . .

SAMWEL (to Max): Solia mai he o iko! Fuck off fuck off uba.
Give it here! Fuck off fuck off out there.

. . .

(Samwel and Sione start pretending to do rap music, imitating an African song, currently popular on television)

SIKELI: I enjoy it! (imitating a Coke ad)

. . .

LUKE: Amu nomu, motherfucker.
Not yours, motherfucker.

These brief excerpts from the slow-motion rugby game illustrate the prominence of mass-mediated sports in their imaginary. They spoke mostly in Ra dialect and interspersed English profanities and terms for rugby moves from television. They frequently called each other "boy." They broke into refrains from popular songs and from TV ads as if imitating the commercial breaks in a televised game.

This creative combination of Ra dialect and English mass-media masculinity indexed a special boys' modernity separate from the more refined world of girls and adults. The use of these English swear words and terms for rugby moves, combined with Ra dialect, indicated an orientation toward an antiauthoritarian world of young men. Ra dialect was the language for formal speeches in the *vanua*, but for children, it was more obviously a code associated with antiauthoritarianism since teachers discouraged the use of local dialects in school. For girls, Bauan appeared to have positive connotations as the code of a wider world where women led more autonomous lives than in the village, but for the boys, Bauan appeared to be a language associated with outsiders and submission to authority. Adults associated Ra dialect with local traditions and commitment to the hierarchical *vanua*. But for the boys, Ra dialect was an in-group code that indexed an imagined transnational world of antiauthoritarian young males.

The same patterns were evident on another day when I happened upon two boys sitting holding a rope, apparently doing a tug of war, each making car noises. When I asked a young woman who lived nearby what they were doing, she said they were imitating a Stephen Segal movie that had recently been shown at the village hall in which Stephen Segal prevented a car from escaping by holding onto a rope tied to its rear bumper. The two boys happily pulled at both ends of the rope making car noises, calling each other "boy" and accusing each other of having smelly yellow teeth, revealing a preoccupation with masculinity as defined by the mass media.

I saw evidence of a similar kind of masculine modernity in other young men who chafed at the restrictions placed on them in the traditional *vanua*, where they served older men. Peter Devine (2004), for example, studied the tattoos of young males in the Rakiraki area and found that many of them had special nicknames and insignia from boarding schools they had attended tattooed on their hands and forearms. They told Pete that these tattoos indicated the special closeness among people who had attended the same school and said that wherever they went, they could find alumni of their schools through these tattoos. Devine also found that many young men had tattoos such as *freedom* written in English on their chests and backs. Both the choice of words and the choice of language indicate an orientation toward a larger world where young men are not subordinate to *vanua* elders.

I saw similar patterns in the lineage among whom I lived. In this lineage all of the young men had left the Methodist church to join Pentecostal churches, a move that allowed them to bow out of almost all ceremonial events, since drinking kava, a central part of all ceremonies, was considered sinful in most evangelical churches. When these young men avoided ceremonial events, they also avoided being placed in a subservient role vis-à-vis lineage elders.

Another Union undergraduate, Brian Card, also encountered a similar orientation toward schoolmates as a substitute for the *vanua* in the young man Josua, who hosted him in Suva. In the course of living with Josua and his family for ten weeks, Card was struck by how seldom the family interacted with relatives. Instead, their social engagements almost always involved alumni of Marist secondary school, an elite school that Josua had attended. Josua told Brian that he disliked his family and his *vanua* because he was illegitimate and had been adopted by his father's sister at a young age. He felt that he had never fitted into the *vanua*. So extreme was his bitterness toward his relatives that when he contracted to play on a rugby team in Japan for several years, he did not tell his mother, who only learned about his move after seeing him on television. Josua said that he had gotten both his current job as a Marist club bartender and his previous job at a bank through school ties and that he had also arranged to play rugby in Japan through similar ties.

These examples show that many young men, like the Rakiraki boys, define themselves as members of translocal communities of young males in order to escape the hierarchical *vanua* where they are subordinate to senior men. As LiPuma (2001, 152) argues, young Melanesian men increasingly seek to distance themselves from a local community that they find unduly constraining but then have difficulty finding a place for themselves in urban professional society. I suggest that identifying with a transnational community of young males is, for many, a resolution to this problem. Social ties formed through schools always transcend local *vanua* and often, as in the case of Marist secondary school, cross ethnic divisions important in larger Fijian society. Young men like Josua make use of school ties to tap into international networks of rugby players.

Conclusions: Gendered Modernities

As the papers in this volume suggest, youth are often at the forefront of defining gendered modernities. Children are distinctively positioned in society and come to conclusions about global forces and ideologies that are quite different from the views of adults. Furthermore, children are often targeted by purveyors of modernist ideologies such as mass media, school systems, and religious groups. As the chapters also illustrate, however, children are not a unified group; boys and girls have different concerns and are impacted differently by discourses of modernity. This point is particularly true because modernity and tradition are gendered in most areas of the world, and so definitions of modernity transform gender roles and vice versa.

Here I have argued that indigenous Fijian village children are preoccupied with the distinction between tradition and modernity even though they are excluded from the discourses on these topics from the adult world. For adults, modernity is equated with chiefliness, and the resulting discourse justifies ethnic- and rank-based inequalities in the larger nation of Fiji. Children's experience of modernity and tradition, however, stems mostly from mass media, schools, contact with urban and international relatives, and Pentecostal churches. Village girls learn to equate modernity with the freedom and privilege they associate with Pentecostal pastors' wives and urban professional relatives. They eschew "chiefly" behaviors such as modesty and instead orient themselves to an imagined nation of Fiji where they can control their own lives and form friendships based on individual preferences rather than ethnic and kin ties.

The girls' experiences are shaped by adults who do not think it is necessary for girls to develop ties with the local community. But girls form conclusions that differ from the views of adults when they perceive urban and Pentecostal women to be autonomous, strong, assertive, and free of pressures to contribute to the *vanua* or submit to parents. Boys, on the other hand, develop a much more localized identity. But closer inspection reveals this modernity also to be an imagined one, where boys orient themselves to local and transnational communities of autonomous young men, free from pressures to bow down to lineage elders.

I suggest that these gendered modernities of youth have potential to transform Fijian society as both boys and girls locate themselves in imagined communities that foreground the importance of autonomy and personal choice and place lesser emphasis on attachment to a distinctive, ranked local polity. As children's identities become less rooted in the local community, it could well also signal a weakening of the strong ethnic divisions between indigenous and Indo-Fijians that currently structure Fijian society.

5

Androgynous Beauty, Virtual Sisterhood

Stardom, Fandom, and Chinese Talent Shows
under Globalization

HUI FAYE XIAO

In the future, everyone will be world-famous for 15 minutes.
    —Andy Warhol, exhibition catalog (1968)

[P]opular culture always has its base in the experiences, the pleasures, the memories, the traditions of the people. . . . Hence, it links with what Mikhail Bakhtin calls "the vulgar"—the popular, the informal, the underside, the grotesque.
    —Stuart Hall, "What Is This 'Black' in Black Popular Culture?" (1993)

Three decades of post-1978 rapid economic growth have made China the world's second-largest economy. Its 2002 integration into the World Trade Organization further affirmed its place in the global capitalist order. The accelerating marketization and globalization of the Chinese economy have changed every aspect of contemporary Chinese society, including its gender ideology and cultural politics. Transnational capital and cultural flows have brought in a variety of imported television programs broadcasting to the single largest national audience in the world. The threat of foreign cultural invasion has propelled a reform of the Chinese television broadcasting system that, combined with an emerging Internet culture and regionalization of visual culture, affects its youthful audience's perceptions of beauty, gender, and sexuality.

In the recent frenzied competition among Chinese television stations in adapting various Euro-American reality shows into localized programs, an arguably first made-in-China idol has been produced. The craze for the androgynous beauty of this unlikely new star has spread from mainland China to Taiwan, Hong Kong, and overseas Chinese communities mainly through the medium of the Internet. This new phenomenon of urban youth culture suggests not only dramatic changes in the definition of femininity in a globalizing China but also the enormous power of the new medium.

In this chapter I will examine how transnational popular imagination and visual pleasure transmute ephemeral televisual signals into universal moral and aesthetic legibility in an age of globalization. I will start with a survey of dramatic changes in China's television program production and consumption with a focus on the sweeping popularity of the talent show *Super Girl (Chaoji nüsheng)* and its winner Li Yuchun, a tomboyish girl with a deep voice and mediocre singing skills. Then I will investigate how the urban-based younger generation within or without the national boundaries of mainland China negotiate their cultural, ethnic, and gender identities through watching the reality show, becoming its fans, engaging in heated debates about it, supporting and imitating the young star, and forming online virtual communities and sisterhood. Tracing a transnational flow of iconoclastic images of androgynous beauty, I also analyze how a melodramatic structure of feeling of the talent show attaches emotional appeal and moral legitimacy to this "revolutionary" image of the "Super Girl."

As Liu Kang (1998) suggests, postreform China often deploys commercial popular culture to disseminate the state-sanctioned free-market ideology. Situating my analysis of the engendering of the *Super Girl* stardom and fandom against the backdrop of China's accelerating marketization and globalization, I propose that the excessive emotional manipulations of the *Super Girl* idol show sentimentalized and reshaped the competition and elimination mechanism of the show into a celebration of a seemingly impossible convergence of social mobility, market individualism, alternative sexuality, and "traditional" female virtues.

Chinese Television under Globalization: A New Trend

Despite the phenomenal expansion of the Internet in recent years, television broadcasting still secures a dominant position in the industry of mass media in contemporary China. Since the production of the debut television drama *A Mouthful of Vegetable Pancake (Yikou cai bingzi)* by Beijing Television in 1958, the Chinese television industry has developed speedily, particularly after the Dengist "Economic Reform and Opening Up" (*gaige kaifang*) launched in 1978. Up to 1987, China had 600 million viewers with 120 million television sets (Guo 2008). In 2005, every 100 urban households owned 130.5 color television sets, whereas every 100 rural households had 109 television sets, color or black-and-white (Landreth 2005). Chinese audiences spent at least three hours in average watching television every day (Ling 2006, 4). By the end of the year 2005, a multilevel and multichannel television-broadcasting network was established with a wide range of broadcasting technologies, including fiber-optic cable, satellite delivery, digital broadcasting system, and the Internet protocol television. There were 2,284 television-broadcasting institutions (including terrestrial broadcasters, educational television stations, and cable stations) that spawned 2,899 sets of television programs for 1.24 billion viewers. The rate of coverage of this enormous television-broadcasting network reached 95.81 percent (Society of China Television Broadcasting 2006).

The extraordinary volume of television programs caused outrageously intense competition among television stations nationwide. Currently, in addition to the state-owned and -controlled flagship news media, the China Central Television (CCTV), with its gigantic and controversial Koohas-designed postmodern headquarter towers lurking against Beijing's skyline, numerous local television stations at provincial, municipal, and county levels vie for a larger market share, which means higher viewers' ratings and commercial profits. In the battlefield of this fiery "eyeball economy," a shortcut proved to be exceptionally efficient and effective in churning out well-received programs at low cost of financial investment and production period. The successful shortcut to attract young urban audiences was to adapt various Euro-American competitive reality shows (à la *Survivor, Big Brother, Extreme Makeover, Who Wants to Be a Millionaire?* and *Dancing with the Stars*) into indigenous programs by making minor changes, adding local flavor and elements, and conforming to Chinese audiences' viewing habits and state-censorship standards. In the past few years, a large number of Chinese reality shows (*zhenren xiu*) have been produced in this way. The widely viewed ones include *Special 6+1 China Dream (Feichang 6+1 mengxiang Zhongguo)* and *Dictionary of Happiness (Kaixin cidian)* by the CCTV, *Lycra My Way (Laika woxing woxiu)* produced by the Shanghai Dragon Television, *Stars Dancing Contest (Wulin dahui)* by the East China Satellite Television, not to mention Hong Kong– and Taiwan-made television programs (Keane, Fung, and Moran 2007).

Overall, the CCTV, with its monopoly on state-controlled resources, still enjoys the lion's share of the television market. However, recently the Hunan Satellite Television (HSTV, or *Hunan weishi* in Chinese), a provincial upstart broadcaster, has gradually risen to challenge the cultural and commercial hegemony of the CCTV. The hinterland province of Hunan has always been regarded as a land with a revolutionary spirit. It has produced numerous reform and revolutionary figures (including Mao Zedong) in modern Chinese history, discussed in depth elsewhere (Platt 2007). In the same spirit of reform and revolution, the HSTV has shown its vitality and determination in revolutionizing provincial-level Chinese television broadcasting network ever since its start on January 1, 1997.

Avoiding politically sensitive topics to bypass the state censorship, the HSTV chooses to focus on the market of young urban audiences between sixteen and twenty-four years old. It spawned a series of popular youth-oriented entertainment programs such as *The Citadel of Happiness* (*Kuaile dabenying*) and *Romantic Date* (*Meigui zhi yue*) that set records in both viewing figures and advertising revenue (Barboza 2005). The sweeping popularity of these programs has not only established its leading position among local television stations but also decentralized the CCTV's hegemonic control of the mass media at a national level. On top of these exceptional achievements, the unprecedented success of the *Super Girl* talent quest by the HSTV planted the seeds of a revolutionary urban youth culture in presenting Li Yuchun, an idol of androgynous beauty, that would be totally unimaginable for CCTV-style reality shows.

This success immediately raised alarm in both the Administration of Radio Film and Television and the Chinese Propaganda Bureau. The latter's full name is the Chinese Communist Party Central Propaganda Bureau (Zhongguo gongchandang zhongyang xuanchuanbu, often abbreviated as Zhongxuan bu). The Propaganda Bureau controls the state apparatus of the official ideological propaganda. It supervises all the mainland Chinese institutions involved in the production or distribution of cultural products and enforces a strict censorship of news broadcasting, press publications, films, and television programs. In order to understand why Li Yuchun's androgyny was both so popular and so controversial at the same time, we now turn to a discussion of the multiple meanings *Super Girl* produced.

The *Super Girl* Myth

Super Girl has set a new benchmark for subsequent Chinese idol shows in the midst of the recent frenzied competition among Chinese television stations. The Hunan Entertainment Channel and the Shanghai-based Sky Entertainment Corporation (Tianyu chuanmei gongsi) coproduced *Super Male Voice Contest* (*Chaoji nansheng*) in 2003, the first attempt at adapting the reality-contest model for Chinese audiences. *Super Male Voice Contest* achieved regional success within Hunan Province, and in 2004, a female version of the idol show attracted even more contestants, viewers, and commercial sponsors. However, it was not until the year 2005 that the "quasi-documentary" idol contest reached its peak with the *Inner Mongolian Cow Sour Sour Yogurt Happy China Super Girl Voice Contest* (hereafter *Super Girl*). This title is a literal word-by-word translation of the Chinese name of the idol show, named after the major sponsor's yogurt product. A TV commercial featuring the 2004 *Super Girl* second runner-up enjoying the "Sour Sour Yogurt" was played prior to each episode of the idol show in 2005.

This show has achieved extraordinary popularity all over China as well as among overseas Chinese communities and has run for six seasons so far. However, owing to fierce competition from idol shows of the same type and the tightening control of the Chinese Propaganda Bureau, the glamour of the idol quest gradually faded out. In 2005, the cultural fever aroused by the second season of the *Super Girl* show spread far and wide, reaching an impressive range of social groups and Chinese communities. Starting from May when the nationwide registration for the singing contest began, a set of statistical numbers sent shock waves through Chinese television audiences: more than 150,000 female contestants between the ages of four and eighty-nine registered in the cities of Guangzhou, Zhengzhou, Changsha, Hangzhou, and Chengdou. Surpassing the popularity of the benchmark CCTV *Spring Festival Eve Gala* (*Chunjie wanhui*) and the national news broadcast (*Xinwen lianbo*), the viewers' ratings of *Super Girl* turned out to be the highest ever in China. Each weekly episode of this most-watched show drew more than 2 million faithful viewers. More than 400 million people tuned in to watch the final contest held on August 25. The Mengniu Dairy Corporation, the show's primary sponsor, invested 108 million yuan (around US$15.8 million) in its commercials that regularly appeared during the broadcasting of the show and unprecedent-edly expensive Chinese marketing effort (Tang Delong 2005). Thousands of reports about the show appeared in various mass media, including newspapers, magazines, radio, television, and the Internet. Google could easily retrieve 2,550,000 web pages featuring news entries related to the *Super Girl* show. Additionally, the largest Chinese-language Internet con-tent providers such as Sina, Baidu, and Tianya designed special forums dedicated exclusively to massive audiences' discussions, analyses, and debates about the show, which generated tens of millions of postings dur ing and after the show season.

This idol show marked a brand-new social and economic phenom-enon (ibid.), with "Have you watched last night's *Super Girl* show?" becom-ing the most often heard greeting phrase on the street. Indeed, *Super Girl* became one of the most frequently used cultural keywords in 2005 (Dai Xiaolin 2005). An album titled *The Ultimate PK* (Zhongji PK),[1] featuring songs by ten *Super Girl* contestants, sold 650,000 copies within just one month, immediately after the final round of the singing game. The DVD version of the show and a book titled *I Am Crazy about "Super Girl"* (*Wo wei "Chaonü" kuang*) also became instant best-sellers. A series of *Super Girl* performances were held in the ten metropolitan cities all over China and drew millions of fans everywhere, beginning on China's National Day of October 1, 2005. Thanks to its sponsorship of the show, the Mengniu Dairy Corporation doubled its market share, particularly among urban-based young consumers. Its products became the top brand in a shrink-ing domestic market, and other principal investors of the show including the HSTV, its collaborating Internet portals, and the telecommunications industry all benefited immensely from the program. With the unifying power of a globalizing market, the show not only boosted the growth of Chinese domestic economy but also caused the Hong Kong Weike stocks

---

1. PK is the abbreviation of "Personal Kill," a term used in video games. It was intro-duced into the *Super Girl* idol show as a central mechanism of instant elimination. In each episode of the show, two girls were selected to demonstrate their singing skills and compete for popularity among the audience members. The one who received fewer audi-ence votes would be eliminated on the spot. Now *PK* has been absorbed in the everyday use of Chinese language to refer to any kind of elimination mechanism and competition in any aspect of social life.

to rise 104 percent (*Economic News Daily* 2005). Reaching far beyond the entertainment industry, *Super Girl* became a synonym with for the most successful marketing strategy in China's globalizing economy to date.

What distinguished *Super Girl* from dozens of other Chinese versions of *American Idol*? One main reason was that its rules were unprecedented in the history of Chinese popular culture. Copied from Euro-American predecessors, the *Super Girl* idol show packaged itself as a singing contest open to any female who wanted to follow her dream of performing in front of a vast television audience and becoming instantly famous for thirty seconds. In the first round of screening (*haixuan*), each contestant was given thirty seconds to sing a song of her own choice with no accompanying musical track. According to Wei Wenbin, the head of the Hunan Radio and Television Broadcasting Bureau, "the 'Super Girl' show indicates the advent of a new age of the masses' self-entertainment" (Tang Delong 2005). He Jiong, a popular young host of *The Citadel of Happiness,* commented: "This show is great because it transforms girls-next-door into pop stars, talented daughters in moms' eyes into talented singers in everyone's eyes!" In other words, both the onstage participants and the audiences in front of the television screen were (self-)identified as "ordinary girls." More significantly, the rules of the singing contest differed radically from conventional CCTV-style evaluations, where the well-educated and senior experts got the unquestionable authority to decide on the contest outcome. Young audiences selected the *Super Girl* winners by sending in cell phone text messages and organizing voting campaigns online and offline.

The text-message voting mechanism triggered a heated discussion in regard to the relation between the Chinese state, civil society, democracy, and text-message voting. One netizen wrote in his blog, "I don't think that I will ever get to vote [for] a president in this lifetime, so I'll elect a girl that I like" (*China Digital Times* 2009). Prominent scholars, public intellectuals, journalists, and anonymous netizens were involved in this intense debate.[2] In addition to innovative game rules in the Chinese context, the show was even more unique and controversial because of its unlikely winner, the

---

2. The articles and online postings are too numerous to list here. To name a few widely read ones, see 2005 articles by Xu Jilin, Wang Xiaofeng, Ren Woying, Reuters, Ni, and Wang Shuang.

androgynous Li Yuchun, whose ultimate victory resulted from massive fan support via text messages and online portals.

The Li Yuchun Phenomenon

Labeled the "most unique and cool 'Super Girl,'" twenty-one-year-old Li Yuchun (also known as Chris Lee) attracted tens of thousands of fans domestically and abroad. Her unequaled popularity whipped up a storm of controversy. The rebellious image of this grassroots idol (*pingmin ouxiang*) defied conventional Chinese criteria for femininity, which aroused a series of debates centering on "androgynous beauty" (*zhongxing mei*) and "Chinese-style feminine beauty" (*Zhonguo shi meinü*). While her fans (mostly young girls) imitated her fashion style and behavioral manner and publicized passionate love letters to her online, more conservative audiences called this visually ambiguous figure "ladyboy" (*renyao*). Never wearing a skirt or heavy makeup, Li was said to be a "very boyish and unfashionable girl" (Zhao Yu 2005).

Li had a lanky figure with no prominent markers of physical sex. Her "masculine" facial features were said to resemble the traits of Yao Ming, the macho basketball player and the embodiment of China's globalizing sports market. Li often performed with her trademark orange-tinged spiky hair, husky voice, and Ricky Martin–style Latin dance steps. Additionally, her most well-known song was "In My Heart There's Only You, Never Her" (Wode xinli zhiyou ni, meiyou ta), a golden oldie originally sung by Liu Wenzheng, a male Taiwanese singer. Well loved for "being herself," a cool and handsome tomboy rather than a pretty and gentle girl, Li, the authorities' least-favored contestant, achieved the ultimate victory of the singing contest. The zealous support of her admirers changed the final outcome with 3,528,308 SMS (short-message services via cell phones) votes of all the 8 million SMS votes in the final week of the show.

Immediately after the end of the contest, Li Yuchun featured in commercial advertisements for domestic and foreign products such as Swatch and Coca-Cola. Within twenty-four hours after Li won the *Super Girl* contest, the "Divine Vehicle" (Shenzhou) Computer Company paid a million yuan (approximately US$150,000) to sign Li to be the spokeswoman for their high-end laptop. The company explained that they had handpicked her to do the computer commercial in the hope that their electronic products could become renowned and increase in value overnight, just as Li herself had done (*Southern Metro Daily* 2005). Capitalizing on the androgynous exteriority of the pop star, the Amoi Cell Phone Company paid Li an even higher price to advertise its new model, the "Straight and Handsome" (*Zhishuai*) cell phone. This innovative marketing strategy grabbed a huge market share, particularly among young urban consumers (Mai Jieying and Fang Nan 2005). These marketing campaigns further commodified and monetized the androgynous image of the youth idol. Meanwhile, they also crystallized the market-oriented competition mentality behind the *Super Girl* singing game.

In addition, Li's androgynous image graced the covers of widely read Chinese and English magazines such as the *New Weekly* (*Xin zhoukan*), *Sanlian Life Weekly* (*Sanlian shenghuo zhoukan*), *South People Weekly* (*Nanfang renwu zhoukan*), and *Time Asia*, and she was listed as one of Asia's heroes in 2005. Put in the category of "iconoclasts," she was said to be "defying pop star formulas" and marking the new trend of being innovative and true-to-self in radically changing times (Jakes 2005). In 2008, she was selected as number one in the "Fifty Most Beautiful People in China" (Sina 2009), sparking an online debate. Li's critics called her "Brother Chun" (*Chun Ge*) or "100% Macho Man" (*chun yemen*), suggesting that Li was too masculine to be considered a beautiful woman. On the other side, Li's supporters praised her "natural beauty" unmarred by trendy makeup or plastic surgery. One female admirer commented, "She is simple, pure, clean and neat. She will never please men with sex."

One of the widely read and much-debated articles on Li's androgynous beauty was by Cheng Naishan, a prominent woman writer. This article was titled "Androgynous Beauty Is a Purely Women's View of Beauty" (Zhongxing mei shi chuncui nuxing xinli de shenmei [2009]). According to Cheng, Li's androgynous beauty represents a global trend for modern women to prefer simplicity: short hair, an austere shirt, pants, and flat-heeled shoes. Cheng suggests that modern women do not admire traditional beauties whose hair is long and who adorn themselves with delicate makeup and exquisite clothing items. In conclusion, Cheng calls androgynous beauty a "feminist view of beauty" because it reflects women's views rather than male desires. However, she adds, this view of beauty is popular only among youth because women outgrow these tastes after their rebellious years. Following Cheng's article, some commentators agreed with her that androgynous beauty gives women more freedom in their lifestyle choices, while others criticized Cheng's "feminist tendency" to erase the essential gender differences between men and women.

A piece of representative criticism of Cheng's view was published by a netizen called Xiubo Shanren (2009) in his or her blog. In this article titled "Cheng Naishan: Why Do You Praise the 'Androgynous Beauty'?" (Cheng Naishan: Fukua zhongxingmei wei naban?), Xiubo Shanren countered Cheng's argument that androgynous beauty is a global trend. The author gave a long list of examples of feminine Euro-American celebrities including Madonna and Princess Diana. Toward the end of the article, Xiubo Shanren concludes, "The groundless excessive compliments on 'androgynous beauty' can only mislead women's view of beauty. Did we lack this 'androgynous beauty' during the Cultural Revolution? Those Red Guards in loose-fitting male military outfits looked so androgynous. You call that beauty?"

Obviously, economic and cultural globalization has shaped contemporary Chinese people's view of femininity. People like Xiubo Shanren celebrate stereotypically feminine Euro-American celebrities as an antidote to the Maoist model of "Iron Girl" or "Red Guard" androgyny. The chaos in sexual politics is also a common theme in post-Mao "Scar Literature" (*shanghen wenxue*), as Kam Louie (2003) suggests. In a similar vein, Mayfair Mei-hui Yang (1999) also argues that China's entrance into a global capitalist system can help liberate women's sexual desire and individual agency long suppressed by the Maoist revolution. Through establishing individual identity grounded in reinscribing the "erased" gender differences on sexualized bodies, women are able to carve out "a space of their own" from the state intervention. However, the overemphasis on polarized gender differences tends to lead to the production of a universal and essentialized gendered subject. Furthermore, this prevailing globalization of consumable feminine images also causes standardization, commercialization, and objectification of women's body and sexuality.

Virtual Community, Virtual Sisterhood

Since the mid-1990s, China has witnessed a revolution in Internet culture. Up to July 21, 2005, the population of Chinese Internet users was more than 103 million (CNNIC 2005). In July 2008, the number of cyber citizens in China was more than 253 million, and China surpassed the United States to become the largest Internet-using population in the world (Zhao Jin 2009). With such a colossal number of users, the Internet has become one of the major venues to spread news, gossip, rumors, and public opinions in contemporary China. It is particularly notable that when the Chinese Communist Party sought to bring more openness and transparency to Chinese society, they chose to charm the web-savvy younger generation by chatting online with them (Cha 2009).

Cyber citizens valued the way the Internet made interactive communication between distant people possible and enabled high volumes of information to be mass disseminated. The anonymity, speed, and illusionary sense of security and equality brought about by the Internet made possible a new virtual public sphere where participants celebrated freedom of speech. Ai Weiwei, an artist who helped design the Beijing Olympic stadium known as the "Bird Nest," hoped that the popularity of the Internet in contemporary China could pave the way to freedom of speech and participatory democracy. He said, "As long as people care about society's problems, they will go to the Web to look for information" (Jacobs 2009).

A netizen calling himself or herself Wen Zhongsi (literally "Thoughts of Writing") posted an article titled "Online Freedom of Speech Is a Good Thing" (Wangluo yanlun ziyou shi ge hao dongxi), stating that the "Chinese Internet has been the testing forum of freedom of speech since its birth" (2007). Similarly, in his January 14, 2007, MSN blog, Kai Guo wrote that the "Internet is the public sphere where we enjoy the freedom of speech to a greatest extent. I steadfastly support maximum tolerance towards all the online comments and speeches." Others endorsed Kai Guo's view. Netizen Xiao Gang wrote: "This is our freedom declaration, made for our freedom of speech. I don't want China to go back to the past era of Culture Prison or Cultural Revolution. What is wrong with China?" (2009). Countless online articles and comments of this type demonstrate Chinese netizens' yearning for the ultimate fulfillment of freedom of speech and their criticisms of China's current policy in regard to this issue.

The largest group of netizens, constituting 30.3 percent of users, is urban-based high school and college students ranging from eighteen to twenty-four years old, also the dominant demographic group of the *Super Girl* audience (Dai Zhikang 2008, 12; Qian Qing 2005). Obviously, the new medium of the Internet has played a pivotal role in the formation and shaping of *Super Girl*. The Internet provided easy access to public debates for marginalized and underrepresented social groups such as women, young people, and minority communities. Many grassroots stars such as Sister Hibiscus (*Furong jiejie*) and Back Dorm Boys (*Houshe nansheng*) achieved instant celebrity in the unbounded space of the Internet.

Similar to Li Yuchun, Sister Hibiscus is a girl-next-door-turned-star. Born in 1977 in a small rural village in the Shaanxi Province, she went to Beijing to take the entrance examinations for the graduate school of the Beijing University and the Tsinghua University. She became famous in 2004 for posting her saucy photos and writings on the bulletin-board system (BBS) of the Tsinghua University and Beijing University, which drew tens of thousands of hits each day. This "Sister Hibiscus" cultural phenomenon characterizes a case of rural women seeking to participate in a global cosmopolitan modernity through their bodily practices.[3] The "Back Dorm Boys" is a parody of the "Back Street Boys." Two college boys studying at the Central Fine Arts Institute (Zhongyang meishu xueyuan) created a series of hilarious videos of their lip-synching to Back Street Boys hit songs and circulated them online. As a result of the wild popularity of these videos, they became leading figures of the contemporary Chinese "spoof culture" (*egao wenhua*).

The Internet also brings stars close to their fans since stars keep blogs, posting pictures of their daily lives, keeping their readers updated on performance information, new hairstyles, and other personal trivia, and sometimes even revealing the daily fluctuations of their feelings and emotions. All these activities successfully bridge the vast distance between idols and their adherents and give readers the impression that stars are just average people. This "everyman aesthetic" (Keane, Fung, and Moran 2007) worked effectively among the youthful supporters of *Super Girl* idols.

Since the release of the first entry on December 23, 2005, Li's blog (http://blog.sina.com.cn/liyuchun) has been read 14,369,709 times. It promotes her latest album and advertises links to her fans' online networks. There are thousands of responses to each blog. The online comments reveal that teenage girls constitute the majority of Li's fans, who gave themselves

3. For a detailed discussion of this cultural icon, see Xiao Hui, 2006. Also see Cody 2005.

the name "corn" (*yumi*). *Yu* is a homophone of the first character of Li Yuchun's given name, and *mi* is a homophone of the character that means "fans." The association with food (corn) rendered the young (and dominantly) female fans consumable as they avidly consumed the star image of their idol. Thus, a virtual sisterhood has been forged between the girl-next-door-turned-star and her numerous adherents who sought a nonorthodox venue to break through the mainstream culture promulgated by the system of mandatory education and school life. Through interacting in online communities, young girls were able to make sense of their daily life and express their dreams, ideas, values, desires, and sentiments about coming of age during a rapidly changing period of time.

For example, responding to the first blog that Li Yuchun composed after the closure of the *Super Girl* show, many of her fans showed their support and enthusiasm. While some elderly commentators such as Qingfeng called Li a young kid and asked if she was male or female, Li's fans used the words *handsome* (*shuaiqi*) and *cool* (*ku*), normally applied to good-looking males, to praise her performance. One commentator, Snay, wrote on December 29, 2005, "I like you because I like girls who are true to themselves." Another enthusiast, Pianzi, wrote on December 30, 2005, "I never thought that I would love a girl so much, even more than I love a man." Some more conservative commentators inquired about scandalous "lesbian photos" (see below) and Li's sexual orientation in their commentary. One netizen, Huadan, wrote on January 18, 2006, "Is Li Yuchun a Lala [Chinese nickname for lesbian]? Why have I seen more and more Lala on the street after TA becomes a superstar?"[4] These comments raised sensitive issues that could never be discussed in school or at home. Li's fans such as Kegie and Zhgzh responded, "We don't mind if you are lesbian or not. We just support you!"

Li's fans also had their own websites. One of the largest fan clubs is the forum called the Li Yuchun Posting Bar (Li Yuchun tieba), established at Baidu.com, the leading search engine in China (CNNIC 2005). The Posting Bar is a new type of electronic BBS invented by Baidu. Unlike a

---

4. *TA* is the Pinyin romanization for both Chinese characters 她 (she) and 他 (he). The online commentator used *TA* instead of a gendered pronoun to emphasize the sexual ambiguity of the androgynous pop icon.

conventional BBS, all the postings on the forum are dedicated to a single subject, such as a megahit television show, a pop show, a pop star, a leisure activity, or a social issue. Theoretically, anyone can start such a "Posting Bar" on any subject matter. The easy accessibility provides technical support for the formation of virtual communities sharing a common interest, goal, or identity. There are hundreds of "Posting Bars" dedicated to pop stars, but the one devoted to Li always ranks the highest with its 2,377,000 topic threads, 46,636,633 postings, and 52,101 members, the numbers of which are still increasing each day. Occasionally, Li herself logs in and chats online with her fans.

Many posts speculated about Li's romantic life and sexual orientation. Many stories concerned Li's possible "homoerotic relationships" with other contestants. For example, in one episode of *Super Girl* broadcast on July 15, 2005, Li sang a popular love song, "You Are the Most Precious" (*Ni zui zhengui*), with Zhang Liangying, another contestant. Fans wrote enthusiastically about their onstage improvisation of holding hands and staring at each other "lovingly." One admirer, who appears from her Internet ID and profile to be a teenage girl, wrote: "I believe at that moment Liangying must have fallen in love with Yuchun. At that moment in Liangying's heart Yuchun is the angel who guards her through the dark night. At that moment in Liangying's heart Yuchun is the most precious one. I was so fascinated that my eyes were glued to them. I wish I could indulge myself in romantic love together with them" (http://tieba.baidu.com/f?kz=114444344). The fantasized female-female homoerotic practices worked as "a disruptor of heterosexuality, a presence standing outside the conventions of patriarchy, a hole in the fabric of gender dualism" (Zimmerman 1992, 4). In other words, the imaginary female-female homoerotic relationship challenges the universal model of heterosexual romance prevailing on television in contemporary China. This homoerotic fantasy does not necessarily cause girls to see themselves as lesbians. Rather, homoerotic romance gives girls a sense of empowerment and agency by undermining the dominant views of love and sexuality that always envision a woman's body as the passive object of male desire. Many of Li's fans revealed that they liked her because she did not make herself "sexy" or "feminine" in compliance with social gender norms. One netizen, Nanyumi, commented on Li's blog on January 4, 2006, "Many of my female friends told me they wish they were boys because they just want to be as free and unrestrained as boys."

Li's success on the Internet and on *Super Girl* both mark and promote a significant shift in Chinese gender ideology. Li's popularity even changed the conventional Chinese preference for boys of at least one television viewer, who wrote, "I always hoped that my wife could give birth to a boy. Watching the show totally changed my idea" (Lu Jun 2005). Many gay and lesbian people chose to come out of the closet online and established virtual communities such as the "Les Posting Bar." Chen Bo, a good-looking young man living in the Chongqing city of Sichuan Province, underwent a sex-change operation and publicly pronounced that he hoped to become another *Super Girl* idol and sing a song together with Li in the future (Zhou Rui 2005).

Yet attitudes clearly do not change overnight, as was evident when a controversy arose involving pictures of a young woman, who strongly resembled Li, kissing another woman that began to circulate online in August 2005. It significantly compromised Li's image as a pure and innocent girl and even jeopardized her chances of winning the contest. The "inside story" that Li was a lesbian quickly sparked a large-scale personal attack on her (Wei Hong 2005), and her previous image of being a pure and innocent girl was on the verge of collapse. This incident revealed the tensions between androgyny as an index of female power and homoeroticism as a radical challenge to family and gender roles.

Melodramatic Structure of Feeling

The unregulated and rapid circulation of information on the Internet resulted in the creation of a whole series of "inside stories" about the *Super Girl* show that were as significant in determining the outcome of the context as were the televised performances. These "inside stories" transformed the relentless competition among 150,000 young girls into a real-time unscripted melodrama that was able to fulfill people's voyeuristic desire and sense of mass participation at the same time.

In her study of melodramatic narratives, Linda Williams defines the melodramatic mode as "a peculiarly democratic and American form that seeks dramatic revelation of moral and emotional truths through a dialectic of pathos and action" (1998, 42). She proposes the three-stage model of "guilt-punishment-redemption" typical of melodramas with female protagonists, and this model fits the story of Li and the lesbian photos well.

In the first stage, Li's carefully constructed image of absolute purity and innocence was threatened by the wide dissemination of the homosexual photographs, which were condemned by conservative social commentators. In response, Li Yuchun made a public speech in the following week's segment of the *Super Girl* show, claiming that she was wronged and had nothing to do with the controversial photos. Confirming her honesty and moral integrity, Li's family stated that she was the same pure and honest girl as before the show.

Subsequently, during the broadcasting of the semifinals on August 19, Li suddenly burst into tears when another contestant, who had been a student at Li's school, was eliminated after three rounds of competition and voting off. Li cried so hard that she almost passed out, and this melodramatic display of emotion further resuscitated her image as a pure, unsophisticated, and honest girl who valued friendship over winning. The tears shed on and off the screen provided audiences with a great sense of moral satisfaction and thus strengthened their support for her. The pathos aroused by the virtuous suffering of a female figure ensured the continuity of the melodramatic narrative of *Super Girl* and made it possible to achieve the final happy ending, in the form of the champion title for Li Yuchun and huge commercial profits for the show's major investors and sponsors. The young audiences took an ambiguous position here: on the one hand, they were drawn to Li's androgynous beauty that defied current polarized gender roles, while on the other hand, they made Li conform to public morals by portraying her as a pure and innocent girl. The girls were clearly trying to reconcile female power with traditional values promoted by a current resurgence of patriarchy. In recent years, the revival of Confucian ethics under state sponsorship has caused gender conservatism and reassertion of patriarchy. Boundaries between male versus female and public versus private have been redrawn. Essential gender difference and traditional femininity that places great value on woman's moral purity, virtues, and civility have been promoted.

Drawing on Christine Gledhill's view on individual ego and performance, Williams adeptly analyzes the reliance on personality in melodramatic mode:

Adapting Peter Brooks's notion that amid the collapse of the sacred as the standard of value, the individual ego became "the measure of all things," Gledhill argues that this reduction of morality to an individual embodiment of ethical forces prepared the way for the psychologization of character and the performance orientation of twentieth-century popular culture. Faced with the familiar dilemmas of modernity—the decentered self, the failure of language to say what it meant—melodrama responded with a heightened personalization and expression of the self. The cult of the star fed into this personalization. The contemporary phenomenon of the commodified star whose task is not so much to act as it is to embody a "truthful" "presence"—an authentic performance of his or her "self." (ibid., 78)

This passage illustrates precisely how the performance of the true self of a *Super Girl* idol was constructed out of the very surface of the televisual representation of her physical exteriority. All through the show time, *self* (*ziwo*), *individuality* (*gexing*), *quality* (*suzhi*) (Keane, Fung, and Moran 2007), as well as *purity* (*chunjie*) and *truthfulness* (*chunzhen*) were the most celebrated buzzwords in Li's "Posting Bar." The strictest moral standards were applied to Li as well as other girl contestants, who were often evaluated not for their singing skills but for their "natural" revelation of their true self, purity, and moral innocence.

Writing about the recent Japanese teenager fad *Sailor Moon*, an anime (animated cartoon) of *bishôjo hîrô* (beautiful girl heroes), Anne Allison analyzes how the teenage girl warriors combine superpower action with attractive and cute appearance. Allison observes that "given that powerful women cause such discomfort for men and for society in general, they can only be tolerated by being assigned, or by themselves adopting, a (traditionally) 'feminine' masquerade: klutzy, inept, sexy, pretty" (2006, 144). Similarly, Li Yuchun's deliberate androgynization undermined prevailing feminine fashion to establish a more powerful female role. However, as in Japan, female power must be muted and cannot appear to undermine men. Thus, when Li appeared to go too far, she was attacked as a lesbian but was able to win back public approval by appearing to be an innocent, asexual girl with conventional feminine virtues of gentility, virginity, and moral purity.

Under such public scrutiny and emotional investment, feminine purity and absolute good are represented as constantly in danger of contamination that necessitates constant cleansing through excessive tears and virtuous suffering. In other words, the magic enchantment of the reality show comes precisely from its moral appeal through portraying young girls' feminized victimhood. Turning a singing contest into a nationwide election for moral models, the great power of affects in this melodramatic account of subject formation transmuted ephemeral televisual signals into universal moral legibility. Thus, "super girls" grew from nobodies to superstars as well as the embodiment of absolute good and innocence that society was said to have lost in an era of dizzyingly fast paradigmatic shift. In this sense, Li's "revolutionary" image of androgynous beauty fell back into the stock gender role of the virtuous victim. The combined forces of commercial culture, renovated Confucian ethics, and state censorship set limits on the rebellious potential of Li's star image. Thus, the gender norms questioned by Li's androgyny are ultimately reinforced in compliance with the demand of a state-regulated popular-culture market.

Feminine Masculinity or Masculine Femininity?

The *Super Girl* show also had a huge base of fans among Chinese diasporas who pointed to Li as the embodiment of Chinese national values. But this discourse on the made-in-China pop star often overlooked the fact that the new idol was aesthetically transnational and culturally hybrid rather than purely Chinese. Talking about androgyny and cultural identity under globalization, Lingchei Letty Chen acutely points out, "As a human figure embodying dual sexuality, androgyny serves as a metaphor for hybridity and the androgynous voice is a voice that articulates alternatives, not erases differences" (2006, 88). In other words, the androgynous image of Li Yuchun defies as much the cultural binaries of "Chinese versus the foreign Other" as gender dichotomies. The warm reception of Li's androgynous image among global Chinese communities revealed constant border-crossing cultural flows and integrations in the East Asian region.

Since the late 1970s, foreign films and television dramas have come to dominate the Chinese cultural market, as well as the popular imagination of a new lifestyle and its accompanying structure of feeling. Through the regional distribution of these seminal cultural products, a media regionalism was spurred by "the development of consumerism and electronic communication technology" (Iwabuchi 2001). Chinese audiences passionately embraced Japanese television miniseries and anime (animated programs and films). Since 1991, the particular *manga* (comics) genre "Boys' Love" (also known as *Yaoi*) has been imported into China and became extremely popular among Chinese urban girls (Welker 2006). The authors and readers of "Boys' Love" comic books are exclusively young girls, while the fictional characters are adolescent homosexual boys (*bishonen*) with seductive androgynous beauty. The new century has witnessed the rapid proliferation of "Boys' Love" comic books, stories and novels, magazines, and anime produced by young Chinese women. Numerous websites including general BBSs, fan clubs, and video-sharing portals were designed to provide forums for the distribution, appreciation, and discussion of these works. The most frequently visited ones include Blgl .cn, Blsu.com.cn, Blmoyu.com, Be-boy.cn, and so on.

Depicting the androgynous-looking teenage boys' romantic love, the palpable craze for this particular *manga* genre seriously challenges conventional gender norms. The chic-looking youngsters with stunning appearances in the "Boys' Love" *manga* transform condemned homosexuality into an icon of "cool kid" (*ku er*, the Chinese translation of "queer"), similar to Li's much-acclaimed cool image. Perhaps coincidentally, many postings centering on imagined romances between Li and other contestants took a similar *manga* form. These romantic and ambiguous homoerotic stories were often released frame by frame, with each frame composed of a well-taken close-up photo of a couple of intimate contestants and one or two lines of caption. This online *manga* format created and circulated among fan clubs provided a new language of visual icons and verbal signs for the young audiences to produce an alternative imagination about gender relationships within the boundaries of cyberspace.

Taiwanese popular culture played a pivotal role in translating Japanese "Boys' Love" *manga* into Chinese. This genre, mediated by Taiwanese translation, spread to mainland Chinese youngsters who look to the androgynous beautiful boys as a new model of beauty and sexual imagination. Similarly, the 1998 Taiwanese film *Bishonen* (*Meishaonian zhilian*, literally *A Love Story of Beautiful Boys*) portrayed a tragic love story between two beautiful young men and was adapted into a "Boys' Love" *manga* by its avid Japanese fans. Based on Kamio Yoko's popular Japanese *manga*, *Boys over Flowers* (*Hana yori dango*), another trend-setting Taiwanese idol drama, *The Meteor Garden* (*Liuxing huayuan* [2001]), featured four male protagonists who were collectively called F4, with *F* standing for "flower."

Famous for their physical beauty, they were called flowerlike beautiful men (*huayang meinan*), a metaphor usually devoted to pretty women. Having witnessed the regional popularity of *The Meteor Garden,* the HSTV invested a mainland Chinese version starring indigenous idols produced by its 2007 *Happy Boy* (*Kuaile nansheng*) talent show, the male version of *Super Girl.* The steady cultural flow and interpenetration helped propagate an emerging model of androgynous beauty, which rewrote the masculinity definition visualized normally by modern (read: Hollywood-standardized) muscular "tough guys." This model captured the pulse of trendy youth culture that yearned to challenge the heterosexual hegemony through experimenting with nonconformist sexual desire and gender identity.

Through the regional production, distribution, and reception of these popular melodramatic narratives, the legitimacy of the conventional sexual division of labor and absolute authority of patriarchs were generally undermined. Li's androgynous look could be read as a Chinese mirror image of the new feminine masculinity (or masculine femininity?) circulated in the Pan-Asian media coverage and popular-culture flows. This new type of androgynous beauty appeals to modern youth in China, first of all because of the glamour associated with the stars' images and their chic lifestyle, which provides the young demographic a space of imagination, identification, and self-expression of a cosmopolitan youth identity through consuming what they view as sophisticated commodities and visual cultural products. Furthermore, the ambiguity embedded in the popularity of feminine masculinity and masculine femininity enables young people to challenge conventional gender norms and explore alternative possibilities for performing gender identities. In this sense, the duality of regional politics and a globalized economy plays a significant role in the subject making of Chinese women through the mechanism of melodramatic representations.

Conclusion

In this chapter I examined the phenomenal popularity of the *Super Girl* talent show, a Chinese spin-off of *American Idol,* in a larger sociocultural context of contemporary Chinese society under globalization. Through a close analysis of audience reaction to the androgynous beauty of the "super girl," Li Yuchun, I explore the possibilities of forging virtual sisterhood in virtual online communities that often transcend the geographical boundaries of Chinese territory. This new type of female bonding centering upon an unconventional image of the new idol rewrites the femininity-masculinity definitions, and provides a powerful venue for young Chinese females to negotiate their cultural, ethnic, and gender identities. As a result, they are enabled to explore possibilities of alternative imaginations of self-image, intimate relationships, and sexual desires.

However, the "revolutionary" force of the model of androgynous beauty should not be overestimated. On the one hand, Li embodies young girls' desire to be liberated from time-honored prescribed gender roles; on the other hand, their phantasmagoric desire projected on the androgynous figure is often articulated in the grammar and vocabulary of melodramas that tend to locate purity and innocence as key female virtues. Additionally, the instant commodification of the androgynous figure in various television commercial marketing campaigns reveals the ultimate neoliberal logic of the idol contest, which makes it "politically compatible" (Keane, Fung, and Moran 2007, 171) with the official ideology of a market economy with "Chinese characteristics."

Under the great pressure of reorientation to survive in the neoliberal market economy, Chinese audiences project their yearning for "traditional virtues," which are supposedly long lost in the alienating and value-disintegrating development of the market economy, on the idealized image of the "super girl." In this sense, the immense appeal of *Super Girl* lies mainly in its melodramatic narrative and emotional investment, which transforms the show into a staging of various desires, sentiments, and fantasies engendered by the subject-making forces of the globalizing market economy, trans–East Asian cultural flows, and state ideology.

6

Teenage Girls and Global Television

Performing the "New" Hindi Film Song

SHIKHA JHINGAN

The image flickering across the television screen features a teenage girl running among the paddy fields in one of eastern India's rural corners. Viewers watch the girl playing with a goat and riding her bicycle in a bucolic setting far from media-saturated urban India. A first-person voice-over reveals the obvious: the girl comes from a small village in the state of West Bengal, a world away from the competitive big city. The girl, whose name is Antara, then appears on-screen, facing the camera, and says, "*Indian Idol* contest is very important for me as I will never get an opportunity to show my talent from this village." We now cut to a glittering studio space. The audience claps as the girl walks toward the stage. The studio lights are dimmed, and the spotlight is now on Antara. Attired in a bright-red chiffon sari with a spaghetti-strap blouse, dangling earrings, and straightened hair, Antara takes position, pointing the mike toward herself, and jerking her body softly with the beat of the music. As rehearsed, she turns her face meaningfully toward the tracking camera, at the right moment. As one of the *Indian Idol*'s top four contestants, it is indeed Antara's big night![1]

Antara's case does not take place in a vacuum: indeed, India is now home to one of the world's largest television markets, just behind China and the United States, attracting global media corporations to reach out to more than a million television households (Mehta 2008; Kohli-Khandekar

1. I would like to thank Ranjani Mazumdar and Sabeena Gadihoke for their thoughtful comments on the first draft of this chapter. I have also benefited enormously from my discussions with Ira Bhaskar on the performance, practices, and circulation of female voice in Hindi film songs. I deeply appreciate the support given by the editors of this volume, Susan Dewey and Karen Brison, for the editing of this chapter.

2006). *Indian Idol* was introduced by Sony Entertainment Television (SET) in 2004, as part of a much larger media phenomenon following the opening of the Indian economy to foreign investment in the early 1990s. Originally based on the British television series *Pop Idol,* this format was introduced by Fremantle media in South Africa, the United States, and Malaysia before it made its way to India. The promotion of the show before its telecast created a stir with the use of on-air teasers and print and web advertisements. The target audience was an age group of fifteen to thirty-four. During the voting period from November 2004 to March 2005, the talent show got more than 55 million votes via SMS (Kohli-Khandekar 2006). In 2007, *Indian Idol 3* caused a stir as two young men from the northeastern states of India won the contest, provoking debates about the show's potential role in bringing the youth of the marginalized northeastern states closer to the mainland.

The eight states of the Northeast in India include Assam, Arunachal Pradesh, Mizoram, Manipur, Tripura, Nagaland, Sikkim, and Meghalaya. Many of these states share their borders with Bangladesh, Myanmar, Nepal, and China. Most of these states are marked by underdevelopment and militant conflicts with the Indian state. The news media rarely report on these states unless they are hit by natural disasters or during the escalation of armed conflicts. As Nalin Mehta writes, "This new 2007 'fever' led to mobilization of a different kind, combining the imagery of television with the democratic process of voting" (Mehta 2008, 3). In the 2008 season, Sorabhee Debbarma, belonging to a tribal community from Tripura, bagged the *Indian Idol* title, a first for any female contestant or member of a tribal community. Many Tripura-based fan clubs campaigned in rural and urban areas to persuade people to vote for their homegrown contestant (Ali 2009). The chief minister of Tripura even used Sorabhee's success to urge the youth in Tripura to move away from the path of militant insurgency.

The expansion of the format market in television has been seen in light of the proliferation of global television in national markets, enabled by deregulation, privatization, and the advent of new technologies of distribution. The Indian television industry today attracts advertising revenue of approximately 1.4 million US dollars (Sharan and Turakhia 2008), a large chunk of which is cornered by reality shows. According to one industry spokesperson, "reality show advertisers pay almost 100 percent premiums over normal soaps per 10 seconds of advertising" (ibid.).

The process of rapid expansion of cable and satellite television in India began in the 1990s, closely linked to the liberalization of the Indian economy with the Indian market opening up for foreign capital and consumer (including cultural) goods. In the initial years, foreign networks including Star, MTV, and CNN dominated the field, evoking fears of cultural invasion. But by the end of the 1990s, "India was transformed from a major receiver to a major supplier" of media content (Mehta 2008).

Singing shows on Indian television challenge the dominance of the "Hollywood Planet" or the idea of the global monoculture. What is unique about a contest show like *Indian Idol* is its content, which is drawn from film music, the largest chunk of the popular music market in India. More important, their accent on heightened notions of performance, with larger-than-life images of teenage singers filmed using dynamic tracking shots and multiple screen projections, imbue the contestant-singer with a corporeality hitherto denied the singer under the playback system in Hindi cinema. Introduced in Indian cinema in 1935, playback technology created a split between the singer and the on-screen actor, or the aural and the visual. By the late '40s this split became official, as gramophone companies and radio stations started announcing the names of the playback singers. The contemporary body of the female contestant-singer is thus particularly significant in that it has become a site of multiple transactions where social mobility and consumption coalesce.

This chapter focuses on television's music talent shows to explore the dynamic of instant stardom available to teenage girls from small towns. Prompted by a desire for mobility, visibility, and success in the world of popular entertainment, these girls, barely sixteen or seventeen years of age, negotiate their own aspirations with the demands of the global television industry. What do these negotiations and mediations tell us about changing experiences of identity in a world dominated by the proliferation of media images? How are these popular shows making available new discourses on the aesthetics of musical performance in "Bollywood" music?[2] These are some of the questions I explore in this chapter.

2. I use the term *Bollywood* as understood to be distinct from the Indian film industry, which represents a diffused cultural conglomeration of films as well as a range of circuits of distribution and consumption activities from websites to musical content that developed only in the 1990s, with its eyes on the global market (Rajadhyaksha 2008).

The Journey of the Film Song on Indian Television

Since the arrival of the talkie (nonsilent) film in 1931, the film song has been an inherent part of Indian cinema. Teri Skillman shows that the technology of filming available in the 1930s, combined with poor-quality microphones, severely limited the movements of the actor-singers while performing a song. As Skillman (1986) notes, 1930s film technology limited movement in favor of improved sound quality. The microphones used for sound recording had to be stationary to eliminate excess machine noise. This requirement limited the movements of the actors while singing.

The introduction of playback technology provided freedom to the on-screen actress to move or dance while she moved her lips to the prerecorded song, in front of the camera. The singer in this new regime was rendered immobile, confined to a studio, making her disembodied voice available for circulation. The "ghost" voice of the woman amplified by the gramophone, the radio, cinema, and other technologies of dispersal became an object of desire, evoking enigmatic fascination. While singers of film songs became stars in their own right with fan followings, it was only on rare occasions that fans could see their singing idols perform onstage. As the state-owned television station and sole channel available to Indian viewers until the 1990s, Doordarshan did very limited recordings of leading playback singers which were shot in a somber manner, with the singers reading the lyrics from their notebooks. This style was especially associated with Lata Mangeshkar, one of the most respected playback singers of the Hindi film industry, whose songs often feature an enigmatic, ghostly quality.

Until the late 1980s, *Chitrahaar* was the only show on Doordarshan that featured film songs with their video clips, but unlike the state-run All India Radio, Doordarshan did not offer any space for requests made by the audience for film songs. The show itself was only a half hour long, too small an offering amid a growing film-music market, the expansion of which has been documented in Peter Manuel (1993). The unmet demand was filled by Metro, a second channel launched by Doordarshan to increase its revenues by selling time to advertisers.[3] Metro introduced *Superhit*

---

3. Metro was also used by Doordarshan to resist the rising popularity of private channels like Zee and Star. In her insightful work, Purnima Mankekar (2000) has shown

Muqabla, a one-hour countdown show of contemporary film songs. *BPL Oye,* hosted by Ruby Bhatia, became another popular show on Channel V. Both *BPL Oye* and *Superhit Muqabla,* produced by private production houses, started including music videos of Indi-pop songs on their shows. In other words, there was an explosion of popular music on Indian television in the early '90s with film songs often lined up with newly emerging Indi-pop songs with artists like Alisha Chinai, Baba Sehgal, Shweta Shetty, Sunita Rao, and Ila Arun performing in their own music videos.

In the cinema of the 1990s, the Hindi film song became an important vehicle for travel in the Hindi film narrative. Disrupting the continuum of the film by taking its characters to spectacular locations in Europe and America, the film songs functioned as "electronic catalogues of the post globalization commodity experience" (Mazumdar 2007, 108). Breaking the split between the heroine and the vamp, Ranjani Mazumdar shows how the song and dance sequences, through fragments and fleeting moments, offered on display desiring and consuming women, laden with performative registers of sexuality. The emergence of cable television generated hypersexual images of popular cinema, through countdown shows like *Superhit Muqabla,* trailers of upcoming films, teasers of music albums, and telecasts of films, accessible to Indian middle-class homes. Shohini Ghosh has shown that film songs such as "Choli ke peechey kya hain" (What's behind the blouse?) were targeted by women activists for depicting "obscenity," "vulgarity," and "indecency," creating moral panics to demand stringent codes of censorship from the Indian state. As Ghosh notes, "The images and representations that have simultaneously provoked outrage from both the Hindu right and feminists have been sexually coded representations primarily articulated around women's bodies" (1999, 236).

Writing on the 1990s, Melissa Butcher highlighted the figure of the socialite, the veejay, the model, the fashion designer, and the cricket star emerging with cable television's expanding space. According to Butcher, "The VJ represents a lifestyle that embodies the acceptability of the desire

---

that in response to the success of transnational satellite television, the Indian state further jettisoned its commitment to development communication by deregulating its operations by launching the Metro Channel.

for wealth and fashionable accessories" (Brosius and Butcher 1999, 175). The re-creation of the film song on television in the post-1990s was marked by a rupture, with advanced mobility, circulation of sexualized imagery, and uneven sound registers on "different overlapping levels such as regional, and national, local and global, individual and collective" (Brosius and Butcher 1999). The music videos on MTV and Channel V showing remixed versions of old film songs offered instant visibility and corporeality to the singer, who danced and moved her body with abandon, breaking older codes of performance.

Private channels were quick to realize the potential of film-based music on television. Zee TV cashed into this popular segment with *Close Up Antakshari* and *Sa Re Ga Ma*, the latter a singing contest show placing considerable emphasis on the quality of singing as demanded from a playback voice for film songs. The singers were judged by veterans of Hindustani classical music, music directors of the 1950s and the '60s, and established playback singers of the film industry. The mood in the studio was somber, with contestants touching the feet of the judges as a mark of respect. Although some contestants chose to sing contemporary and off-beat songs, the majority of film songs on the show were from the repertoire of old and classical film songs, evoking a nostalgia for the past, very much in tune with Zee's market positioning toward nonresident Indian (NRI) audiences. Bringing in a convergence of Indian entrepreneurship and NRI capital, Zee TV was also producing the idea of India for the NRIs, targeting the South Asian diasporas in Africa and the Middle East. After 1995, Zee was also beaming into South Asian homes in Europe and North America. Purnima Mankekar shows that "the centrality of NRI capital to the marketing of 'India' via transnational television crucially mediated the production and reterritorialization of Indian culture" (2000, 349).[4]

In 1995, Doordarshan's Metro commercial channel introduced *Meri Awaz Suno* (Listen to my voice), produced by Metavision, a company jointly

---

4. To target NRI audiences, Zee produced special episodes of *Close Up Antakshari* and *Sa Re Ga Ma Pa* that were shot in Dubai and London, inviting the NRIs to the studios. The themes of these episodes were patriotic; close-ups of teary-eyed audiences as patriotic songs evoking the feeling of exile, shared memories, and loss of home and loved ones formed a common refrain of these special episodes. The singers were used to evoke the idea of "India" through popular nationalistic film songs.

owned by singer Lata Mangeshkar and film industry elites Yash Chopra and Sanjeev Kohli. The lineup in the contest separated female singers from the male contestants. This move was in line with the practice of Bombay's music industry of creating separate codes for judging male and female voices. The contest was projected as a platform to search for an ideal playback voice that would match with a Hindi film hero and the heroine. The studio backdrop in *Meri Awaz Suno* was lined up with large posters of legendary playback singers like Lata Mangeshkar, Mohammed Rafi, Manna Dey, and Asha Bhonsle. In an important section in the contest, singers were expected to sing along with a running video clip of a song sequence (projected on-screen), matching the performance of the on-screen actor (lip-synching) as well as the vocal register of the original playback singer. In my personal communication with Sanjeev Kohli, the idea of the show was to select some talented singers who could do playback. Some of the contestants who made their mark were given an opportunity to sing for *Mohabbatein,* a film by Yash Chopra.

In other words, what was expected from the singer was a re-creation of the original song in an *imitative* framework. The body of the singer was masked by having the singer face the screen rather than the audience. The need was for a disciplined body, kept at a distance from the television viewer, producing the voice in sync with the projected song. In many ways, it caused a dissonance with new cultural practices and performance codes on Indian television as seen in channels like MTV and Channel V and shows like *Superhit Muqabla*. As shown by Brosius and Butcher, television audiences by then were already familiar with the use of dancing gestures, suggestive body movements, and facial expressions of the singer, enabling her to leave her *own* unique trace over a particular song. *Meri Awaz Suno* lasted for only two years (two seasons), but its rival, *Sa Re Ga Ma* on Zee, ran successfully until 2005, when it was reintroduced in a new format as *Sa Re Ga Ma Pa Challenge*. This remodeling was clearly exacerbated by the arrival of *Indian Idol*, introduced in 2004 on its rival channel Sony Entertainment Television.

Indian Idol was the first talent contest show that introduced public voting through SMS and direct phone lines, garnering the votes of fifty-five million viewers. The auditions for aspiring singers (held in four metro cities) evoked a huge response. The Indianization of the show was cleverly created by introducing animated visuals of all the major national monuments such as the Taj Mahal, Qutub Minar, and Lal Quila in one single frame. This sequence was followed by the familiar credit sequence of the international *Idol* format with animated robots (the idols) walking across a fabricated, acrylic walkway with one significant change. In this case, the walkway was lined with bright-colored Indian flags, elements removed from *Indian Idol 2,* the later version of the show. According to Vipul Shah, representing the creative team of Optimystix, "It's not a cake-walk to adapt foreign shows. They have to be modified to suit Indian sensibilities" (Unnikrishnan 2005). The duet song rounds, for instance, were unique to *Indian Idol,* in accordance with the show's excessive reliance on popular Hindi film music. This dependence is owing to the extreme popularity of romantic duets sung by the male and female leads in Hindi films.

Female Mobility and the "New" Hindi Film Song

The *Indian Idol* auditions were shot with rawness, using static, frontal camera work, no makeup on the contestants, and very little editing. The show's key strategy was to locate the aspiring contestants in a particular milieu; audiences were never allowed to forget the "ordinary" girl who was picked up from the auditions, a strategy deployed to court teen spectators. The journey of a singer from a small town, struggling to make it big in the world of music, was depicted using cinema verité–style grainy images, simulating the life of the contestant before she or he entered the *Idol* platform. Each time a contestant appeared to sing, a small video showed her journey to the *Idol* platform, sometimes a rags-to-riches story. In case of Prajakta Shukre, who came from Jabalpur, the video showed her with her friends in her school uniform, followed by a shot revealing her at the iconic marble caves of Jabalpur. Images of the contestant's mother or grandmother praying for her success on the show were a common refrain. A few shots of the neighborhood or a small-town street were edited together with the contestant speaking in first person as a voice-over. Stylistic devices like electronic noise were added to highlight the humble background of the singer and impart a home video aesthetic.

As the show progressed to the piano round, the contestants went through a makeover; accoutrements like hairstyle, designer outfits, and accessories were foregrounded by using camera tracking movements and giant back-projected screens. Farha Khan, one of the judges of the show, was especially hired to highlight the look and presentation style of the contestants. She said to Prajakta Shukre, "Oh my God! What a transformation! Are you the same girl we picked from the audition? I can't believe this!" To another contestant she remarked, "You were looking like an aunty when you came for auditions. Now you look like a star." Unlike the invisible body of the singer in *Meri Awaz Suno,* the singer's body here was clearly on display.

As the show moved to its gala round, props, designer clothes, and accessories highlighted through studio lighting were used to depict the journey that the contestant had made through the *Idol* platform. "With each week, we make the show more sophisticated," as Albert Almeda, the creative head of SET, explained to me. In *Idol 2,* the split screen was used to track each female contestant's makeover. Often all the contestants were shown shopping in malls with cash gifts that they had received from the show's sponsors. Clothes, accessories, makeup, shoes, and bags were all part of the shopping list. In another short vignette, which worked like a built-in advertisement, some of the contestants experimented with hair color products on camera. These images were mobilized to draw the female spectators to desire different adornments and an "enhanced" lifestyle. In one episode of *Idol 2,* Antara, who was always introduced as "a girl from a small village of West Bengal," asked Farha Khan, "Is *Indian Idol* only meant for good-looking girls?" Khan replied in the negative and then told Antara how attractive she was, while the screen was split into four vertical frames, each depicting Antara's improved look, starting from the audition to the gala rounds. This construction was clearly influenced by fairness-cream advertisements, deploying images of weekly step-by-step "improvement" of skin color. The show presented the mobile, visible body of the singer, adorned and "improved" by the luxurious offerings of a consumer society. As Nivedita Menon and Aditya Nigam write, "The new economy was not simply about consumption; it was equally about desire, pleasure, and production at a dispersed and molecular level" (2007, 86).

Thus, unlike the veejay or the socialite of the 1990s, singing shows like *Indian Idol* mobilize "ordinary" girls to speak to the youth about the aspirations that guide them to seek mobility. These transformations demonstrate how "ongoing changes in the imaginations and practices of a range of stakeholders" are involved in the global flows of Bollywood music (Kavoori and Punathambekar 2008, 6). Arjun Appadurai suggests the importance of imagination as a social practice and a form of negotiation between sites of agency (individuals) and globally defined fields of possibility (1996, 31). In her work on the Miss India Pageant, Susan Dewey (2008b) shows how the contestants use the intensive training program under the expert eyes of the celebrity trainers to seek social mobility. The trainees undergo a monthlong rigorous workshop, lending their bodies to experts from the world of fashion, fitness, film, and the beauty industry to not only build networks and resources that will provide them a quick entry into the glamour industry but also help to transcend their middle-class background.

Performing the Self on Global Television

I use the idea of mobility in an expansive sense that covers social, spatial, and aspirational mobility as well as mobility encoded in the aesthetics of performance. Yet this unlocking of imagination also has its pitfalls, as these contest shows are about "performing the self" in ways that necessitate the transformation of contestants into global consumers. However, my own observations point toward a complex set of negotiations undertaken by the female contestants to maintain some control in presentation of self against a powerful media industry.

Ankita Mishra, an eighteen-year-old contestant from *Indian Idol 3*, epitomized the convergence of singing and performing on live television, drawing a huge response from viewers on blogs and websites. Hailing from the provincial North India town of Kanpur, Ankita covered up for her weak singing by a unique style of performance, using the stage with great confidence, sometimes moving close to the judges. By pushing a tomboyish image, sporting jackets, hats, belts, and other accessories, Ankita explained to me how she carved a niche for herself:

> I told the producers from day one, "I want to move on the stage." They kept telling me to wait. . . . They knew I would not stop, so they would ask me, "What are you planning this time? How are you going to move on the stage?" Then there was this picture of mine on a motorbike in Kanpur. They starting using that. I always had lots of jackets and told the costume designers, "I will not wear sleeveless [garments]." It is not my style. For my performance of the "Chamma Chamma" song [from

the Hindi film *China Gate*], they gave me a butterfly dress. I refused to wear that and asked for a gypsy dress. For Helen's "Piya Tu" [originally performed in a cage by Helen, a Hindi film star], I demanded a cage and performed with it.

What we get from this account is a heady cocktail that combines singing with a mobile dancing body, available for consumption and endorsement on prime-time television across geographical boundaries. "Light has gone out from Indian Idol," wrote fan Pooja Sharma in 2009 following Ankita's elimination from the show. "Remember her. . . . *Piya tu ab to aa ja* performances that had a *big cage* on the stage. Did I notice that she had few of her notes up and down? I was too captivated to notice while I watched her. The audio of her performance heard stand-alone retains that special enthusiasm and confidence. It is contagious."

In a way similar to the young women working in call centers, teenage girls like Ankita use music (and dance) contests as a way to move out of the rut and "perform the self." As shown earlier, the emphasis in *Indian Idol* on locating the singer in her humble social milieu becomes a clever strategy to draw younger audiences. With the dramatic rise in the income and fortunes of the urban elite in postliberalized Indian, contest-based television shows offer an easier and perhaps the only route for small-town contestants from middle-class backgrounds to be part of this new aspirational world. Like the malls in suburban Indian, contest shows provide the "tangibility, the materiality, the facticity of desire that democracy needs" (Vishwanathan 2006). Attracted to the idea of glamour, stardom, and a good life, the contestants are ready to observe and play along with what the television industry demands of them. Shukre had been trained in Hindustani classical music in Jabalpur and had also participated in an earlier version of *Sa Re Ga Ma,* but she was quick to learn that *Indian Idol* was not about singing but about performing. As Shukre explained to me,

In *Sa Re Ga Ma* the performance was not very important. I remember we used to bring our own clothes, though it was a TV competition. There was a little bit of makeup just at a basic level, for the camera. And we used to sing standing at one place, and not much importance was given to expressions. But in *Indian Idol* format you have to be a rock star; you have to perform like that. If you look good and you carry yourself well, then people will like you more. Of course, you have to connect with the audience. So that those who do not understand music get moved by the use of hands, gestures, and performance.

Many of the girls who come from small towns remain in Bombay after they are eliminated from the show. Shukre, for instance, has bought her own flat in Bombay and is getting offers to sing for Marathi (a local language) films. As she explained to me, "I like to go back to Jabalpur for a few days to meet my friends and can see that the town is changing rapidly, but Bombay is where I want to be."

Saptaparna, a contestant from Star TV's *Voice of India,* came to Bombay to get training in Bollywood music at a well-known music academy when she was only sixteen. She cleverly chose to go back and give her audition for *VOI* from Guwahati in her native state of Assam. The television industry has been pushing the regional identities of contestants not only to pull in more votes, but also to deepen the reach of their networks in peripheral areas. This strategy suits the contestants, as they unabashedly use visual identity markers and often speak in their regional language to ask for more votes.

Defying any easy conceptualization, Saptaparna showed many facets to her personality, often speaking her mind on the show. In an episode dedicated to the theme of wedding songs, Saptaparna wore full bridal regalia as she sang a popular film song about the feelings of a young bride. After her rendition was over, she was asked what her ideal notion of a husband was. She was quick to reply that she never wanted to get married and was happy being single, thus destabilizing the impulse with which the episode on marriage songs had been presented. In another episode, Saptaparna chided Anju, a fan in the audience, who was being propped up by the producers as a love interest of a fellow contestant, a strategy deployed to pull in more viewers. Each time Ravi sang a romantic song, the camera showed Anju's reaction shots in close-ups. In what turned out to be a classic cat fight between two women on a reality show, Saptaparna confronted Anju in one episode. "Why are you wasting your time on Ravi? He is not even interested in you. Why don't you focus on your own life and career?" Anju protested, "You won't understand. You have never been in love." Saptaparna responded, "How do you know I am not in love? I have already fallen in love. My love is *my* music." The producers cleverly used this spat to spice up the show, highlighting it in the teasers. Yet, as Saptaparna explained to me, both incidents happened spontaneously and were not scripted. About the spat with Anju she said, "I had noticed that Anju always praised the boys' singing. She always said she enjoyed Ravi's or Vipul's songs. She never praised me or Rithisha. I never planned to say this, but somehow that day I could not stop myself."

Contest-based reality shows play with fact and fiction, drama and documentary often blurring the boundaries between these binary oppositions (e.g., Roscoe 2001). In the episode cited above, all these categories seem to have become fuzzy, including the one between text and the audience. I would suggest that this episode makes visible the anxieties of teenage girls living in conventional social arrangements. Yet what gets articulated is an ordinary middle-class girl's desire for mobility and escape from the predictable route of "finish your undergraduate degree, get married, and have kids."

In her work on teenage girls in the context of changing contours of youth cultures and femininity in Great Britain, McRobbie (1994, 172) reads *Just Seventeen,* a magazine targeted at teenage girls, as projecting a new diffuse femininity, far less invested in romance. This emergent femininity is a "product of a highly charged consumer culture which in turn provides subject positions for girls and personal identities for them through consumption" (ibid., 173).

Saptaparna's articulations on the *VOI* show are not so much about the "dislodging of romance from its place of cultural prominence" (ibid., 167) as they are about achieving success by presenting a self that is willing to be constructed, improved, and customized. Teenage girls like Saptaparna from small-town India look for opportunities to get away from gendered roles in order to access the glittering world of urban desire and high consumption. What motivates their desire to break out are proliferating images moving through the expanding circuits of global media.

The push for democratization on contest-based television reflects "the new economies of desire that include a series of new aspirations" (Menon and Nigam 2007, 85). With the liberalization of India's economy, sectors like banking, insurance, and the airline industry, hitherto controlled by the state, were opened up for privatization. The resultant transformations created conditions for the expansion of the Indian market for global consumer products often targeted at segmented audiences (D. Page and

Crawley 2001). Advertisements of numerous beauty products on television gave expression to young women's desire to enter the burgeoning service industry, selling the dream of upward social mobility with the help of consumer goods at their disposal. In her insightful work on media and mobility, Mankekar (2008) has suggested that young men and women working in the business process outsourcing industry rely on the codes of Hollywood films and other media produced in the West to better deliver their services to Western clients. In an essay on call centers, the Raqs Media Collective writes, "From [this] history has emerged a body, more specifically a larynx that is gifted at learning—very quickly—diverse accents, styles and manners of speech in the English language" (2003, 177–82). The information technology industry in India has been successful in creating an image of its workers as autonomous, flexible individuals whose work is synonymous with a youthful and cosmopolitan lifestyle (Sandhu 2008).

Popular Hindi cinema of the recent past has not shied away from staging such aspirations for mobility. In *Delhi 6* (2008), Sonam Kapoor plays the role of Bittu, a girl who aspires to make it big through the *Indian Idol* platform, "to become somebody from nobody." Indeed, *Indian Idol 4* cleverly used this film to showcase its own popularity by inviting the cast and the director to its show. *Bunty Aur Babli* (2005), directed by Shaad Ali, can be read as allegorical, bringing into sharp focus the aspirations of small-town youth who want to escape their mundane life, opting instead for mobility, adventure, and a wealthy lifestyle. The film begins as its protagonist, Vimmi Saluja (Rani Mukherjee), runs away from home to escape an arranged marriage with a head clerk to enter a supermodel contest. During the journey, she meets Rakesh (Abhishek Bachchan), who has also left his home in search of his dreams. The train is a constant motif, and the film begins with the song sequence titled "chhote chhote shehro se" (literally, "we've come from small, small towns"), which is itself filmed on a moving train.

Marked by absurdity, humor, and a self-mockery, *Bunty aur Babli* makes direct references to talent contest shows as Vimmi lines up to register for the Miss India contest. When denied entry, Vimmi picks a fight with the big-city girl by mocking her pretentious style. In their onward journey to Bombay, Vimmi and Rakesh take on the identities of two fictional figures, Bunty and Babli, ripping off people to make quick money. Their victims are those individuals who have become symbols of wealth in small-town India, such as the nouveaux riches who crassly display their wealth by showing off their luxury cars and ostentatious fashion garments. In several sequences, Babli caricatures the obsessive play with makeover as she is shown trying on face packs, hair curlers, and other beauty products. Babli plays with several identities, mastering the accent, the attire, and the persona in each performance.

When Bunty and Babli finally decide to move to Bombay, the train becomes a motif to set forth on imaginary journeys. Sitting in a freight couch of a moving train, Babli starts dreaming of her life ahead in Bombay as a song fades into the soundtrack. We are transported into a dark tunnel, with the camera tracking slowly toward the end, revealing a large studio space, with overhead lights, steel architecture contoured with grids, and a simulated Manhattan skyline as the backdrop. The journey to Bombay melts into a global arena, a simulated space, in which Bunty and Babli dance with abandon and hyperbolic energy to "Nach Baliye," a Punjabi bhangra number mixed with English lyrics. Bunty and Babli's fantasies are framed by the media, enabling them to inhabit spaces that are at once phantasmagoric and intimate.

Music contest shows such as *Indian Idol* produce the logic of globalization to create a sexualized imagery drawing on universal notions of beauty. The subject is produced through makeovers, improvement packages, grooming, and self-presentation. At the same time, these shows make room for teenage girls to produce a self that is encoded with mobility and performance. More important, contingent and emerging identities get imbricated in changing notions of femininity, as the singer acquires the freedom to move her body through a performative power that was denied to her in playback singing. Transnational television thus becomes a site for projecting imaginary journeys to simulated spaces, through the use of a mobile body.

Mauli Dave and the Changing Notions of Female Stardom

While the *Idol* format was making inroads into the Indian market through Sony television, Zee was still eyeing its audience base overseas, enabling a countermovement. In 2005, one year after the launch of *Indian Idol,* Zee introduced *Sa Re Ga Ma Pa Challenge,* an interactive music contest show based on audience polls. To give the show a unique touch of Indianness, each contestant was identified with a *gharana,* which was steered by a guru who would mentor the contestants and work on their strengths and weaknesses. *Gharana* is a school in Hindustani classical music representing a specific musical tradition. According to Ranade, it is the formulation of the basic music philosophy or ideology that influences conception, teaching, learning, performance, and codification of music.

The *gharanas* were represented by well-known and popular music composers of Hindi films, prompting a sense of competition between the composers and the contestants under their wings. In the second season of *Sa Re Ga Ma Pa Challenge, 2007,* the show was introduced as the "first world war of music," and auditions for the show were conducted in Dubai, Johannesburg, London, Pakistan, and the United States. The logo of the show depicted a globe with headphones. The unique synergy between transnational television and the Hindi film song on the Zee show enabled several interesting possibilities. Contestant singers from Pakistan, Dubai, and South Africa entered the show and generated a considerable amount of popular support.

Mauli Dave, a seventeen-year-old of Indian origin from Houston, became a rage on *Sa Re Ga Ma Pa.* Mauli had already won the crown of Miss Teen Texas and was rechristened as India's Shakira by her mentor on the show. Though eliminated in the thirty-seventh episode, Mauli Dave got a huge response on YouTube and other online forums, with several fans writing detailed blogs on her singing and style of performance, while others criticized her for just being a glamorous doll, with no singing talent. Here are two examples taken from the show's website:

> hi Mauli I am big fan of yours. And I love your voice, personality. And u r also very good dancer. u r mind blowing. When you sing there is fire on the stage. I think u will win Saregamapa 2007.

> Mauli, you cannot sing. Listen to your own past performances, and you will realize this. All you are good at doing is "oo"- and "aah"-ing, and dancing. I'm surprised that you have made it this far in the competition, because quite frankly you really do not deserve to be there.

Performing an identity as a second-generation Indian American, Mauli spoke with a heavy American accent, often speaking in Gujarati to appeal for votes. "I want to be a performer. I want to be an entertainer. I want to please everyone. I want to give the audience what they want. I want to give the composers what they want," announced Mauli on the show. Dressed in tank tops, short skirts, and leather boots, with her tall frame, Mauli Dave did not need a makeover, nor did she require a video to show her humble background. Yet Mauli presented herself as someone who was flexible enough to do everything required to woo her audience. Mauli's performance involved a mobility that stretched between two sites of identification: home and abroad. The following online exchange between viewers, taken from a website aptly titled "The Rise and Fall of Mauli Dave," clearly points toward this fluidity:

How does an American-Indian find popularity with the Indian masses? Mauli played the prodigal daughter. We aren't talking *Scarlett Johansson* here, but *compared to the rest of the girls on SRGMP*, Mauli did carry a corked carnality that set her apart and allowed her to stand out (Aspi)

Good post Aspi, while I was never a fan of her singing, she definitely made me take notice of the show. (the judges eye-popping reaction to mayya mayya promised oodles of future fun). Also all the contestants had a really great rapport with her, they weren't in awe of her ABCD [*American Born Confused Desi*/Indian]-ness but genuinely liked her as a friend (Leera)

Yes, Mauli was definitely the "u can love her, u can hate her, but can never ignore her" sorts. Her baby-voiced-talk along with her very cool-babe-looks, yet presenting herself as a very i-have-the-bharatiya-naari [idealized Indian female] values, kept people confused as to what the real Mauli is like. And everyone does like enigmas!!! (Anu G)

As early as the second episode of the show, Mauli created a sensation by singing "Mayya Mayya" (Dear Dear), a popular song composed by A. R. Rehman from *Guru* (2007). The lead vocals of the song, with liberal doses of Arabic words, were given by Maryam Tollar, a Canada-based Arabic singer, with backing vocal support provided by Chinmayee, a Tamil singer. The film version of the song "Mayya Mayya" featured actress Mallika Sherawat performing the sensuous number in an Istanbul bar. An upcoming star, Sherawat is known for her sultry performances in nightclub or item songs of Bollywood. A few weeks after its release, the song track of "Mayya Mayya" was cleverly edited to Shakira's music video for "Whenever, Whatever" and placed on YouTube. The coming together of a pool of talent as diverse as A. R. Rehman, Maryam Tollar, Chinmayee, Mallika Sherawat, Shakira, and now Mauli shows how deeply embedded Bollywood music is in transnational circuits of consumption. The intermeshing of languages, genres, vocals, and sound registers creates an enigma around the song but also enables it to reach out to global audiences. By performing this song in an impeccable style, Mauli managed to create an aura around her own persona.

Xiao (this volume) shows how online forums spread news, gossip, and inside information around a television contest show, exacerbating the democratization of *Super Girl,* as well as the show's melodramatic impulse. Mauli's presence on *Sa Re Ga Ma Pa Challenge* got an unprecedented response by online communities, with her fans claiming that her "Mayya Mayya" performance was the most viewed clip among singing shows on YouTube, outnumbering Sherawat's original performance. Those viewers who disliked Mauli scoffed at the idea of her being called India's Shakira, mockingly referring to her as "Shakira Ben," using the Hindi and Gujarati language term for "familiar sister" as a way to demean what her critics saw as overly affected efforts to appear sexy. What also needs to be emphasized is that Mauli's performance had given a new lease of life to "Mayya Mayya."

What is common to Mauli, Mallika Sherawat, and Shakira is the style of performance that relies on a dancing mobile body. In analyzing talent shows based on music on television, I have tried to draw attention to the process of democratization enabled by media technologies, as teenage girls, in conjunction with producers and audiences of television shows, intervene in the re-creation of the musical mode. By mobilizing new circuits for the consumption of popular music, singing shows on global television have completely transformed the aesthetics and the formal structure of the Hindi film song. With shrinking sales of film music in retail showrooms owing in part to piracy, the music industry is on the lookout for new sources of funding, and television has become one of the most important sources of revenue. Film producers and music composers target youth to yield songs that could become popular on television shows. The repetitive use of the hook line through television promos, singing shows, award nights, and other spin-off events leads to obfuscation of the original song. In this new formulation, the film song not only gets unhinged from the narrative of the film but also becomes a vehicle to evoke responses from dancing bodies.

It would be useful here to borrow the concept of redundancy (Fiske 1982) in interpersonal communication that is understood to keep the channels of communication flowing. In normal day-to-day conversation, phrases like, "you know," "I mean," "I am like," "What the hell," and "you see" are redundant or low information fillers that help maintaining the flow of communication. More important, these phrases add layers of meaning to conversations, enabling the insertion of an individual style. In a similar vein, the repetitive use of hook lines in songs like "Mayya Mayya" or "Nach Baliye" allows style to seep in, creating spaces for the singer-performer to make the song her own. The hook line in the contemporary songs work through this enunciative capacity of redundancy, opening up the song to express a unique style of performativity. Repetition also helps in creating an intensity of performance by making the live audience energized and responsive. This repetitive structure gives certain figurability to the dance movements, especially through the medium of television. Second, the repeatability of the song through hook lines creates an excess of repetition, allowing the singer-dancer the chance to create a spectacle in which the voice, orchestration, and a dancing body come together through heightened codes of visuality. The visualization of the song in the cinematic text creates a prophecy for its dispersal through an afterlife that is marked by fluidity; mined by transnational television as well as the Internet, the song can be reenacted anywhere in the global sphere.

The Indian music industry relies heavily on television shows and live events for the creation of value through a deferred economy of monetization. A whole range of stars have emerged through this new formulation. New stars like Mallika Sherawat, Malaika Arora, and Rakhi Sawant pose a serious challenge to film stars, emerging as parallel icons with a huge television fan base, but such stardom is not stable, as each star faces constant challenges from newcomers. Mauli Dave fits well into this lineup, as she carries with herself an aura of an American-born Indian with a unique persona.

I would suggest that the use of repetition (hook line) and heightened codes of visuality have allowed a large number of teenage girls to actively intervene on reality television and play with the *re-creation* of the musical mode. Having grown up listening to Lata Mangeshkar, on the one hand, and Shania Twain and Mariah Carey, on the other, teenage girls on singing shows are staging new codes of performance. The emphasis on style (props, gestures, and attire), a fluid dancing body, and a unique voice suggests a scenario where the global interacts with the local, creating complex circuits of fashion, beauty, music, and dance on global television.

Music contest shows dispersed through the circuits of global television may look similar in many parts of the world. It is important to interrogate how the local and the national popular forms mediate with the global, embedded as they are in specific industrial and technological practices. Format-based singing shows have engendered a whole new way of projecting the voice in Hindi film songs, in conjunction with the body—unleashing in its wake an inventory of images of teenage girls. In their quest for mobility, young girls are not only negotiating the terms for their own visibility on global television, but also questioning the disembodied voice and disciplined body of the playback singer.

PART THREE

Youth as a Symbol of Modernity's Contentions

7

Xenomania

Globalized and Gendered Discourses of the Nation in Cyprus

MIRANDA CHRISTOU

A typical scene at an urban mall in Nicosia resembles what Augé (1995) terms "a metropolitan non-place" devoid of localized features in favor of now familiar western European and North American styles. Clutching mobile phones, sporting the latest Puma athletic shoes, and pierced in trendiest of places, Greek Cypriot urban youth look much like their peers in any other European capital city. Yet on a different day of the week, these same youthful figures are equally likely to be found marching on the streets. Social scientists often deal with such disparate scenes in the lives of youth as distinct phenomena, focusing upon either the spectacular ubiquity of youth consumerism or the popularity of nationalist movements. My goal in this chapter is to span the conceptual gap between this customary division of disciplinary labor in order to analyze how "youth" is partially constructed through the intersections of discourses on globalization, nationalism, and consumerism. I argue that discourses of young people's consumer prac- tices—*xenomania*—reveal gendered constructions of indulgence and national resistance that dominate intergenerational dynamics in Cyprus.

This chapter is based on ethnographic material from a study on mem- ory and history in Cyprus where I explored how the educational system in Cyprus handles the issue of the 1974 Turkish invasion and continuing occupation: what kinds of stories students bring from home, what history is taught in schools, and how students, teachers, and parents negotiate their historical responsibility (Christou 2002, 2006, 2007).[1] My initial purpose

1. This paper is based on an ethnographic project that focused on the negotiation of memory and history in the Greek Cypriot educational system and the intersections

147

was to analyze how young people understand the national problem, and as the study progressed it was obvious that the generational gap was central in constructions of collective memory and history. I use here the concept of youth as a generation not in the strictly biological sense but in Mannheim's (1952) thesis that a generation is formed through the shared experience of historical and political changes. The older generation of Greek Cypriots has been through the anticolonial struggle in the 1950s and the turbulent years after the 1960 independence and, of course, remembers the events of 1974, whereas the younger generation has experienced the post-1974 semi-occupation. These different political experiences along with the changing landscape of economy dictate intergenerational dynamics and, I argue, show that, as in other postcolonial settings, youth are discursively constructed in the intersections of consumption and the nation.

The responsibility of maintaining the memory of the occupied part alive is explicitly communicated to the younger generation. Since 1974 schools have been decorated with the phrase "I don't forget and I struggle," and almost all national celebrations are linked to the continuing occupation and the new generation's duty to maintain the memory of those places as well as the desire for return. The "Cyprus Problem" consumes the everyday political, social, and educational life in Cyprus, and no reference to youth by politicians or educators misses the opportunity to emphasize their national responsibility to continue the struggle. For example, in his welcoming letter to all students in September 2004, the minister of education and culture reiterated, "Especially you, the new generation, ought to

---

between school and home narratives. During an intensive four-month ethnography (September–December 2000) I conducted high school classroom observations (of history, Greek language, and citizenship courses) and observations of national celebrations and interacted daily with students and teachers at the school. Apart from the ethnographic material, this paper is also based on fifty-five interviews with students (ages sixteen to eighteen), ten teachers, and eight parents as well as four focus-group discussions with students. All of the student interviews were conducted in the afternoon at student hangouts (mostly cafés) and at the students' homes when the interviews included the whole family. Analysis of the interview and observation material was based on the method of Critical discourse analysis as it was adapted for the study of national identities by de Cillia, Reisigl, and Wodaket (1999). See also Wodak et al. 2000; and Fairclough 1995. See Christou (2006, 2007) for findings from this project related to the construction of nationalism and national identity in Cyprus.

always be at the forefront of the struggle for reunification of our homeland and the establishment of peace and justice in our martyred island."[2]
This chapter analyzes how discourses of struggle are refracted through
discourses of globalization, fears of foreign-oriented consumerism—*xenomania*—and gendered constructions of resistance.

Nation, Youth, and Gender

"Youth" and "nation" are historically located in the eighteenth-century
socioeconomic transformations of Western societies and the emerging
political, social, and economic realities. The concept of the nation has
been linked to the material realities of modernity both in Ernest Gellner's (1983) modernist position that emphasizes standardized education
and increased mobility and in Benedict Anderson's (1983) seminal thesis on the spread of "print-capitalism" and the formation of "imagined
communities."[3] The concept of youth[4] appears at a similar moment when
the Industrial Revolution enforces social and educational restructuring

2. http://www.schools.ac.cy/dde/circular/data/Doc4501.pdf (accessed June 20, 2009);
translation by the author.

3. Definitions of *nationalism* vary and are usually reflected in the division between
"civic" and "ethnic" kinds, where nationalism is defined either as a form of civic loyalty to
one's national group or as a primeval drive to unite people of the same cultural heritage as
a single political entity (see A. Smith 1998). These various typologies of nationalism relate
to the different historical developments that have led to the rise of nation-states around
the world (from eighteenth-century movements to anticolonial struggles in the twentieth
century). Chatterjee (1986), for example, argues that the West's liberal-rationalist model
has defined Western nationalist movements as the norm and designated all other nationalisms as extreme and pathological. For the purposes of this chapter, I refer to nationalism in Cyprus when referring to the anticolonial struggle in the 1950s.

4. The concept of youth is often used interchangeably with the terms *adolescent* and
teenager, but their disciplinary loyalties in social sciences are easier to discern. Usually,
adolescent and *teenager* are associated with research in developmental and social psy-
chology and focus on the study of human behavior during a period of physiological and
psychological transformations that are considered important in preparing a person for
the final stage of adulthood. *Youth* is a term mostly used within the sociological and cultural studies literature where young people's lives are investigated as part of the larger
societal context and in relation to constructs such as ethnicity, gender, and sexuality. My
use of *youth* in this chapter reflects the perspective that the lives of young people cannot
be studied independently of how *youth* is constructed and debated, both in society and

that influences the way societies understood and distinguished concepts such as education, work, and leisure and private and public domains (Ben-Amos 1995). Youth is also rather obviously related to the concept of the nation through the idea that youth represents the future of the nation. In the "Great Leap Forward," China harnessed the power of youth for national reform. Similarly, the "Young Turks" were central in forming a powerful vision of the emerging Turkish nation. As Griffin argues in her 1993 book *Representations of Youth*, "Youth is ... treated as a key indicator of the state of the nation itself. ... Young people are assumed to hold the key to the nation's future, and the treatment and management of 'youth' is expected to provide the solution to a nation's 'problems'" (cited in Griffin 2001, 149). Not only have youth historically functioned as central to struggles or revolutions leading to the "birth" of the nation, but "youth" has also become the nominal category through which the dreams, hopes, and aspirations of a nation are realized.

This high national investment in youth alternates between adulation of young people's drive for change and the destructive potential of this drive. Indeed, the rebellious nature of young people has been identified not only in nationalist narratives but also in research: from G. Stanley Hall's (1905) early "storm and stress" model to Erikson's (1968) "identity crisis," youth have been portrayed as disruptive and defiant. Young people are expected to challenge authority and test societal limits by breaking rules or taking risks, oscillating between the view of "youth as fun" and "youth as trouble" (Hebdige 1998). In the history of the nation, this rebellious nature often appears to serve the national body because it is against the foreign, imperial, or invading authority that young people are fighting. This portrayal has certainly been true for Cyprus, when young Greek Cypriots took on the anticolonial struggle in the 1950s against the British colonial powers that had been ruling the island since the late nineteenth century.[5] The guerrilla war, fought mostly on the mountains, was the epit-

---

in academic research. For a literature review on youth and an argument for the use of the term *youth* instead of *adolescence,* see Bucholtz 2002.

5. The 1955–60 struggle against the British was not an independence struggle (as was the case with most British colonies) but a demand for union (*enosis*) with Greece, mainly supported by the Greek Cypriots on the island. The Turkish Cypriot minority (20 percent) present in Cyprus since the Ottoman era (1571–1878) was not in favor of union with

ome of defiant youthfulness that, on the one hand, exhibited faith in the nation but, on the other hand, disobeyed the law. Violations of curfews, bombings of colonial supply stations, and clandestine activities such as raising the Greek flag in schools became the mark of youthful national heroism. In this case, a deviant act was interpreted as righteous struggle and the defiance of law as resistance to an oppressive regime.

National rebellion, however, is gender coded, not only in the male-female representation of heroes but most important in how the construction of a national "hero" or "heroine" reflects prevailing gender norms and performances. For one, violence and defiance of law invariably concoct images of young boys' destructive and dangerous acts, as the male gender has become synonymous with risk taking. In the anticolonial struggle in Cyprus, it was young men who took on the role of fighting for freedom, and it was the young men who became icons and symbols to be imitated by the younger generation. Women's contribution was recognized in their practical support for these fighters but only in a generalized manner. Furthermore, national commemorations of the anticolonial struggle also honor the heroes' mothers—which is as much an acknowledgment of the work of motherhood as it is an explicit placement of responsibility on the mother for the nurturing of patriotic sentiments (see Anthias 1989).

In the context of the nation, gender is not simply a metaphor in the familial identification of the homeland (motherland, fatherland) but also a seemingly natural organizing principle in the social realm. Feminist critiques of the nation have pointed out the role of modern nation-states in legitimizing and reproducing patriarchy through policies of exclusion and exploitation (Anthias and Yuval-Davis 1989). The modern nation-state

---

Greece. In 1960 Cyprus became an independent country, cogoverned by Greek Cypriots and Turkish Cypriots. The period 1963–74 was dominated by intercommunal strife. In 1974, after a Greek-led coup overthrew the Greek Cypriot president, Turkey invaded Cyprus, claiming to protect the Turkish Cypriots on the island. The one-third northern part of the island has since been occupied by Turkish troops. About two hundred thousand Greek Cypriots became internal refugees in the South as Turkish Cypriots flew to the North. In 2004 Cyprus became part of the European Union, but the *acquis communautaire* (EU laws and regulations) is suspended for the occupied areas. A few days prior to EU accession (May 1, 2004), a UN-sponsored plan (the Annan Plan) for a resolution to the Cyprus Problem was voted favorably by Turkish Cypriots in a referendum but rejected by Greek Cypriots. Talks for a solution to the Cyprus Problem continue even today.

was constructed upon the exclusion of women (noncitizens) and the denial of sexual difference, while simultaneously the nation-state itself valorizes and universalizes "ethnic" difference (Alarcón, Kaplan, and Moallem 1999). On the other hand, the nation's reproduction rests on the biological, cultural, and symbolic role of women (Yuval-Davis 1997). National birth-rate levels and policies on population control employ women's reproductive role to articulate national survival. At times of war, women have either been excluded from decision making or become the site of militarization, domination, and control (Oliver 2007; Enloe 1989). Culturally, women are also appointed as the carriers of traditions and customs, bearing the responsibility of representing the purity of the nation's cultural expressions. As I will point out, discourses of the nation in Cyprus reflect not only the older generation's anxieties about youth's *xenomania* in a divided country but also both generations' gendered encodings of what constitutes struggle and resistance in the midst of these cultural challenges. I argue that just like the national youth hero is a gendered concept, so are current discourses on resistance that enmesh anxieties of a globalized culture with culturally organized concepts of a gender order.

Youth Consuming and a Nation Consumed

Xenos means foreigner in Greek. Perhaps the most widespread derivative of this word is the term *xenophobia,* which is defined as "fear of strangers or foreigners," and it is considered an indication of racism. *Xenomania* is a less common term in English, and its usage designates fascination—if not obsession—with foreign products. One could argue that the two terms stand on the opposite ends of a continuum, but there is no guarantee that someone who obsessively follows a country's brands and fashions will not hold negative attitudes against its people. As I will show in my analysis, *xenomania* is often used disapprovingly by the older generation in Cyprus to denote youth's consumer obsession with everything foreign. My purpose is to point out that this word is not simply a descriptive term but a concept underlined by national fears about youth's dedication to the nation.

Consumption is an activity that maintains an ambivalent position in the repertoire of human behavior because it is hailed at once as an indication of the healthy functioning of a "free" market economy, and at the same time it constantly begs the question of human agency in relation to corporate structures. The enveloping culture of mass consumption in the West has prompted concerns about the erosion of civic culture by private interests. From "conspicuous consumption" (Veblen 1965) to "competitive consumption" (Schor 1998), the desire to own more and better products has raised a putative conflict between democracy and the function of the free market that seems to be an integral part of Western democratic societies. In the case of children and youth, debates about the consumer desires and demands of young people often evolve into questions of morality and adult responsibility (Cook 2004). Young people are usually perceived as the scandalous casualties of market wars, seduced and deceived by advertisements, helpless to distinguish, disregard, or defend themselves. Consumerism remains a troubling behavior, especially when young people constantly express a desire for new products, thus raising questions about processes of socialization, cultural homogenization, and the maintenance of class lines.[6]

In other words, the consumption practices of children and youth are as much about personal choice as they are about the collective meaning of the producer and consumer identity. Clearly, the move from a society of producers to a postmodern society of consumers (Bauman 2005) also implies that every individual act of consumption is an indication of status and cultural capital (Bourdieu 1984); thus, consumption may be less about satisfying needs than about showing how we satisfy our needs. Consumerism represents not only the ambivalence of individuality versus collectivity but also collective dilemmas about the implications of having citizens absorbed by material possessions. Constantly purchasing goods is viewed both as the function of a healthy economy and as the possible sign of a nation in decay.

Furthermore, the state of the nation is often measured against citizen consumer patterns through what has been called "consumer patriotism," that is, preference for domestic versus foreign products. In his book *China Made*, Gerth (2003) describes the early-twentieth-century campaign in

---

6. A consumerist society is one in which "many people formulate their goals in life partly through acquiring goods that they clearly do not need for subsistence or for traditional display. They become enmeshed in the process of acquisition—shopping—and take some of their identity from a procession of new items that they buy and exhibit" (Stearns 2006, vii, cited in Deutsch and Theodorou 2009, 2).

China to promote the purchase of Chinese products and explores the ways in which consumerism contributed to nation building and the rise of modern nationalism in China. In Britain, the 1960s slogan "I'm Backing Britain" was launched as a government effort to promote British industry and British-made products. The campaign flopped when it was discovered that T-shirts with the "I'm Backing Britain" logo were actually made in Portugal, presumably because they cost less. As recently as 2002, UK manufacturers created the label "British Made for Quality" with the hope that it would boost consumer confidence in British products. In the United States, the slogan "Buy American" appears regularly, from bumper stickers in Detroit, Michigan—where the General Motors headquarters are located—to the Wal-Mart aisles. Evidently, in the age of globalized economies and transnational corporations, the country-of-origin distinction may be purely emblematic given that parts, materials, and even labor are imported. Consumer patriotism, however, remains a relevant issue both in its symbolic capacity as well as in the actual financial benefits derived from supporting the "local" economy—a point that is especially true at a time of economic downturn.

On the other hand, the phenomenon of globalization, defined as the transnational flows of people, goods, and information in an increasingly borderless world, has brought forth the question of how "consumer patriotism"—that is, preference for products produced in one's country—is inflected by the perceived dangers of cultural imperialism (Tomlinson 1991). Globalization is often referred to as another form of Americanization, especially in the ubiquity of McDonald's, Nike, and Coca Cola in virtually every corner of the world. Fascination with these products has ranged from the Hong Kong urban middle-class passion for fast-food birthday parties to Brazil's street kids' unparalleled knowledge about authentic Nike products despite their lack of access to them (Diversi 2006). Alternatively, this fascination has been met with opposition, both against the perceived unethical practices of transnational corporations (child labor, health risks) and against the idea of the powerful few controlling the fate of the rest of the world.[7] This interplay between obsession for foreign

7. Young people and youth organizations have been at the forefront of antiglobalization protests (World Trade Organization or G8 summit meetings in Seattle in 1999, Genoa in 2001, and Cancún in 2003), which aimed at curbing the influence of transnational

products and steadily growing resistance against them (Hooper 2000; Li 2008) has produced contradictory reactions. In cases such as China and India, the mobilization of consumer resistance against the infusion of foreign imports has employed cultural nationalism arguments by emphasizing the economic survival of the nation as well as the need to protect its spiritual superiority. The response has fluctuated from steadfast, organized resistance against purchasing foreign products to the valorization of local goods through approaches that often reproduce Orientalist images of Asia (Juluri 2002, Hooper 2000)

In this new arena of consumer indulgence and resistance, youth play a pivotal role not only as a site of investment by the media and advertising market (Kjeldgaard and Askegaard 2006; Juluri 2002; Deutsch and Theodorou 2009) but also as the prototypical exhibition of hybridity in a culturally globalized world. Young people are constructed in the intersections of consumerism and the nation whether they are organizing antiglobalization protests, negotiating the Indianization of MTV (Juluri 2002), or articulating through their consumer practices a glocalized identity in Denmark and Greenland (Kjeldgaard and Askegaard 2006). What these "youthscapes" (Maira and Soep 2005) demonstrate is the complex negotiation of globalizing forces that brings the heterogeneity-homogeneity question into new light. Consumption is a privileged site for the study of globalization and youth (Lukose 2005) exactly because of its capacity to engage the tensions in nationalism and cultural imperialism. Furthermore, the rise of the cosmopolitan urban middle class in postcolonial contexts highlights the centrality of youth's hybrid taste in the construction of class based dispositions (Grixti 2006; Fernandes 2000). Youth's *xenomania* or resistance to it is a pivotal issue in questions of globalization, and, as I argue, youth's consumer actions are fraught with anxieties about national identity.

Xenomania: Youth as a Locus of Adult Critique

Older Greek Cypriots often criticize the younger generation for being too absorbed by their everyday consumer needs instead of being more active

corporations in regulating the function of the world economy in order to maximize their financial interests.

in the national cause. However, if the national cause is to end the occupation through political negotiations, not armed conflict, it is unclear exactly how the new generation is expected to show its determination for a resolution to the problem. During my school fieldwork, I observed students in their preparations to demonstrate on the streets against the anniversary of the illegal declaration of the occupied part of Cyprus into a separate state (called the Turkish Republic of Northern Cyprus, a state recognized only by Turkey). This tradition has existed since 1983, but teachers felt that even though the students were taking this decision by themselves, they did not possess the necessary fervor that would stimulate them to protest passionately about what was going on in Cyprus: "Our babies are mild," said one teacher commenting on the demonstration. Other teachers chimed in to validate the semisarcastic comment and compared the students' behavior to their own "fighting spirit" during the anticolonial struggle. Most teachers argued that this demonstration was a habit, devoid of any true meaning for the students. Others predicted that students went in order to cut class and expected them to end up at the shops or the cafés before the demonstration was over. In fact, the younger generation's consumer indulgence became the main approach for explaining their commitment to the national cause. As one teacher told me:

> The new generation . . . grew up with more luxuries. They didn't go through the experience of being a refugee. They didn't have the experience of living in a tent and have the tent leak during the winter and you don't know where to sleep. We spent two months in a bus, and we were sleeping on the seats—from my grandfather to the youngest child—two months! We are another generation. We went through this hardship. But . . . these kids are used to luxury, and so they get used to easy money. And the parents give money too easily because they were deprived of it growing up.

Such critiques are constructed on multiple levels of comparison between the new and the older generation. First, the experience of being a refugee remains, for the older generation, an important point of reference in the gap between hardship and indulgence. Even though this teacher and mother would not wish on anyone to suffer in the same way she did as a child, she still holds that experience as emblematic of what young people today should need or desire. Second, the concepts of "luxury" and "easy money" are constructed around the experience of losing one's home, having to endure substandard living conditions, and being deprived of basic means to survive. These dynamics are not exclusive to the troubled island, despite the fact that Cyprus faces a unique political situation; the idea that young people are impossible to satisfy compared to the disciplined and austere upbringing of their parents seems to be a common intergenerational exercise. For example, a poignant argument in Malta is that young people today are never satisfied with what they have, compared to the older generation that used to be happy with less (Grixti 2006). The 1990s generation in Turkey is perceived as "turning the corner," moving away from the intensely "political" past and brandishing a rather individualistic and consumption-oriented lifestyle (Neyzi 2001). Juluri (2002) makes a similar point about the nation-building, Nehru-generation Indian parents who vicariously experience the contemporary uncontainable consumer culture through their children. Parents indulge their children's consumerism since it does not directly challenge traditional values, even if they are apprehensive of the highly sexualized images on the glocalized MTV Indian channel.

To make sense of these statements, however, one has to examine the larger historical and economic context of Cyprus. Following transition from British colonial status to the 1960 founding of the Republic of Cyprus, the island's economy functioned, for the first time, under the status of an independent state and slowly began to expand its agricultural and tourism sectors. The 1963–74 interethnic conflicts and the Turkish Cypriots' withdrawal from the government fostered uncertainty but also increased the socioeconomic gap between the two groups, with Greek Cypriots advancing economically compared to Turkish Cypriots (Kedourie 2005). The major and abrupt setback was the 1974 events that brought all major functions of the economy to a halt. Nicosia's airport, the only airport on the island at the time, was caught in the buffer zone between the two sides, while a third of the population lost its entire livelihood means and the tourist industry's major hubs came under Turkish military occupation. For Greek Cypriots, this transition forebode a future of dark economic times, but with a steady stream of foreign aid the economy in the South recovered at an unprecedented rate during the 1980s—a development that has been dubbed the "Cyprus Miracle"

(Christodoulou 1992).[8] Cyprus became a member of the European Union in 2004, in an awkward agreement that recognizes suspension of EU law in the northern part of the island currently not under the control of the Republic of Cyprus. The thirty-eight-year-old shift from refugee tents to a booming economy was met with a collective Greek Cypriot pride for the hardworking ethic that paid off. Nevertheless, the new comforts became an uncomfortable reality that contradicts the need to maintain the determination for a solution to the Cyprus Problem (Christou 2006). The younger generation exemplifies a materialist turn that, for the older generation, is at odds with the existential need to preserve this "fighting spirit."

To the eyes of the older generation, therefore, young people are ignoring the national problem through a seemingly constant obsession with foreign fashions. To be sure, a cursory look at the styles of the new generation would prove such a trend: showing off the latest fashions in clothing, music, and accessories or even adopting the now internationalized "minority" or "rebel" styles—Che Guevara T-shirts and dreadlocked hairstyle—seems to be an adequate indication of youth's *xenomania,* which is read as disregard for local products and traditions. What is interesting to consider, however, is that, beyond its descriptive capacity, *xenomania* is an ideologically loaded word that reflects an impossible dilemma. Taken literally, *xenomania* means a preference for foreign products. This meaning is certainly true for Cyprus, not because foreign products are chosen over domestic ones but because local alternatives are scant. As a small country that does not feature any kind of heavy industry—its economic mainstay is tourism—Cyprus is bound to be oriented to foreign markets. Despite a relatively prosperous economy in the southern part of Cyprus, the island is still dependent on foreign imports for all the major consumer goods such as cars and electric appliances and does not provide a competitive alternative for clothing or furniture. In other words, to buy foreign products is not a choice in Cyprus, but mostly a necessity and a way of life—everyone is a *xenomaniac* by necessity.

8. It is important to emphasize, however, that this outcome was not the fate of the northern part of the island inhabited by Turkish Cypriots. The lack of an internationally recognized status caused the economy to suffer, and development has been at a much slower rate.

Nevertheless, young people today are products of the new economic reality in Cyprus, shaped by the opening up of the economy to foreign markets in the 1990s. Their display of such prosperity, however, becomes an uncomfortable sight for those Cypriots who went through the experience of war, even when the experience of war is what they tried to overcome by focusing on building a new life and a new economy. Not only does *xenomania*, therefore, describe consumer trends, but it is a term that exemplifies the national fear of forgetting one's commitment to the national cause and being absorbed, indeed "consumed," by the pleasure of buying new and foreign things. In this way, *xenomania* moralizes youth's consumer behavior in relation to the national body and especially the problem of semioccupation. The older generation's drive for survival and prosperity in the face of hardship seems to have created a generation that can only take the hardship of nonstop shopping.

One of the most frequent comments about today's generation in Cyprus is that even the compulsory army service for young men has become too easy, catering to their increasing inability to face daily adversity. As one female student said, "The only thing missing from the army today is air-conditioning!" The younger generation of warriors is considered too "soft" to take on the challenge of an unwelcome but possible war. Commenting on the globalizing (or Americanizing) forces in Israel, Sznaider (2000) makes a similar point when he contrasts the different moral order of the "citizen warrior"—ready to fight, face hardship, and poverty—and the "citizen shopper" who is attuned to consumption and pleasure. In recounting the plot of *The Jewess of Toledo*, Sznaider (2000) points out that the book creates an opposition between knightly ideals and the Jewish woman who represents submission to worldly, material pleasures. In this scenario, the "citizen warrior" is an aggressive male, willing to use violence to defend the nation, whereas the female "citizen shopper" is kept busy with frivolous affairs.

This danger of the "citizen warrior" being feminized by the "citizen shopper" is a recurrent modernity theme. In her book *The Gender of Modernity*, Felski argues that the critique of commodity fetishism in modernity presents a persistently gendered subtext in that women are seen as weak and passive enough to be manipulated by the market: "Women are portrayed as buying machines, driven by impulses beyond their control to squander money on the accumulation of ever more possessions.

The familiar and still prevalent cliché of the insatiable female shopper epitomizes the close associations between economic and erotic excess in dominant images of femininity" (1995, 62). In the context of collective responsibility, therefore, the opposition between pleasure and sacrifice is nuanced by gendered undertones. This gendered opposition is what the older generation suggests when commenting on the lack of "fighting spirit" for the new generation. The implicit comparison is usually between the male heroes of the anticolonial struggle and the new generation's presumed inability to sacrifice for the nation the way these men did in the 1950s.

Furthermore, if youth's *xenomania* is an effeminizing feature, youth are also seen as dangerous because of their potential corruption by "Western values" (sexual behavior, drugs, consumerism) and often become the focus of social panics (Swedenburg 2007). In Cyprus, the panic is also a national one, given the need to preserve both tradition and the "fighting spirit" necessary for the solution of the political problem. Interestingly, some young people also argued that consumerism and materialism were responsible for Greek Cypriot's dwindling interest in the national problem. One sixteen-year-old student was especially caustic: "Cypriots like showing off. We take on foreigners' customs, their entertainment, their cars, their food. Ever since McDonald's opened up in Cyprus a lot of restaurants closed down. We don't go out to eat Cypriot food. We buy foreign clothes. Not that we have Cypriot companies making clothes. Whatever foreign people say, we do. We drink Pepsi Cola and Coca-Cola. Americans brought them here." He went on to explain to me that countries like China resisted importing McDonald's and told me that he avoids drinking soft drinks or going to McDonald's to make a political statement. Overall, the threat of *xenomania* did not remain limited to the sphere of economy (e.g., the problem of exporting domestic currency, stifling local economy) but evolved into a discussion of tradition and national responsibility. Foreign products were not problematic in and of themselves—given that some are necessary—but became symbols of national degeneration. As another parent told me, "We are obsessed with foreign things. We are obsessed with fashion and foreigners. Young people need to have deep roots, and they need to have tradition, to know their tradition." The question of tradition, pitted against the proliferation of foreign products and customs, is central in the construction of youth's ideal image: young people are expected to hold on to tradition even as they are revolutionizing their society. Tradition in this case is defined as attachment to the nation and its religious values, often referred to as the "Greek Orthodox tradition"; as one grandmother told me about her grandchildren, "They should be good Christians and good patriots." A prominent Greek Cypriot educator, Dr. Michalakis Maratheftis, argued that the "good life" has made the role of education today more difficult, indeed even more difficult than it was during British colonial rule, because it has absorbed people into a self-centered way of life instead of getting them involved in the national problem. He maintains, furthermore, that one of the biggest dangers to national identity is the "negative outcomes on the Greek Orthodox tradition and way of life brought about by foreign customs which are imported through tourism and the media" (1992, 145; translation mine).

At the cusp of a nation's survival, young people represent both hope and anxiety: they are potentially the generation that will solve the national problem but also the generation in danger of losing sight of the problem. Youth are constructed as the promise of the nation and as the obstacle to the nation's survival. Their consumer behaviors are alarming to the older generation at a time when the nation's hopes rest upon them. When young citizens focus on the pleasure of consumption and self-fashioning, they are not seen as likely to surrender a comfortable life for self-sacrifice. Young people, therefore, are seen as caught between the gendered opposition of the "citizen shopper" and the "citizen warrior" (Sznaider 2000).

National Resistance and Gendered Collective Memory

When you have the group of mothers of the missing people who go and demonstrate at the Green Line, I think that's a big achievement because for [thirty-eight] years they have been persisting in this, and they don't let it go. But to have some young men go over there with picket signs to show their machismo, I don't think this shows interest in the cause. Or to have people killed at the Green Line, I don't think that this is interest. They did not do those things because they felt them. They did them because they wanted to show off.

—Eleni, seventeen years old

In August 1996 the Cyprus Motorcyclists' Federation organized a symbolic ride to the Green Line in Cyprus in order to protest the continuing occupation in Cyprus—a trip that had originated in Berlin and ended in the easternmost town of Deryneia, adjacent to the buffer zone. The ride brought together leather-clad, unshaven youth who fashioned their motorcycle lifestyle as rebellion to conventional social norms and whose long hair and tattooed arms signaled a stereotypical form of masculinity. The male-dominated procession derailed when some, acting spontaneously, entered the UN-controlled buffer zone, chanting slogans. One man who was not part of the motorcycle ride was caught in the barbed wire and bludgeoned to death by a group of Turkish Cypriots. Following his funeral a few days later, a crowd gathered again at the scene. His cousin managed to swerve by UN soldiers and attempted to climb the Turkish flagpole. He was shot dead.

These events were exceptional in that such violence at the buffer zone is uncharacteristic of the quiet yet fragile truce in Cyprus since 1974. The two men who died in 1996 are considered martyrs, but for the students, who watched these events unfold live on television when they were thirteen years old, the most powerful symbol of the occupation has been the persistent weekly protests by the mothers and wives of the missing persons. In my question as to how they understand the meaning of "struggle" in the phrase "I don't forget and I struggle," almost all of them brought up the women's struggle for the memory of missing persons and the fact that maintaining this memory is a collective indication of a "fighting spirit." Eleni's comment goes a step further to contrast the "machismo" of the motorcyclists' ride to the peaceful protests of the black-clothed women who bring the pictures of their loved ones at the Ledra Palas checkpoint in Nicosia every week to demand the truth about their fate.[9] For the new generation, accused of *xenomania* and obsession with global fashion, these women who embody the shopper antidote have come to symbolize the national struggle. Interestingly, the national struggle was gendered, first, in the identification of "real" national heroes in the faces of the 1950s male

9. In July and August 1974 it was estimated that about 1,619 Greek Cypriots were officially missing persons. This estimate has been continuously revised, especially since the beginning of exhumations by the Investigative Committee for Missing Persons (established in 1981) in August 2006, something that had been a constant demand by the missing persons' families since 1974. DNA testing on remains found in mass graves and other locations identified by witnesses have, to date, led to the identification of more than 160 missing persons (both Greek Cypriots and Turkish Cypriots).

fighters and, second, in the designation of the wives, sisters, and mothers of missing persons as the purest symbol of national struggle in the current political context. As I have noted elsewhere (Christou 2006), the younger generation identifies with the older generation's nostalgia for the 1950s struggle against the British and the genuine "fighting spirit" of that time. In the post-1974 context, however, it is the mothers of the missing persons who truly embody the purity of the struggle. Schoolbooks are decorated with pictures of these women, and many posters that circulated in the 1970s presented images of Cyprus as a grieving mother and reflected the trauma of 1974 through their pain.

Women's protest, often in the form of peaceful demonstrations against the state itself, has provided alternative political spaces to contest both nationalism and prevailing gendered norms. From the Plaza de Mayo mothers of Argentina's *desaparecidos* to the women in black and their antiwar protests in many parts of the world, including Israel, Colombia, and Serbia, women have performed political resistance by embodying not only suffering and struggle but also hope (Sutton 2007). The demure and persistent presence of wives and mothers of missing persons at the checkpoint in Cyprus evokes the personal extent of a national tragedy and constitutes a powerful statement of the relatives' determination and hope to find the truth. Young people talked with admiration about these women and identified the meaning of national struggle with the women's resolve to hold political leaders accountable for the fate of the missing persons. At the same time, however, such admiration confirms women's designated national role as the "natural" proprietors of peaceful sentiments that do not challenge the nation-state's legitimacy. Whereas there have been incidents of wives of missing persons publicly challenging the government to be more active in searching for the missing persons (see Cassia 2005), in most cases, these women's presence at the Green Line corroborated the official state rhetoric that named them tragic victims of 1974. The articulation of their pain is also one of the few times when women in Cyprus can be seen in the media talking about the Cyprus Problem. As Vassiliadou (2002) argues, women in Cyprus have acquired political consciousness not by struggling against patriarchal structures but through participating in peace groups that address the "ethnic" conflict, failing to recognize the double oppression of nationalism and patriarchy (see also Cockburn 2004; Hadjipavlou 2006).

What is interesting, furthermore, is how the mothers and wives of missing persons represent for young people a form of pure struggle epitomized in the fact that their regular presence at the checkpoint, black-and-white photographs of their relatives held up front, calls attention not to themselves but to the painful collective loss of human life. Unlike the 1996 events, which became a battle of muscle and arms—one man attempting to lower the enemy flag, another man shooting him from a balcony across the street—the women's struggle is an act of self-effacement, where the focus remains on the missing persons and the pain of being suspended between mourning and hope. Youth's iconization of the wives, mothers, and sisters of the missing persons as symbols of the national struggle reflects the gendering of memory not only in what women remember—pain and suffering—but also in how the memory of this suffering is represented through women's bodies. As gender becomes the performativity of suffering, women are identified with sacrifice that is defined through their black-clothed, mourning figures.

Conclusion

Both discourses of national struggle and fears of globalizing forces of *xenomania* expose gendered understandings of what constitutes sacrifice or self-indulgence. The question of whether the nation suffers or indulges itself in unfettered consumerism is refracted through the everyday consumer practices of young people, and it is also reflected in how youth is identified with the self-denial and selfless sacrifice of the women relatives of missing persons. In the same way that young people themselves are constructed through fears of *xenomania* and global homogenization, discourses of struggle and national resistance are played out in the dimension between sacrifice and self-serving pleasure. Furthermore, at the center of these dynamics lies the construction of youth through the discourses of consumerism and national struggle that respond to the recurrent problem of youth as a political and ideological force. In the case of postcolonial societies such as Cyprus, the cultural-ideological domain is shaped by the legacy of colonialism, anticolonial nationalism, and their negotiation in the new global order that throws questions of tradition, modernity, and Westernization into sharp relief (Lukose 2005).

The implicit nostalgia for tradition and purity is evident in the critique of *xenomania,* in the longing for a (male) heroic youth and the discovery of chaste struggle in women's silent bodies. This romanticization of the past by Greek Cypriots lies in viewing 1974 as a major rupture that not only divided society into two generations but also divided historical time into two starkly different periods: the simple, idyllic, and presumably peaceful pre-1974 time that was followed by destruction, pain, and the decadence of consumerism. The occupied areas symbolize not only the land that is no longer accessible but also a time of tradition and roots that has given way to the indulgence of modern times. For the older generation of Greek Cypriots, "modern" is what came after 1974; therefore, the invasion of 1974 is narrated as the invasion of modernity that unsettled people, mores, and fundamental identity values. The post-1974 context is vilified as national degeneration both politically and culturally; foreign products, images, and ways of life are seen as a form of cultural invasion. In this nostalgic critique, the female gender becomes a metaphor of purity: on the one hand, the female is identified with the dangers of self-indulgence and frivolity, but, on the other hand, it holds the possibility of redemption by carrying a pure and selfless struggle against the invasive enemy. In the context of globalizing forces in Cyprus, youth's *xenomania* reveals gendered constructions of national resistance that dictate intergenerational dynamics.

Children as Barometers of Social Decay

Perceptions of Child Sex Tourism in Goa, India

SUSAN DEWEY AND LINDI CONOVER

"Enjoy our beautiful beaches," reads a billboard on the palm-lined road that ferries arriving European and Israeli vacationers from Dabolim Airport to resorts in the western Indian state of Goa, "but remember that Goa is not a pedophile's paradise." This jarring statement, accompanied by a photograph of a young ethnic Goan[1] child's smiling face juxtaposed against a sweeping backdrop of blue skies and sandy beaches, raises a number of troubling questions about the social costs exacted by an economy heavily dependent upon the whims of its foreign visitors, many of whom carry independent conceptions of Goa that are rather incongruent with the beliefs of local people.[2] Accordingly, this chapter describes the complex ways in which conflicting cultural norms and gendered discourses on sexuality and migration intersect in institutional responses to child sex tourism.[3]

---

1. We use the term *ethnic Goan* specifically to refer to individuals who self-identify with the term *Goan* not as an indicator of their state of residence, but rather a complex constellation of ethnocultural markers, including Catholicism, consumption of certain foods (particularly seafood and *feni,* an alcoholic beverage made from cashews), and a sense of distinction and separateness from predominantly Hindu and Muslim India.

2. Such incongruency is particularly problematic given the state's dependence on tourism. According to statistics gathered by Dewey at the Goa Ministry of Tourism, tourism-related revenues constitute 34 percent of the state's gross domestic product. However, the volatility of the tourism market became painfully obvious to Goa residents following the Mumbai attacks in 2008, after which some Goa residents estimated tourism-related visits and associated revenue went down by 90 percent.

3. The Optional Protocol on the sale of children, child prostitution, and child pornography of the UN Convention on the Rights of the Child defines child prostitution as "the use of a child in sexual activities for remuneration or any other form of consideration"

Goa has a unique position in India as a predominantly Catholic state and former Portuguese colony that attained independence in 1961, nearly a decade and a half after the rest of the country. Since its forcible incorporation as an Indian state following an invasion by the Indian Army, Goa has witnessed sweeping socioeconomic changes that resulted in increased economic dependency upon tourism and emigration, both of which have been accompanied by new ways of thinking about gender roles. In order to understand the complexity of these realities as they are experienced by many ethnic Goans, this chapter asks two interrelated questions: what do responses to child sex tourism reveal about the complex realities inherent in a tourism-based economy, and where, how, and why do individual actors assign blame in sex tourism cases? In answering these questions, we argue that discussions about child sex tourism have become a locus through which Goans express discontent about the state's failure to effectively manage tourism in ways that directly benefit ethnic Goans.

Methodology and Brief Synopsis of Findings

Findings presented in this chapter are the collaborative result of independent research in Goa by Dewey on tourism and nongovernmental organizations for three months in 2002, two months in 2004, and one month in 2007, as well as independent research by Conover specifically on nongovernmental organizational responses to child sex tourism for two months in 2007. Our independent research methodologies focused upon a variety of actors, most notably including orphans and other children in institutional care, ethnic Goans who work in the tourism industry, tourists, and NGOs that include child sex tourism in their portfolio of prevention activities. The strategies of these NGOs vary widely based upon the national origin of their leaders, and the most disturbing consistency Conover in particular found in speaking to such NGOs was the tendency of individuals, charities, and established organizations to assign blame to members of another ethnic group or community.

(United Nations 2000). The full text is available at http://www.unhchr.ch/html/menu3/b /k2crc.htm.

Charities and NGOs founded in Goa to combat sex tourism and protect children often repeatedly mention ethnicity in conversations about their work. For example, NGOs staffed primarily by ethnic Goans and other Indians typically insist that pedophilia is the exclusive domain of white foreign tourists, many of whom fit a narrow profile of aging, middle-class western European men who knowingly exploit to their advantage the financial and other inequalities between Goa and their home countries. Other NGOs established by western Europeans in Goa often express sentiments that domestic Indian tourists and Goan locals are responsible for the vast majority of child sexual abuse. Through her participant observation research, Conover was privy to a number of conversations in which Goan NGO employees and volunteers expressed particular frustration about the unequal relationships between tourists and locals that underlie at least some of this assignation of blame.

Findings presented here also draw upon Dewey's longer-term cross-cultural research on sex work, NGOs, and the international organizations that help to regulate both has shown that the way social problems are constructed reveals a great deal about the state of contemporary societies in ways that are often less about the actual crisis under discussion than the cultural context that frames it.[4] As this chapter will repeatedly argue, discourse among nonactivist ethnic Goans and NGO representatives regarding child sex tourism frequently represents children's bodies as a sort of metaphorical stage for the enactment of these "modern" inequalities.

A "Paradise for Pedophiles"?:
Gendering the Repercussions of Tourism

How do so many widespread social anxieties become manifested around a single social issue of unknown proportions? Sociologist Zygmunt Bauman argues that such patterns are symptomatic of what he terms "liquid modernity," in which people "have no choice but to try to reach some sort of completeness and order in their lives out of all the in-betweens with which they are confronted so that they can make some sort of sense of the world in all its contingent excess" (cited in Blackshaw 2005, 11). Bauman

---

4. For a more in-depth discussion of this phenomenon, see Dewey 2008a.

argues that an increased sense of insecurity worldwide combines with the declining ability of nations to effect positive change in individual lives and in doing so creates a seemingly chaotic condition that does little more than cleverly disguise the interests of the powerful.

Bauman believes that globalization manifests itself through a widening sense of polarization between the minority who have freedom of mobility and choice and the majority who do not. He describes the latter group as "dark vagrant moons reflecting the shine of bright tourist suns and following placidly the planets' orbit, the mutants of the post modern evolution, the monster rejects of the brave new species" (1998, 92). Indeed, he notes that the condition of liquid modernity has in no small part been prompted by the growth of neoliberalism. This economic and moral philosophy is one in which, as Bauman notes, "the responsibilities for resolving the quandaries generated by vexingly volatile and constantly changing circumstances is shifted onto the shoulders of individuals—who are now expected to be 'free choosers' and to bear in full the consequences of their choices" (2007, 3–4). The state thus has little to offer individuals in such a situation, and accordingly responds with "the promise to protect its citizens against dangers to personal safety. The specter of social degradation against which the social state sought to insure its citizens is being replaced in the political formula of the 'personal safety state' by threats of a pedophile on the loose, of a serial killer, an obtrusive beggar, a mugger, a stalker, a poisoner, terrorist, or better still by all such threats rolled into one in the figure of an illegal immigrant" (ibid., 15).

Bauman essentially argues that neoliberalism's deceptively seductive offer of increased individual choice comes at a heavy price, in which individuals find themselves increasingly vulnerable. This point is particularly true of those persons who already inhabit the margins of social life because of their poverty or status as labor migrants. We argue that the way in which a social problem is constructed and responded to is an equally powerful index of this condition. In the Goan case, we see that "exploited children," as victims of sexual abuse are often delicately described, in many ways have become the ultimate symbol of modernity betrayed through the failure of the state to protect its citizens from predatory outsiders and to prioritize their needs above the needs of the Goan elites and privileged long-term expatriates who benefit from tourism. When viewed in this way, it becomes clear that many ethnic Goans see the global modernity they experience in everyday life as a condition that subverts appropriate behavior as dictated by indigenous age and gender norms. In a social environment in which many men (and, increasingly, women) must migrate to affluent Gulf countries to support families, a heated social debate surrounds perceptions of changing family and parenting norms.

Concomitantly, debates continue to rage about popular perceptions that Goa is becoming what newspapers frequently term a "paradise for pedophiles." Newspapers and popular-cultural sources that use this disturbing expression are far too numerous to count, and the use of the term has also been incorporated into anti–child sex tourism campaigns. Certain restaurants and other places of business located on the beach sometimes feature small, handwritten signs that read, "No drugs or pedophiles allowed." What is causing this level of popular concern regarding child sex tourism? Why have so many ethnic Goans, among others, seized upon this issue as particularly worthy of attention in the face of so many other tourism-related social ills? As we shall argue, both the level of local discussion about and the national and international media coverage of the child sex tourism phenomenon in Goa reveal a great deal about how modern childhood and its meanings are currently the subject of particularly contested terrain.

Certain gender roles and perceptions of youth both affect and are affected by sex tourism in Goa, and although NGOs insist that the number of girls and boys harmed by sex tourism is nearly equal, it clearly has gendered consequences. This point is particularly true in the case of girls, for whom the looming social threat of prostitution ignites a discourse on female purity and the need for society to protect them. Alternatively, when young boys are harmed by older men, the discourse focuses on the feminization of Goan males. Thus, the overall debate leads to subtle shifts in gender norms as well as the image of youth that, as we shall see, speak to the ways in which ethnic Goans and others envision broader relationships between individuals, society, and the state.

In addition to the gendered repercussions of child sex tourism, the discussions among adults regarding the state of their children have shifted as well. While adults portray children as victims of predatory outsiders, children are often extremely adamant that they manipulate tourists. The discourse of pure and innocent children who need protection is one that, to a limited degree, children employ to increase their own power in a bad situation. Just as Heather Montgomery (2001) has argued in the case of Thailand, at least some of the child sex workers in Goa see themselves as helping their families and avoiding more dangerous work, such as begging or stealing. These findings are not meant to justify child prostitution, but rather to illustrate that children see themselves as having some control, while adults portray them as victims.

Implicit in these discussions about shifting gender roles, parenting, and the increasing presence of tourism and the state's dependence on it is an undertone that privileges ethnic identity. Ethnic Goans often see themselves as morally superior to non-Goan Indians and European tourists, while resident non-Goan Indians blame the social ills on ethnic Goans and are preoccupied with economic stability in a burgeoning tourist industry. Many ethnic Goans believe that European and Israeli tourists share a sense of superiority that defines their relationship to the state of Goa and with the people who host them there. Although many dynamics are at work in this situation, one of the foremost among them is Goa's unique position within India.

Goan Life in "Incredible India"

Contemporary Goa is the product of complex historical interactions among an eclectic set of actors: indigenous Hindus, Portuguese traders, Jesuit missionaries (including, according to many ethnic Goans, Jesus himself), Indian nationalists, hippies, Israeli motorcyclists, and European package tourists. This complex history informs the current phenomenon of and response to child sex tourism. The region has an equally complex history of racialized Othering. Goa was the first part of India to experience Western contact as early as the twelfth century, with European interest in the region peaking at the zenith of Portuguese rule when it was termed "the Rome of the Orient" (Axelrod and Fuerch 1998, 440). Although Goa has a unique place in India as "an 'island of Western civilization' in an Indian sea" (Newman 1984, 429) as a result of four and a half centuries of Portuguese colonization and mass religious conversion to Catholicism, Goan history has often been written by outsiders, so that even in the region's earliest written records, "Native Goans are mainly peripheral, appearing as palanquin bearers, galley slaves, petty traders, deceitful feudatory chiefs, and heathen savages requiring the ministries of the *Padroado,* the state-sponsored church establishment. . . . [I]ndigenous Goan villagers are variously conceived as targets for conversion, resisters of Portuguese rule, practitioners of devilish and barbaric religious activities, and sources of tax revenue" (Axelrod and Fuerch 1998, 443).

This unfortunate tradition continues today through discourses and practices that situate Goans on the peripheries of life in the service economy that dominates their home state. The income of many people in Goa has long been dependent upon contact with outsiders through trade and migration, particularly to Africa, the Gulf states, and the South Asian cities of Bangalore, Mumbai, and Karachi. The region never experienced the kind of radical nationalist movements that characterized the rest of South Asia, and although many ethnic Goans feel nostalgic toward Portuguese rule, which they regard in hindsight as a period of stable prosperity, the reality is a bit more complex.[5] Portuguese rule in the region deteriorated considerably over time, so that by the 1950s, "the Goan economy was doubly colonial: subject to a do-nothing Portuguese administration" and dominated by Japanese and German interests in its iron-ore reserves, 70 percent of which were imported by the latter in 1960 alone (Newman 1984, 431).

It was partly in response to this sustained lack of Portuguese interest in the region that the Indian Army invaded Goa in 1961, ousting the colonial administration and causing massive infrastructural and demographic changes, including the departure of many Portuguese-affiliated ethnic Goans for Brazil, North America, and, of course, Portugal. Indian citizens poured into their newly acquired state, in part to administer infrastructural projects and also in search of economic opportunity, particularly in construction, mining, and the nascent tourism sector (ibid., 433). Simultaneously, Goa began to develop a reputation among free-spirited western European and North American travelers as an inexpensive destination inhabited by local people more willing to tolerate drug use and seminudity on beaches than other communities in the rest of India. This countercultural movement, populated predominantly by white western

---

5. For instance, some ethnic Goans who are old enough to remember learning Portuguese in school recall with great bitterness the difficulties that the instant transition to English-language instruction created following India's acquisition of Goa in 1961. Such individuals often use *Indian* as a pejorative term, although (paradoxically) they are citizens of India themselves.

European and North American individuals who called themselves "Goan Crazy" or "Goa Freaks" (Odzer 1995), has its contemporary avatar in the all-night beach parties frequented by expatriate visitors. These tourists hail particularly from Israel and the UK, and D'Andrea (2007) and Saldanha (2007) have extensively documented the continuities between the groups of the 1970s and their current counterparts in terms of drug use, open attitudes toward sexuality, and disrespect for authority as well as local cultural norms.

This influx of outsiders both Indian and expatriate somewhat paradoxically coincided with increased Goan emigration, so that by the 1970s and 1980s, approximately one-third of the total population was living abroad either permanently or for work (Newman 1984, 434). This pattern has continued to the present day and has dramatically altered family dynamics and gender norms, as large numbers of men (and, increasingly, women) engage in long-distance parenting through remittances. Recent anthropological work on the families left behind during the labor migration process in areas as diverse as Ecuador (Pribilsky 2007), the Philippines (Parreñas 2005), and Sri Lanka (Gamburd 2000) suggests that a sense of social disintegration is often perceived to accompany the overseas residence of one or both parents, despite the fact that their migration is necessary in order to support their families. Pribilsky, for instance, describes *nervios* (anxiety) as a formerly female affliction that now also affects Ecuadorian children and men following male outmigration, while both Parreñas and Gamburd have noted the high degree of suspicion that surrounds the behavior of women who migrate as well as those women who stay in the home country to receive remittances from their husbands.

These patterns are similarly in operation in Goa, where ethnic Goans often wax eloquent about what they believe to be the infinitely superior standards of family life that characterized their state prior to its acquisition by India. Two primary factors exponentially compounded the need for Goans to migrate in the 1990s: the rise in land prices owing to expanded tourism and the need for capital to become involved in the tourism sector. Tourists from Europe and other parts of the world began to buy up and develop land in Goa, building apartment complexes that are lived in only four weeks out of the year. The prices of this land have skyrocketed, making it harder and harder for Goans to purchase land and establish homes or businesses.

As more and more tourists began to buy land and thereby became long-term expatriate residents, and increased numbers of Indians from other parts of the subcontinent invested in hotels and rental properties, ethnic Goans increasingly found themselves faced with difficult choices about the future of their home state. The greatest problem is that the government of India and various other parties continue to make many of these decisions for them (see Routledge 2002). However, recent initiatives led by ethnic Goans have begun to push out long-term tourists by limiting their visas, making it harder for them to purchase apartments and vehicles. This action is part of the larger struggle for self-determination that many ethnic Goans seek.

In 2001, the government of India embarked upon a new long-term strategy designed to boost tourism revenue by marketing the country as an exotic land of diverse cultural practices and fabulous geographical features accordingly dubbed "Incredible India."[6] This plan is an integral part of India's post–structural adjustment economic policy, which seeks to attract as much in foreign exchange earnings as possible. "Incredible India" advertising campaigns actively capitalize upon tropes of escape and spiritual rebirth in numerous ways, the least obvious of which is evident in a series of scrolling images on the initiative's official website. One such advertisement features a photograph of a white woman in a yoga pose above a series of short phrases that read, "Country of citizenship: USA. Motherland: India. Julie Martin lost herself in yoga. And found eternal peace. Embark on a spiritual journey. Visit India." A second shows a woman with South Asian features dressed in the costume of *bharat natyam,* one of India's classical dances, and reads, "Anne Chaymotty discovered *bharat natyam.* And became Devayani. For peace and fulfillment, visit India. Your search ends here."[7]

This discourse, with its impossible yet seductive promises of everlasting bliss and discoveries of the meaning of life, in itself is characteristic of Bauman's liquid modernity, in which "the more lonely we feel, the more

6. This government of India–sponsored tourism initiative continues to provoke a vibrant scholarly debate over whether it is offensive in its inescapable orientalist imagery or simply an attempt to "sell" India to the outside world (e.g., Bandyopadhyay and Morais 2005).

7. See http://www.incredibleindia.org.

we speak of community (which invariably stands for slowing down in the world of mind-boggling acceleration) . . . [so that] the gaping void is hastily filled by . . . ad hoc communities . . . and other disposable substitutes meant for an instant and one-off consumption. . . . [T]hey quench the thirst for security, albeit briefly. None is likely to deliver on the hopes invested, since they leave the roots of insecurity unscathed" (2001, 2). Indeed, a vibrant literature documents the elaborate connections between tourism and notions of escape that function to naturalize preexisting socioeconomic inequalities. As Gmelch (2003), Strachan (2003), and Chambers (1999) have observed in the islands of the Caribbean, the unequal pleasure-labor exchanges that characterize interactions between tourists and "natives" all too often replicate colonial patterns of servitude. Also in the Caribbean, Kempadoo (1999) and Brennan (2004) observe how sex tourism renders such inequalities glaringly obvious, and reports of child sex tourism are often cited as particularly egregious examples of such abuses.

In her analysis of sex tourism cross-culturally, sociologist Julia O'Connell Davidson argues that it is dangerous to so clearly separate adults from children in discussions of sex work. Instead, she recommends that discussions about child sex tourism be analyzed "against the back-cloth of much deeper anxieties about the ordering of social and political relations in late-modern Western societies" (2005, 2). O'Connell Davidson believes that because children and young people represent "innocence, dependency, helplessness and asexuality," popular culture seizes upon examples of child sex tourism as a particular type of horror that is actually symptomatic of something infinitely more profound. Her critiques strongly resonate with our research findings in Goa, which also suggest that something much deeper is afoot and speak to broader Goan social debates surrounding conceptions of childhood, gender, and modernity.[8]

Goa has a long history of contact and exchange with the outside world, yet contemporary tourism has undeniably changed the region in ways that are otherwise historically unprecedented. By depicting Goa as a sort of backdrop for the enactment of personal pleasure, tourism reinforces a number of preexisting hierarchies at work in the region and simultaneously

---

8. In many ways, the same sorts of arguments might be made regarding child labor, as recent ethnographies have begun to do (see Kovats-Bernat 2008; and Offit 2010).

raises powerful questions about the sort of existential crises described so eloquently by Bauman. Ethnic Goans often point to what they view as an enormous rise in tourism-related social ills as examples of the need to be particularly vigilant over their children because of the vast catalog of what they perceive as negative cultural changes that have taken place in recent decades. The most frequently cited of such troubles relate to the belief that visitors to Goa import a number of undesirable problems in addition to the much-needed revenue they bring. These problems include drug use, prostitution, and the reality that the presence of tourists with money to spend in turn fuels continued in-migration of impoverished, unskilled families from the nearby states of Andhra Pradesh and Karnataka. Such migrants, whose children often work as beach peddlers, are the subject of much suspicion and hostility because of their status as transients as well as their cultural differences from predominantly Catholic ethnic Goans.

Ethnic Goans are also acutely conscious of less glaring but nonetheless painful inequalities: ethnic Goans are sometimes discouraged from using their own beaches, or altogether refuse to bring their families because of the culturally inappropriate behavior of seminude foreigners who engage in public displays of affection that most South Asians, including ethnic Goans, find extremely offensive. Such disparities are also evident in the number of strikingly handsome young ethnic Goan men who become "beach boys," catering to the racialized sexual fantasies of middle-aged white women from western Europe and North America, and, of course, insecure job conditions that vary based on the number of tourists and thus further encourage emigration (Noronha 1997, 3254). All of these factors coalesce in unmistakably stark form in public perceptions of the particularly abhorrent practice of child sex tourism and responses to it.

These conditions have rather unsurprisingly sparked a debate about shifts in gender norms among ethnic Goans. As labor emigration by both genders increasingly physically separates parents from their children for lengthy periods of time, many ethnic Goans find themselves asking profound questions about the nature of expectations surrounding appropriately gendered behavior. Tourism dependency compounds the seriousness of such inquiry because of the regular interactions many ethnic Goans have with relatively privileged white foreigners who regard Goa as a state where the moral and ethical rules of their home countries simply do not apply. Some young people increasingly see themselves as able to take advantage of this situation through interactions with tourists in the absence of parental control, thus opening new avenues for gendered youth agency in ways that have powerful repercussions for all concerned.

Assigning Blame

The whims of tourists and migration patterns intersect and play out atop the lives of children in many places throughout the world, and Goa knows well its effects. In the same way that ethnicity underlies the dynamics between tourism and migration, so do ideas about childhood. Tourists, ethnic Goans, and children alike construct ideas of childhood in relationship to tourism and migration patterns in the area. This point is particularly significant given that most organizations that address child sex tourism consider it a unique situation that typically involves travel from a country with a high gross domestic product to a nation with a relatively lower standard of living (ECPAT 2002, 3). This issue speaks not only to the exploitation of inequalities between individuals, but also to the conscious exploitation of these disparities by individuals who know that their greater privilege diminishes their likelihood of punishment.

Despite the level of concern devoted to the exploitation of children, childhood itself is a relatively recent historical construction that many scholars date to the publication of Jean-Jacques Rousseau's *Émile* in 1762. In this text, Rousseau contends that childhood is a state of innate purity that is later sullied by the onset of adulthood. It might be argued, as many others have (see Lancy 2008), that this idea is very much a culture-bound concept that varies enormously from place to place. Nonetheless, as global NGO discourse begins to disseminate such western European and North American discourses of rights and empowerment, thus providing new languages for subaltern populations to use as they see fit (Puri 2008), we see child sex tourism in particular emerge as a site of telling social debate unilaterally opposed by activists and governments alike.[9]

9. The UN Convention on the Rights of the Child (United Nations 2000) argues that the age of consent is eighteen years, an age at which many women throughout the world have already given birth. Nonetheless, we see that constructions of "child" and "adult" remain little questioned in the academic literature, thus reinforcing the sanctity of childhood originally espoused by Rousseau.

Popular discourse about child sex tourism in Goa stems from the early 1990s case of Anglo-German pedophile Freddy Peats, a long-term resident of the state who held an Indian passport and was the highly respected founder and manager of an orphanage for more than two decades. Peats successfully cultivated an image of a benevolent godfather to children in need, and in the process sexually abused untold numbers of them. When the father of one such child reported the abuse to the police, a subsequent raid uncovered 2,305 pornographic photographs and 135 strips of film negative featuring young ethnic Goan and Indian boys having sex with much older white men, most of whom were German sex tourists who paid Peats for their activities. Convicted of pedophilia in 1996, Peats died in 2005 at the age of eighty-one in Goa's Aguada Jail (Nair Sen 2005, 482).

The Peats case and the way it is described speak volumes about the conditions of what many gloss as "modern life" for children in Goa, who grow up in a society characterized by economic insecurity and the constant migratory flows of tourists, parents, and relatives for more lucrative work abroad. For some older ethnic Goans, this response takes the form of frustration with India and nostalgia for Portuguese colonial rule, as it did for João, a fifty-three-year-old proprietor of a small guesthouse who often referenced the Peats case in his complaints about what he viewed as the ongoing degradation of his home state:

> Life was basically very good with [the] Portuguese, not like with these Indians [i.e., post-1961]. Indians like to cheat and steal; it is their nature only. Before [under Portuguese rule], anybody rape, anybody steal, [the] Portuguese beat them or kill them. So then [in those times] there was no problems in Goa. Today these very dirty foreigners, like that Freddy Peats, they know no harm will come to them in Goa. Indians [nonethnic Goans], they are like that only. They are cheating and stealing only. This is why pedophiles and all those types come spoil our beautiful Goa.

João evocatively recalls the memory of Portuguese domination as a period of relative order (albeit through fear of physical harm), and attributes contemporary ills to the inability of the Indian state to regulate disorder. As Bauman suggests, the neoliberal agenda has prompted the government to perform a smaller role in the lives of its citizens and favors individuals who find solutions on their own. This paradigm shift has caused many individuals to distrust institutions like the ones established in Goa to combat child sex tourism. During her field research, Conover conducted a phone interview with a guesthouse owner and father of two. When asked if he was interested in cooperating with NGOs to battle child exploitation, he responded vehemently: "No! I will not work with any organization. Organizations do nothing! If a foreigner hurts my children, and the NGO or police do something, they will only give him a slap, fine, or jail time. He will not think twice, and will do it again. But if he hurts my children, and I break his legs, he will think twice and not do it again." This example highlights the ways that individuals lack trust in their government or other institutions. Here then is the model man for neoliberalism: rejecting governmental and institutional aid in personal affairs, he truly takes matters into his own hands. And while Bauman argues that the modern condition is a "personal safety state," one that protects citizens from the loose pedophile, we can see in these comments that the modern state fails to do even that. Further, these sentiments echo João's, suggesting that perhaps under Portuguese rule, the sexual exploitation of children would not happen to the degree that it does today. Of course, the only terms on which he is able to reject governmental aid are themselves indicative of the extremely unequal power relations that shape everyday life in contemporary Goa.

This deep sense of resentment, particularly among older adults, about Goa's increasing reputation as a repository of social degradation so pervasive that children are particularly impacted definitely shapes youth perceptions of prospects for the future. Many young people aspire to eventually own a "beach shack," a small thatched construction filled with plastic tables and chairs that serve Western-style snack foods to tourists. Aspiring to this form of servitude, one preadolescent girl explained to me, "is basically all we Goans do if you are unwilling to migrate."

A growing body of scholarly and activist literature addresses the means by which sex tourism among adults and children is a manifestation of the sustained replication of postcolonial power relations between the global North and South that, as Kempadoo notes, "depend upon the eroticization of the ethnic and cultural Other" (1999). Child sex tourism clearly does not take place in a vacuum and instead exists because of a number of factors that permit it. As Jude Fernando notes, it is "the present system of [inequitable] distributive justice . . . responsible for the vulnerability of children" (2001, 8). Yet the susceptibility of children and young people is directly dependent upon a number of factors, including race, migrant status, and the absence of support networks for the informally employed, many of whom are under the age of fifteen and in constant contact with much older, wealthier foreign men. Such contact often takes place alone or in secluded areas, particularly on beaches where migrant children and youth earn money for food by selling trinkets, handicrafts, and massage services.

These types of social interaction are part of much larger and more pervasive patterns of thinking about race in Goa. For instance, Saldanha (2007) argues that among contemporary visitors to Goa, particularly the ones who seek an experience akin to the "Goa freaks" of Odzer's generation, race remains a salient category that "functions to consolidate whiteness." We clearly see how this situation manifested in the case of Freddy Peats, who was able to sustain his nefarious activities with no discernible source of income for nearly two decades without incurring public suspicion. Although Peats claimed Anglo-Indian ancestry, his ethnic ties to the subcontinent were dubious at best, and he clearly used his whiteness as a marker of authority in ways that, as we will see, disturbingly mirror the infantilizing orientalist discourses presented by many western European NGOs.

Yet not all instances of racialized power in Goa confine themselves to cases as extreme as Freddy Peats. For instance, geographer Paul Routledge has noted the propensities of highly touristic locales such as Goa to become "dispensable space" in which local norms and people are secondary to the adoption of policies that privilege multinational capital and wealthier foreign visitors. Routledge further notes, "The discourse of tourism focuses on 'going away' to places rather than 'going towards' them. Tourist destinations thus become the cultural thresholds where the tourist leaves behind his or her social roles, rules and norms. Such destinations become commodities where the tourist finds a timeless, workless paradise" (2000, 2652). Whereas public discourse portrays children and women as innocent victims of corrupt Europeans, these actors, while aware that their relatively powerless position limits their options, often perceive themselves to be morally and intellectually superior agents who manipulate foolish tourists. Ethnic Goans distance themselves morally from migrant workers whom ethnic Goans see as dishonest and suspect because of their status as poor and unskilled migrants. Yet they equally distinguish themselves from many visiting expatriates, whom they view as reprehensibly weak and lacking in moral fiber.

Of course, subscribing to such a discourse necessarily ignores the reality that a vast amount of work (and, by default, inexpensive labor) is required to maintain this illusion. Goans are only too aware of the way these inequalities frame their lives. Ethnic Goans often comment on these inequalities, thus asserting their moral superiority-in-poverty in direct opposition to "immoral foreigners" in ways that closely mirror Brison's (2007a) discussion of some indigenous Fijian notions of their (reified) tra ditions as righteous despite their lower economic status vis-à-vis other ethnic communities. A clear example took place as Dewey was walking to a presunrise Catholic mass with an ethnic Goan woman and her two young sons. "See," noted the woman, "at this hour only Goans are awake. All these dirty foreign types are still happily sleeping in sin and aren't bothered." Her clear association between superior ethnic Goan moral- ity through rising early for church services and what she perceived as the hedonistic, spoiled character of most Western vacationers manifests itself in their relegation to the category of "dirty."

Yet ethnic Goans are equally quick in attributing any number of social ills to the numerous labor migrants, who come primarily from the South Indian states of Karnataka, Kerala, and Tamil Nadu in search of informal work selling trinkets and offering oil massages on Goa's beaches. These migrants are also often labeled "dirty," and many ethnic Goan parents consider their common practice of sending children to beg from and sell services to tourists particularly reprehensible. Such migrant children are generally readily distinguishable from ethnic Goans by their darker skin, ragged clothing, and often, true to the ethnic Goan stereotype, unwashed state. Begging and hustling for small-denomination bills, these children are often suspected of engaging in survival sex and prostitution to survive. Dewey met Anju, an eight-year-old girl, as she was introducing herself to male foreign tourists on the beach. A Hindi speaker like Dewey, Anju immediately requested that Dewey convince an English tourist in his mid- forties seated nearby to pay her the equivalent of one US dollar to give him a massage. Anju responded angrily when Dewey refused and asked Anju to return to the beach shack–cum-restaurant her mother was work- ing in nearby. In rapid-fire Hindi, she told the researcher that what she termed "old white men" had a lot of money to spare, and her mother later expressed an identical sentiment. A few moments later, Anju managed to convey her offer in limited English to the tourist, who responded with disgust by saying, "No, I most definitely don't want a massage from a little girl!" and then provided her with a few small-denomination bills to "go get something to eat." Foreign visitors such as this horrified man on the beach are acutely conscious of the existence of pedophilia owing to the numerous reports of it that periodically surface in the Western media. Whereas the man on the beach might respond with shock and pity to less-than-subtle sexualized offers of contact by children, ethnic Goans often describe these sorts of relatively commonplace exchanges as further evidence of the status of such children as cunning miniadults unworthy of sympathy.

Ethnic Goan women also appear to acquiesce to tourists but know how to play on tourists' sympathies by pointing out the inequalities inherent in their interactions. Like the man on the beach, most nonethnic Goans visiting the area from western Europe cannot help but notice the economic inequalities between themselves and Goans, but their common interactions with Goans do not suggest that they are willing to equalize the scales. This fact is evident at the Anjuna flea market and many instances in the informal economy. As Conover observed in her ethnographic research, an English long-term resident regularly walked the streets of Goa's capital, Panjim, hoping to find fake Pashmina scarves. When a female street peddler offered her a scarf for 150 rupees (about US$3), the long-term resident said, "I know I can get that for 100 just down the road . . ." and began walking away. The peddler then said she would sell the scarf for 100 rupees (about US$2), and the woman purchased it. Within an hour, however, the same woman was lamenting to Conover about what she termed "global poverty" and the stark contrast in her own wealth and the resources of her gardener, an ethnic Goan woman whose house consisted of a lean-to on the side of another edifice. The Englishwoman then caught herself and reflected, "But I suppose I could have given that woman 150 rupees for that scarf . . ." Tourists and long-term expatriate residents like this woman are thus quite aware of the differences in their wealth and power, but many are simultaneously rather content to maintain their superior position.

Children have also managed to exert some limited control over a situation that is stacked against them, learning how to manipulate interactions with tourists. Many children, particularly those kids with parents of modest means, are acutely conscious of their position vis-à-vis wealthy tourists. Visitors walking down the streets of Goa will find many children asking for candy, pens, or plastic bags that could be traded for money. Volunteers to orphanages and other charities might easily find themselves teaching English and being waited on by Goan children. On Conover's first visit to an orphanage, the director insisted that Conover sit as the children performed Christian praise songs as she was served tea by an adolescent girl from a nearby informal housing settlement who was employed as a casual laborer. This awkward situation was part of a regular routine for the children, whereby they would perform for visiting tourists, who in turn would be expected to leave a "donation" with the orphanage director. Indeed, children from economically disadvantaged backgrounds often learn through such experiences that they hold positions of relative power vis-à-vis their "pitiable" condition and quickly learn to manipulate that status.

When asked why economically underprivileged children are particularly susceptible to sexual and other exploitation by Western and foreign tourists, individuals in NGOs and charities overwhelmingly responded that it was because ethnic Goan children are "too trusting," yet at least some children also managed to reverse the situation to a small extent by playing on this image of the innocent, trusting child to extract small favors from tourists. Interestingly, this explanation through notions of ethnic Goan naïveté is part of a much broader discourse typically employed by ethnic Goans themselves to describe outsiders' abuse of Goan hospitality, natural beauty (both environmental and individual), and migrant labor. "We Goans aren't sharp like . . . ," many ethnic Goans often say in explanation of why tourists, labor-recruiting agencies, and the government of India rather disproportionately benefit from their state's wealth, with the latter part of the sentence filled in with any number of national descriptors.

Actively employing this discourse, several NGOs circulate pamphlets and flyers throughout Goa's beaches and guesthouses that create a discourse of distrust toward outsiders. This literature is heavily informed by Western discourses on child protection, such as police and community responsibility to protect children. The researchers did not encounter any material for distribution that was localized in content, nor did they find reference to nonstranger sexual abuse, which proved the sole point of departure from a strongly Western social-work orientation. The researchers noted a disturbing lack of acknowledgment that a significant number of children need to earn an income in order to support their families. After all, English-language pamphlets that exhort children and young people to "remember it is not your fault" and advise them to avoid speaking to strangers to avoid the potential for abuse are of little use to the children who depend upon the income they receive from their interactions with much older and infinitely more privileged tourists they encounter on the beach.

Childhood on Whose Terms? Constructions of Child and Parental Authority in a Tourist Town

As with any social problem, the question of how to properly define child sex tourism and its practice is a contentious one that sometimes obscures the real issue through debates about mandates and implementation. Some critics of global donor-aid policy and NGO practices have even contended that examining the abuse of children separate from the cultural context in which it takes place is little more than "a convenient means of avoiding direct engagement with the political and economic realities of the emerging global economy" (Fernando 2001, 12). There is also the even more disturbing argument that the efficacy of NGOs is directly dependent upon donor aid and state recognition, which in turn makes it very difficult and even dangerous for any social service to find itself relegated to that sector (Fisher 1997).

Yet the vast majority of efforts to halt what many NGOs believe is a significant problem with child sex tourism has paradoxically fallen to NGOs. As a consequence, NGO leaders and employees are often quick to note that it is their "responsibility" to single-handedly tackle a problem of unknown scope and impact. This sort of belief is not completely without precedent, as the prosecution of Freddy Peats was successful only because of the tireless efforts of Mumbai-based child rights activist Sheela Barse. A journalist by trade, Barse wrote constantly about the reluctance of both state and local governments to investigate charges of abuse in Goa, and widespread public outrage finally led to an increased number of prosecutions related to crimes against children.

Newspaper accounts often blame "a strong tourism lobby with its own vested interest in playing down such incidents in the beach areas" (D'Mello 2004). Children's Rights in Goa president Nishtha Desai states in her book on the subject, *See the Evil,* that there exists "an organized network [of pedophiles] that is institutionalized" in the state (2001, 26). Yet politicians are reluctant to agree, because tourism is such a lucrative source of state revenue and because to aggressively pursue the arrest and prosecution of a minority of undesirable visitors may be akin to alienating the majority. As the minister for women and children in the government of Goa told Dewey in the course of an interview, "Unless and until I see or hear about the cases of pedophilia and get it confirmed, why should I believe it?" This government employee found himself in a difficult position without the presence of concrete statistics on child sex tourism in an economy strongly dependent on tourism, and many NGOs conversely orient their programs specifically toward combating this problem of unknown scope. As such, it is hardly surprising that the two frequently disagree about whether the lore surrounding child sex tourism in Goa is the product of actual abuses or a much deeper social reality.

The purpose of established charities and NGOs is to curb child exploitation, but often the relationships between individual agencies are fraught with suspicion and competition, which often function to inhibit cooperation toward the intended goal. Moreover, these suspicions and competitive attitudes often correspond with ethnic and nationalist identities and are seemingly fueled by global socioeconomic inequalities. One established and ethnically Goan NGO at which Conover conducted participant observation stood out as particularly suspicious of similar charities and NGOs and was characterized by a strong antitourism and anti-Western sentiment. It is likely that their suspicions and negative sentiments toward other organizations are fueled by past experiences whereby established charities in Goa were actually running brothels (Children's Rights in Goa 2006), but for other reasons related to ethnic self-determination as well. For instance, Conover observed a conversation between an employee of an ethnic Goan NGO and an ethnic Goan working in the tourist industry. The NGO worker said to the tourism worker, "If we do not temper [the behavior and influx of] tourists, we will become their slaves!" This example illustrates that some antitourist sentiments are fueled by a understanding of global power relations and a fear that ethnic Goan autonomy is waning in the region.

The suspicions that certain agencies have about one another often correspond with national identity and ethnicity. For example, the prominent ethnic Goan NGO stood in sharp contrast to its counterpart in North Goa that is similar to after-school care and is completely managed by British nationals (with the exception of the bookkeeper and the cook). While conducting participant observation at the former, Conover mentioned that she was going to interview managers at the latter, to which the director of the ethnic Goan NGO said, "Be sure to keep your ears perked up for anything suspicious." The same attitudes were evident when the researcher spoke to the same director of the ethnic Goan NGO about the time she had conducted participant observation at an orphanage managed by non-ethnic Goan Indians.

Ethnic and nationalist differences manifest themselves in ways other than suspicion and competition, highlighting global socioeconomic inequalities. Each agency tends to blame a racialized Other for the atrocities committed against children, following global patterns on sex trafficking–related discourse observed by Jo Doezema (2000) and Nandita Sharma (2005). Indeed, promotional and informational literature by the ethnic Goan NGO often featured a cartoon pedophile that was conspicuously non-Goan: named "Uncle Raju," the character wore a large turban and a beard, explicit markers of non-Catholicism and non-Goan ethnic identity.

Following this pattern, the ethnic Goan NGO stressed that it is non-ethnic Goan Indians and Western tourists who primarily commit these acts; individuals at the English-run NGO emphasized that primarily ethnic Goans and other Indians exploit children. Other organizations operated by western Europeans and interviewed by Conover highlighted the ways in which Goan parents are inferior, raising their children in substandard conditions. This sentiment is visible on any website, newsletter, and often public brochures and pamphlets. These organizations frame Goans as unfit and their own organization's work as necessary, often harking back to colonialist images of the maternal West and infantile East. One such example was the newsletter that one western European–managed NGO, Children Walking Tall, disseminates every few months. Under the "Medical Update" section, the March–April 2008 newsletter reads, "Wherever possible we try to encourage the parents to be more responsible and in most cases they take their own children to the hospital now. This is a great improvement from when we first arrived when some parents were just leaving their children with no checkups even with severe burns." To the British nationals who manage this charity, medical care is a matter of responsibility rather than ability. This message also conveys that Western-ers have knowledge and the individuals who live there do not, and without the maternal hand and superior knowledge of these western Europeans, the children would be neglected. This attitude parallels almost any colo-nial account in which the colonizers bestow knowledge and civilization upon the colonized.

Yet the situation in Goa is not quite so simple and in fact involves complex relationships of agency, resistance, and manipulation by all par-ties involved. Underprivileged children and young people, particularly the ones who work on the beach, often express a clear preference for expatri-ate western Europeans and North Americans over ethnic Goans or other Indians, not only because of the obvious economic benefits such friend-ship might offer, but also because such tourists are outside the norms of caste, class, and gender that otherwise mark them as oppressed. It is not at all uncommon to see older tourists seated at restaurants and beach shacks with an entire table of underprivileged children, who are obviously delight-ing in the experience. Certainly, not all of these visitors are pedophiles, and many genuinely believe that they are helping what they believe to be, as in the aforementioned case of the English tourist, poor Indian children.

Yet the fact that these inequalities both exist and subvert traditional hierarchies greatly bothers many ethnic Goans, such as Maria, who cited the ability of tourists to attract large crowds of children and young people with their seemingly endless amounts of money to spend as a major rea-son she felt she had to keep her twelve-year-old son, Lorenzo, at home with her as much as possible. As she noted in reference to a scantily clad group of white tourist women on their way to the beach, "These women don't like the men in their own country. They prefer our Goan boys, because they are not so smart [manipulative] like [Western] foreigner men. Goan boys are lazy also and quite happy to take advantage of them. It's best avoided [for Lorenzo]." This statement indicates that there is a dimension of feel-ing that ethnic Goan men are reduced to a feminine status by European tourists, thus combining what many ethnic Goans perceive as the worst character traits of both groups.

Although Maria did not explicitly mention sex, she alluded to the inverted power hierarchies that might accompany such a relationship, in which older white women have economic power (see Phillips 1999) and young ethnic Goan boys receive money without working. This inversion of appropriate gender roles is seen as extremely undesirable and is the subject of much humor and pity for women who engage in such relationships, which many Goans believe is a symptom of both the decadence of western European and North American societies and the weakening control of ethnic Goan adults over their children. Conversely, sexual or sexualized relationships between young children of either sex and much older expatriate men are never the subject of humor, but rather examples of the degree of decay that has eroded familial and social structures in Goa. As Maria elaborated, "Young [migrant] girls [selling things] on the beach give foreigners a wrong impression of Goa. These people are not Goans only. Their families don't care a damn for them, and so these [expatriate] men do whatever they want with them. Sometimes the families are so lazy that they even demand this [prostitution] of the girls. This is why people say bad things about Goa. It is because of these girls only."

In situating the impoverished migrant girl prostitute as the culprit rather than the victim, Maria employs a typical strategy that conveniently skirts the broader socioeconomic issues that create even the possibility of such a situation in the first place. We propose that part of the reason ethnic Goans blame migrants for the presence of child sex tourism is because so many ethnic Goans are themselves dependent upon transactional relationships with tourists that inevitably take place upon extremely unequal terms. During the tourist season from December to March, many ethnic Goans open extra rooms in their homes to tourists for less than ten US dollars per night, making such an arrangement an ideal option for budget travelers and those visitors in search of a more "authentic" Goan experience. Some visitors develop long-term emotional relationships with ethnic Goan families and return year after year, exchanging phone calls, small gifts, and even money after they return to their home countries.

One interesting consequence of these fictive kinship bonds between tourists and locals is the strong sense of ownership ethnic Goans display toward such people, often calling them "my foreigner" in casual conversation with other ethnic Goans. The ability to attract many "good foreigners," as ethnic Goans term older visitors who, like them, rise early in the morning, do not use drugs or drink excessively, and have stable professional jobs in their home countries, is a significant marker of status in the community. Some of these expatriates come from fragmented or troubled families and feel deeply comforted by what they see as the Goan propensity toward a generosity of spirit and willingness to spend long hours talking, and thus return each year as part of a sort of annual family reunion. It is not at all uncommon for such ethnic Goan families to have entire photo albums dedicated to major life events such as births and weddings experienced by their expatriate visitors, none of which they have actually attended, that have been mailed to them from abroad.

Although these relationships definitely fulfill an important social function for all parties involved, the fact remains that the boundaries of appropriate financial and emotional exchange between ethnic Goans and their expatriate friends are never clear. Tourists, even the ones who have been visiting for years, are expected to pay for all activities undertaken with their ethnic Goan friends because of their higher economic position, and ethnic Goans are expected to treat such people like members of their families.

There is a high potential for such relationships to rapidly turn extremely awkward, as became painfully obvious during one protracted dispute Dewey was privy to during her fieldwork. Guesthouse co-owner Estella was both furious and mortified as she recounted an exchange that took place between her neighbor Clementine and Simon, an Englishman who had been staying in Estella's family guesthouse annually for nearly a decade. Clementine's husband was a contract laborer who spent all but three weeks of the year working in the Gulf and sent home remittances that she frequently complained to all who would listen were not enough to support her two young daughters. Simon had taken pity on Clementine's plight the year before and had provided enough money for a year of school fees for both girls, who were seven and eight years old. When Simon returned to Goa on his honeymoon with a woman who had never been outside of England, he was accosted outside his rented room in Estella's house by Clementine and her daughters. As explained by Estella:

> Clementine's girls then said to Simon, "Uncle, how will we pay our [school] fees? We will end up working on the beach only," and Clementine loudly said that the children were his responsibility [because he had paid the previous year]. All the while, that poor woman he had just married stood there looking shocked. She must have been thinking, "Who is this fellow I married, who is carrying on [behaving inappropriately] with Goan girls?" Probably she thought Simon was acting funny [sexually] with those young girls. Actually, if you ask me in all truth, I think

that was Clementine's intention so she could remove his money. Imagine what those girls will grow up to be.

Estella's anger was unmistakable as she recounted this story of double betrayal by Clementine, who in Estella's view was eager to exploit Simon's shame and embarrassment in front of his new wife. Yet this scene outside Simon's room is painfully revealing in its layers of violated trust by all parties: Estella was livid that her friend Clementine would exploit "her foreigner" by using her daughters as innocent pawns to take his money, Simon felt humiliated that he had implicitly been accused of pedophilia, and Clementine believed that Simon's greater wealth and previous willingness to pay her daughters' school fees meant that he was responsible for doing so in the future. Above all, however, Estella's greatest anger was at what Clementine's daughters had learned that day about appropriate modes of gendered economic exchange. "Imagine what those girls will grow up to be."

Conclusion

Child sex tourism in Goa is a topic of frequent discussion because it is a crime with terrible consequences, but also because it draws particular attention to contemporary crises in the region, many of which stem from the negative consequences of a relatively unregulated tourism-based economy. It is self-evident that child sex tourism is an abhorrent and despicable practice, yet the amount of attention it receives relative to more pressing tourism-related dilemmas indicates that something deeper is at work in public discourse on the matter. It is telling that the NGO sector and public discussion focus on child sex tourism to the exclusion of more contentious issues that affect a wider range of parties, such as environmental degradation, skyrocketing housing prices, overcrowding during the high season, and general disrespect for the law among some visitors to Goa. We have argued that these realities are enabled by a set of circumstances as part of Bauman's liquid modernity, a condition peculiar to our times that makes it far easier to address symptoms rather than treat the deeper social disease.

PART FOUR

Agency and Refining Youth Identities

9

Negotiating Agency

Local Youth Activism in Aotearoa–New Zealand

FIONA BEALS AND BRONWYN WOOD

Reflecting statistics in the United Kingdom, United States, and Australia, youth in Aotearoa–New Zealand are reported to have falling rates of political and social engagement. In 2005, the New Zealand Electoral Commission (2005) noted that rates of political participation in New Zealand are "trending down." These trends have prompted two responses: a public perception that youth engagement in "citizenship" activities is low and that they are apathetic compared to previous generations as well as a range of adult-led and -controlled initiatives to promote a greater level of youth "voice," representation, and participation in prescribed areas of society (such as local government) and schooling. The adult response has been like a two-edged sword: while some young people are given an opportunity to have a voice, what is said and how it is said tend to be restricted within the boundaries determined by the initiative. With this thought in mind, the emergence of two "activist" youth-led organizations in 2005–6 in Aotearoa–New Zealand came to our attention as a phenomenon worth noting and exploring. These organizations demonstrated that young people were engaging in citizenship-activist activities beyond the scope of adult-led initiatives.

In this chapter, we explore youth agency by examining the actions and voices of these two activist youth organizations, Radical Youth and Youth Organised and United (YOU). Radical Youth was established in 2005 by a network of anticapitalist Auckland students and young people. The group gained media prominence in March 2006 for its involvement in a protest march to increase youth wages that occurred during school hours, called "Supersize My Pay." YOU was formed in 2007 by a number of students who attended the national Youth Parliament event that year.

Both groups have a presence in Aotearoa–New Zealand's mass and middle media. The organizations both make press statements on issues and participate in online and social networking communities. We consider how and where young people in these groups "perform" agency and examine the gendered middle- and mass-media responses to their actions. We draw on this analysis to build toward a conceptualization of youth agency as "performative," in a complex state of negotiation between the liminal position in which adolescents find themselves, the actions of resistance that they take, and the boundaries imposed on them by adult society.

Conceptualizing Agency and Situating It in Aotearoa–New Zealand

A clear definition of agency can be found in the work of Rob White and Johanna Wyn (1998, 315), who argue that agency is something that is "done." It is a verb rather than a noun, an activity not a state of being (Amit-Talai and Wulff 1995). In this sense, young people do not "have" agency; they "perform" agency. To White and Wyn (1998), effective agency involves three dimensions—the personal, the collective, and the transformative. Personal agency is linked to achieving private goals within personal circumstances; collective agency concerns the young person involved with others in small, but limited, changes to society; and the third dimension is transformative agency, where young people work together on collective projects to bring about positive fundamental change in the overall social order. White and Wyn stress the "contextual" nature of agency, as constrained or made possible through the social and structural contexts in which the young person is situated.

White and Wyn's (1998) concept of agency is closely connected to the concept of cultural agency found within anthropological literature (Wulff 1995b; Bucholtz 2002). The concept of cultural agency acknowledges that actions of agency may not necessarily be "positive" in nature, but they are, following Judith Butler (1999), "performative," as they bring the subject into being. They may not challenge and change structural and social conditions, but in any action of agency, they rewrite and reconstruct culture. The concept of cultural agency therefore moves beyond the notion of agency necessarily leading to positive structural change and acknowledges that agency may involve actions and voices of resistance exercised by young people in an attempt to find a space and identity in their culture and world. Hence, some acts of agency may seem irrational, and some acts of resistance may not be conscious choices made by the individual actor. Framing agency in such a way acknowledges that some youth do not have access to the resources needed to do transformative agency, and others are permanently excluded from this position because of who they are and where they live. However, a key theme in anthropological understandings of adolescence is that young people are situated in the liminal, a moment in between childhood and adulthood in which the young person is "becoming" an adult. Bucholtz (2002, 534) argues that we are able to read the performance of cultural agency only when we challenge our understandings of the liminal and begin to see young people as "cultural and political actors" in the "here and now" (ibid., 532).

In Aotearoa–New Zealand, acts of cultural agency can be read through moments of *tino rangatiratanga* (or self-determination) (Williams, Edlin, and Beals 2010). That is, activities of agency occur in spaces where a subject can stand, speak, and be oneself; they are performances of identity just as much as they are moments of cultural creation. In reality, for some young people, the only time a young person may have access to *tino rangatiratanga* is in a voice or action of resistance, either positive or negative. Once we acknowledge the role of resistance, we can also see the power of the liminal. Often the liminal nature of the construct of adolescence is seen as negatively affecting the experiences of agency available to young people (Bucholtz 2002; Lesko 1996, 2001; R. White and Wyn 1998; Wyn and White 1997). It is possible to reconstruct the liminal moment of adolescence as one of contradiction, indeterminability, and possibility (Beals 2008). Acknowledging that agency has elements of liminality and resistance allows us to read some types of activities of agency (such as the activities of Radical Youth and YOU) for what they are: activities of activism and resistance and as the rewriting and re-creating of today's and tomorrow's world.

Young People Exercising Agency in Aotearoa–New Zealand

In order to understand how Radical Youth and YOU performed agency in political, media, and social spaces in Aotearoa–New Zealand, there is a need to "learn to talk again" (James, cited in Wulff 1995b, 10) and to listen to the voices of the activist young people as they describe their agency and identities. This awareness means listening to the voices of youth and not overreading an adult perspective into the texts. Fundamentally, in Aotearoa–New Zealand, both Radical Youth and YOU express a strong sense of purpose in their respective organizations and a strong commitment to empower all young people. However, the way this vision is performed through moments of *tino rangatiratanga* differs for both groups.

Members of Radical Youth voice a strong definition of themselves as independent activists. The organization views itself as youth inspired, developed, and led, where young people can have a voice unlimited by adult expectations. "Radical Youth originally began with a few people who had a feeling that youth needed to be more active in their communities to work for social justice. We also thought that youth should organize independently from adults to defend our interests and make our voices heard" (nineteen-year-old female, Radical Youth). Radical Youth views young people as a "marginalized group" and believes that empowering of all young people is a key toward social change. Gender and race appear to not be huge barriers to the membership or leadership of Radical Youth. Leadership is shared between males and females. Among its leaders are Nista Singh, a seventeen-year-old female Nepali; Omar Hamed, a Palestinian male; and Joseph Minto and John Darroch, both European males (Loudon 2006). According to one Radical Youth spokesperson, Eliana Darroch, their key issue is not gender or racial discrimination in the workplace but age: "We've outlawed gender and racial discrimination in the workplace, are our bosses permitted to subject us to age discrimination? It only works to benefit the rich, while over 3 in 10 young people in New Zealand live in poverty" (Radical Youth 2007b).

Whereas an adult reading of Darroch's statement would suggest that this young female is yet to understand that gender still plays a part in many social and cultural inequalities, the reality of gender, race, and class for Radical Youth is not just balanced through the organization's membership but on the streets of Aotearoa–New Zealand. During the "Supersize My Pay" campaign, diverse groups of youth amassed on the streets outside of fast-food restaurants in city centers. It was a moment in which the privileged mixed with the disadvantaged in a single act of performative agency.

Radical Youth's strong assertion of its independence from powerful adults, such as teachers, unions, and socialist organizations, is one aspect of consistent media concern. At the time of the 2006 Radical Youth protest march, Anon (a member of Radical Youth contributing on Clint Heine and friends' blog) defended accusations of being bought by the unions in the following statement: "I have been reading political theory since the age of 12 and by the age of 15 had a solid grasp of the issues, I have never been led into activism and have instead had to work hard to get involved. It would be nice if there was a conspiracy with teachers and socialist organizations empowering young people but we have had to do it for ourselves. The youth are only uneducated because they are not given the opportunities they deserve" (Heine and Friends 2006a).

Anon defends both his/her knowledge of political issues and his/her independence from adults, unions, and teachers by reacting to a post that depicts him/her as a "good lackey" (ibid.) for the unions and reinstating his/her independence. In fact, she/he has had to "work hard" to get involved in activism, rather then been led into it. Added to this fact, the young people were criticized heavily for their actions—in particular for the timing of their protest during school hours. In contrast, young people spoke out to redefine their action as one of activism and protest, as heard in the words of one young female radical youth activist: "This morning on the radio they tried to discredit us. They said we were here to get out of school. They said this was truancy. This is not truancy—this is activism! No more youth rates!" (Young 2006).

Radical Youth shows a cynicism and distrust of some more conventional methods of activism (petitions and donations). Although these methods created a space for agency in the past, Radical Youth has actively carved out a space for its voice to be heard on the streets and on the Internet. This claiming of new spaces by young people has been observed by other researchers in this area (Coleman 2005; O'Toole et al. 2003; A. Harris 2008). "We don't want you to sign useless petitions or give a monthly donation. We want you to come along to participate in the creation of a world based on peace, liberty, solidarity and equality" (female supporter from Radical Youth). This comment by a female Radical Youth supporter on Myspace highlights the group's active conceptualization of agency as one that is "active" in the real sense of the word. It is also transformative and unpredictable—their voice is not in a simple vote but an actual statement. It requires participation and action and does not see the position of adolescence as a space of powerlessness but rather possibility.

Although YOU has had less public critique, it also asserts its independence from adult interference and its nonpartisan nature, something that is critiqued heavily by writers on the conservative Kiwiblog: "We formed YOU because we identified the need for a non-partisan group that is run both by youth and for youth. We see this independence as our greatest strength. It is our independence that sets us apart from other groups as it means that the possibility for outside influence or coercion is nil" (Youth Organised and United 2007a). The formation of YOU received adult support from the start, with a grant from the J. R. McKenzie Trust in 2007 (Casinader 2008). Their preferred mode of agency is more "traditional" sites and processes of democratic participation (such as submitting bills and building relationships with members of Parliament). From looking at profile names on blogs and in the media, their leadership appears to be composed of mostly males in their late teens. For example, Dan Luoni, a spokesperson for YOU, is profiled on the website Celebrating Young New Zealanders as a "driving force behind the creation of YOU" and "an aspiring politician who wants to help young voices get heard" (Ministry of Youth Development n.d.). Another young member, Rick Malcolm, was profiled in a similar fashion. It is possible that, in traditional politics, the public may be more likely to comment that a young male will make an effective politician than a young woman—hence the presence of a gendered identity.

Further, although the Internet did not reveal the presence of female members, what we do know is that Youth Parliament was composed of both males and females, and it is highly likely that some of these young women joined YOU, as many of them were vocal about the token nature of Youth Parliament. It is also possible that the profile names used could actually be created by young women in an attempt to assert a position to speak from in a predominately male forum; as noted by other researchers in this area, there are definitional challenges relating to attributing gender rendered by the blog names chosen online (A. Harris 2008).

The Space of Agency: The Moment of *Tino Rangatiratanga*

In *tino rangatiratanga*, the performance of agency can occur only if the subject is given a space and, even further, if the space has an element of the social. That is, in the case of Radical Youth and YOU, young people need to have a space to speak—and, in order to be effective, someone has to listen. This implies that the relationship between the spatial and social in moments of agency is intertwined—each cannot be seen separately, as each evokes, and needs, the other (S. Jones 1990; Massey, Allen, and Sarre 1999; Prout and James 1990). If we add a gendered perspective to this understanding of agency (as encouraged by Amit-Talai and Wulff 1995, 231), we see some interesting patterns emerging in the "youthscapes" (Maira and Soep 2005) of agency. In the case of Radical Youth and YOU, the gendered youthscape in agency also has an interesting appearance in adult responses. Radical Youth and YOU's performances of agency took place in both physical public places (such as the street, civic meeting areas, malls, and mass media) and the cyber realm of the Internet (online places of blogging, media profiling, and media releases).

Youth Agency on the Streets and the Initial Adult Response

Research examining the "territory" and use of space by young people in a city suggests that young people experience limited geographies and spatial constraints within public spaces of the city. Rob White (1996, 37) suggests that there are "no-go zones of the fortress [adult] city" owing to excessive policing of young people in public places in recent times. However, rather than viewing young people as passive in this process of negotiating public spaces, "it is important not to lose sight of young people's ability to actively resist such impositions, and to carve out new meaningful spaces for themselves" (Hil and Bessant 1999, 41).

   In the examples of the actions taken by the two groups, we can see that both groups used public spaces to voice their messages. Radical Youth's choice of Queen Street, the street marking Auckland's major commercial district, for their protest march in 2006 highlighted their strategic choice of public space. Their protest site was in keeping with the actions of many other "adult" protests in the past and heightened public awareness and media attention. The protest march followed a rally in the central public square (Aotea Square). The choice of marching during school hours also illustrated an act of reclamation of territory that would otherwise (during schooltime) be classified as an example of a "no-go zone" (R. White 1996) in the city. In this way, it became an act of "resistance" that was heavily opposed by adults—including teachers, principals, and politicians. The march included a specific focus on fast-food outlets where the protesters stopped and chanted and conducted an impromptu sit-down, blocking a major intersection until they were moved on. Young women took a high profile is this march, and both males and females represented Radical Youth in media interviews. The protest march of around a thousand young people was reported extensively by the mass and middle media.

In contrast to the actions of Radical Youth, the choice of YOU to visit the New Zealand Parliament to meet members of Parliament and present a voice for youth received far less media attention. It was also generally viewed very positively by a number of commentators in adult society as an acceptable place to perform agency, although "there have been a few skeptics," states Ricky Malcolm, the group's president (Casinader 2008). Their visit included one-on-one meetings with eight members of Parliament. In response, the group was offered support to set up a website, media training, and use of office space (Casinader 2008). This group was rewarded for following traditional process and places of expression and resistance in a democracy. Descriptions of the young males heading this organization as "aspiring politicians" (Ministry of Youth Development n.d.) and as politicians in the making (Malcolm 2007) by politically inclined older males also point to the more acceptable practices of this group. It is interesting to note that the origins of this group (in a government-sponsored Youth Parliament) possibly encouraged this group to act within adult-approved processes and places of agency.

Youth Agency Online

There is a growing interest in youth agency online and an emerging body of research on the ways in which young people use the Internet for acts of activism (Coleman 2005; A. Harris 2008; A. Harris, Wyn, and Younes 2007). Cyberspace offers a new public space in which young people have opportunities to organize socially, culturally, and politically (Hil and Bessant 1999). It has been described as a "liminal space between the public and private" (A. Harris 2008, 485), making it an effective separate sphere where those individuals who might feel excluded (including young women) can go to enter into acts of personal and social transformation. Furthermore, active participation in online communities may be in part a reaction to the limited spaces young people can occupy in physical spaces owing to the increased privatization and regulation of public spaces (Wyn and White 2008). The unofficial discourse of blogs allows young people to engage in the public domain with fewer limitations to age, gender, and personal attributes (Hil and Bessant 1999. The rise of web 2.0 and freely available blog pages on the Internet means that individuals can have their own voice on issues without having to have access to mass media (or corporate-controlled media).

Anita Harris's research into young women's use of online blogs and social networking sites suggests the emergence of new forms of activism on these sites. She calls for an expanded definition of participatory practices and activism to account for the opportunities presented by new technologies. Although research is still inconclusive about the degree to which women are using the Internet for activism in comparison to men, it would appear that how young women use the Internet differs. Young women tend to mix up the personal and the political, often focusing on having a voice rather than agitating for change. Harris concludes that young women are using online do-it-yourself (DIY) cultures and social networking as sites of activism and political subjectivity, but also an "unregulated public space for peer communities and to construct public self" (2008, 492).

Both activist groups used technology-enabled practices to participate in online DIY cultures (websites, blogs) and profiles on social networking sites. Before July 2009, both groups had an active website. However, both groups have engaged in blogs, and Radical Youth is very active in social networking sites. Emerging research (Gregg cited in ibid.) suggests that women (and young women) occupy more marginalized spaces within blogging culture. Whereas political blogs written by males are supported and seen as serious, women's blogs are taken less seriously and are less likely to draw comment. Our findings lend some support to these ideas, with YOU and its male members being the subject of the political blogs, especially those blogs written by males.

Young women from Radical Youth preferred to use social networking sites such as Myspace and Facebook in their creation of a community of youth activists. These social networking sites have generated few adult responses. In effect, these sites have appeared to be a "no-go" zone for adults, effectively providing young women with a new space to connect with their peers away from the eyes of adults (see ibid.). Additionally, Radical Youth has also used independent online media sites to make press releases about issues they wish to comment on (for example, youth gangs [Radical Youth 2005] and police raids in the Urewera [Radical Youth 2007a]). YOU has also made independent press releases to comment on issues such as the voting age and the discrimination of young taggers and gang members (Youth Organised and United 2008).

The Adult Reaction

When it comes to youth activism, the voice of adult interpretation and reaction traditionally would have been limited to newspapers, radio broadcasts, and television programs. The rise of the Internet in the past twenty years has allowed for new interpretations of youth issues and problems or even the rehashing of old interpretations through contemporary and fresh means. Additionally, the Internet has allowed for extremist perspectives to be shared and discussed with others, and, as in the case with some of the YOU blogs (Malcolm 2007; Youth Organised and United 2007a), it became a place of personal attacks (especially by adult males) on the young people involved, their agendas and aspirations. Hence, although the geographical space of the media may have expanded, young people continued to be talked about by some commentators in almost subhuman terms.

For YOU and Radical Youth, the types of media and the ways in which the media responded were very different. When it came to the case of Radical Youth, the participation of the group in the Supersize My Pay campaign and the successful facilitation of school strikes stirred a reaction both in traditional media and on the Internet. Through print media, such as newspapers, reporters went in depth to develop an understanding of the organization: its members, philosophy, and participation in extremist causes. On the Internet, although Radical Youth facilitated a number of blogs, adult responses were really limited to a "Capitalism bad; tree pretty" post by Maia (2006). In contrast, the media response to YOU occurred mainly through blogs posted by members, supporters, and critics on the Internet. Although YOU has released press statements to independent media on youth issues, New Zealand's mainstream media showed little interest in carrying the YOU message and gauging public reaction to it (we could find only one archived newspaper article and radio broadcast). However, their blogs attracted many comments, criticisms, and attacks.

Activism or "Naughty" Behavior? The Liminal in Radical Youth

Across public discourse, reporters and commentators drew upon an understanding of the liminal to reframe the activities of YOU and Radical Youth as not quite activities of activism. Indeed, the media made continuous subtle calls to a clear space of uncertainty between adulthood and childhood. For example, the young people in Radical Youth clearly could not, through the words of the media, conduct a strike (implying only adults can effectively strike) and come en masse in support of each other. Rather, young people were skipping classes, playing truant from school, coming together to have fun, not a voice. This opinion was clearly shown in a headline and byline of a *New Zealand Herald* article in which the female reporter reframed the actions of the young people as a real and possibly effective strike by putting the word *strike* in quotation marks to encourage the reader to think twice about the accuracy of such a term in this context: "A 'school strike' to raise youth pay rates saw around 1000 young people storm down Queen St yesterday where they staged an impromptu sit-in and chanted outside fast-food outlets" (Beston 2006).

Even when the young people themselves were interviewed by reporters, they were confronted with the message that their actions were an inappropriate use of schooltime, which would effectively see large numbers of young people engaging in the activity—not for the sake of activism but for the sake of getting time off from school. For example, one interviewer, Sean Plunket from Radio New Zealand (the national public broadcasting network), insisted on referring to the strike as "wagging" (the Aotearoa–New Zealand colloquialism for truanting):

SEAN: How many people do you expect to be wagging school with you to be at the protest?

NISTA SINGH (female representative of Radical Youth): First of all it's not wagging schools it's striking.

SEAN: What do you mean? You don't get paid to go to school.

NISTA: Yeah, but it's an issue. . . . [I]f we were wagging we would have done something else like gone to the beach or something. (Plunket et al. 2006)

In such reports, media commentators were able to reframe the young people as naughty little children. This bias also diverted the focus of the protest away from the central issue (youth wages) to an issue of deviance against the schooling institution.

Most schools attempted to stop the young people from attending the protest march. At Auckland Girls' Grammar teachers stood in a line to block the students from walking out. Students at Takapuna Grammar were banned from attending the march, and the principal instead offered to pay for three students to fly to Parliament to talk to politicians about their issues. Many students who did attend were threatened with an after-school detention, and some threatened to suspend students who attended (Hamed 2006; Beston 2006). Most adult commentators agreed that young people and students should be in their "proper place," in school, not marching on the streets.

These children did have a message, which was seen by the media as authentic and timely, but their actions were perceived as far from appropriate. Indeed, the Secondary Schools Principals' Association at the time, Graeme Young, while having sympathy for their cause, paradoxically advocated for a clear-cut boundary between politics and the playground: "On the one hand, if youth are being exploited through youth wages then it is appropriate that some adjustment should occur. But on the other hand, I just don't think that politics should enter the playground at school" (Plunket et al. 2006).

Even the New Zealand prime minister of the time, Helen Clark, known as a former protester herself in the seventies, was quick to acknowledge the cause but play down any actions of the young people. "Prime Minister Helen Clark says while we live in a democracy where students are able to express their rights, they also have obligations to their school community and shouldn't be leaving school for a protest" (One News and Radio New Zealand 2006).

What was overlooked by these media commentators was the purpose of the strike. These young people were not only trying to lift wages across a variety of employers, but also trying to provoke political change by bringing awareness to, what they perceived as, the unfairness of New Zealand's minimum wage policy. In order to effect this change, the young people involved realized that political change had to come through political means—what better decision but to make their voice heard in the political institution they attend daily, the school? In all of this reportage, the general push of some mainstream media, especially by television and radio, was to read the activities of activism and agency as transgressive and deviant behaviors that called for public reaction.

"Too Young" to Protest? Getting Behind Radical Youth

Further to framing youth activism as naughty behavior, adult commentators also felt that these students were "too young" to be acting on their own. Blogger Clint Heine dismissed the political aspect of the protest march by describing the young people as doing something for the sake of fitting in or garnering peer attention. These young people were, to Heine, too easily led and so immature that they would not understand the meaning behind their actions and the ethos of Radical Youth: "I know for sure that high school students do not get all lathered up about something like this unless they are led into it. They are too young to be spouting anti capitalist slogans and marching against the right. They most certainly are too unaware of how taxation and wages are to join up with the Unite and 'Supersize My Pay' campaigns" (Heine and Friends 2006a). Heine argued that the young people were the lackeys of adult union organizations (one of which, Unite, features several 1970s civil rights campaigners).

In Sean Plunket's interview he asked the young female leader continuously about union involvement (Plunket et al. 2006). On four different occasions, Plunket spoke about funding, insinuating that it was not a youth initiative but instead union initiated and led. His questions included: "Do you have affiliations that give you money or support?" "And they what . . . give you money?" "Who's paying for all that?" He also said, "Some people are going to say that really it's just the Unions funding you people . . ." (ibid.).

Similarly, comments made by police officer Donovan Clarke also belittled the protesters, describing their actions as "ineffective" (One News and Radio New Zealand 2006). Although the young people involved were from secondary schools across the Auckland area and no one was hurt during the protests (in contrast to the injuries that frequently occur in adult protests), Clarke informed the public that the protest was poorly organized and involved the leadership of a twelve-year-old child.

Another blog responder questioned whether the protests were even run by young people, evoking an illustration of an adult lobby group using young people to achieve political means. "We should not forget that these are impressionable schoolkids, easy to whip up. The Salvation Army employed the same tactic when whipping up opposition to homosexual law reform in '86" (Graham Watson in Maia 2006).

In what initially appeared as a supportive article for Radical Youth in a major New Zealand newspaper, Nick Venter (2006) spent the bulk of the article discussing a union that supported Radical Youth. Rather than portraying the campaign as a joint campaign, Venter described how Unite achieved a settlement with Restaurant Brands, meaning that youth wages had gone up. It was as if Venter had placed two bookends around the article that mentioned Radical Youth in the beginning and end, but within the bulk of the article, he concentrated on the adult actions of activism. Other reporters directly attributed the actions to Unite, not Radical Youth. For example, Kate Monahan (2006) argued that a young worker should thank Unite for her recent pay raise with no mention at all of Radical Youth.

Notably, other adults who spoke out in support of the protest included prominent left-wing activists and former members of Parliament. Traditionally, the New Zealand media have viewed these people as liberal extremists and (in the case of one female MP and another civil rights activist) troublemakers. Although their voices of support were included in the media, they were often embedded in expressions of caution and concern: should we really support these young people, and are they really old enough to be activists (e.g., Casinader 2008)?

Other news media (e.g., Loudon 2006; E. Page 2006) claimed that Radical Youth was led not by a group of young teenage activists but one of Aotearoa–New Zealand's most "notorious" activists, John Minto. Minto spearheaded an antiapartheid protest in the early 1980s and since then has been blacklisted by many conservative groups as a communist and troublemaker. In Radical Youth, Minto's son Joseph played a leadership role. Although one reporter, Emma Page (2006), acknowledged that Joseph might be merely following in his "father's footsteps," blogger Trevor Loudon (2006) was explicit, stating that Minto was more than just a father but a corrupter of a new generation of young people.

Activism, or Only "Becoming" Active? YOU in the Liminal

Whereas the media response and reaction to Radical Youth was to portray them as naughty little children in the space of the liminal, the response to YOU acknowledged their activities as activism-in-the-making (rather than activism-in-the-now). YOU was seen as a positive sight in the face of falling rates of youth political engagement, but, yet again, their activism was still not quite activism—just a whisper in the development of tomorrow's activists.

Explicitly on one blog, contributed to by predominately male commentators, one of YOU's leaders, Rick Malcolm, was initially described positively as a "politician in the making" (Malcolm 2007). However, later on, commentators were quick to downplay the ability of Malcolm to lead in the now, and even the future, and attention was drawn to his sexuality, which one blogger cynically linked to future success within a liberal political party. Hence, in an attack on Malcolm, the commentator effectively intends to attack his sexuality and, covertly, implies that Malcolm is not male enough to be a "real" politician: "We hear it all the time from Labour, he has great skills and is also a HOMOSEXUAL. If this is what got them into parliament it shows what sort of agenda they wish to carry out" (adolfpowell in Malcolm 2007).

In another blog created by YOU (Youth Organised and United 2007a), commentators went further by attacking YOU's mission statement, in which a key role of the organization is to provide a voice to young people who have none. Bloggers were quick to claim that YOU was fighting to lower the voting age to sixteen and that this aim was far from ideal because young people just do not and cannot behave like adults because of a liberalized and less demanding educational system. "We definitely should NOT lower the voting age, seeing our whole education system is dumbing kids down so that at 18 they're now about as switched on as a 13-year-old a few decades ago (if that)" (PhilBest in Youth Organised and United 2007a).

Within the mainstream media, the general response to YOU was positive. The young people's aim to be an effective lobby group was warmly greeted by politicians and reporters, and in one report (Casinader 2008), YOU was welcomed as a fresh alternative to the "blunt" and "antiauthoritarian" actions of Radical Youth. However, the media also voiced some doubt over whether the group could ever be truly effective—they were just too young.

Looking Within the Liminal: Encroaching on the Adult Fear

The unpredictability of the adolescent liminal tends to make it a space of adult fear. Rather than being seen as a space for an agency of resistance (and, therefore, new forms of activism), it is viewed as a space that needs to be controlled. Often this restraint occurs through stripping agency from young people and, in a way, taking advantage of the space—trying to reclaim that space on adult terms. Looking across both the examples of Radical Youth and YOU, we can see an adult attempt to reclaim and redefine by first asserting the "childish" character of the young people involved: they were either naughty or becoming but never complete activists.

The examination of the restricted and gendered spaces occupied by these young activists highlights the liminal place young people occupy in society—as "potential adults" (Amit-Talai and Wulff 1995)—in which they can participate in some places but not others. YOU occupied rather more "acceptable" places for their choices of agency (mostly in male-dominated online forums and at adult-approved forums such as meeting members of Parliament), whereas the "more blunt" (Casinader 2008, E2) actions of both male and female members of Radical Youth received more attention and greater levels of critique by adult society and the media (for the protest march). Actions of young men and women in the public and private spheres of online blogs and social networks appear to occupy a gendered landscape, with young men more active than young women in political blogs. In this way, the young people continue to negotiate, reconstruct, and redefine meaningful spaces for themselves (Hil and Bessant 1999).

Another way a fear of the liminal unpredictability of adolescence manifested was also in the fear that the young people involved were being exploited by the liberal Left. In the case of Radical Youth, the media attributed leadership to unions and adult activists. Similarly, despite a strong bipartisan stance, YOU was accused of having affiliations with the political Left. Another commentator, libertyscott, argued that having apathetic youth was better than having youth with an agenda: "To say it's good for young people to be more involved in politics PER SE, is valueless. The Cultural Revolution in China had almost all young people involved in politics, and blood was spilt daily by their hands. While apathy is rarely a good thing, I'd rather 1000 apathetic young people getting on with their own lives, than 1000 Green Party activists actively trying to mess with other peoples" (Youth Organised and United 2007a).

In all of this debate, both middle and mainstream media paid some acknowledgment to the ways in which young people were engaging in activism in fresh and vibrant ways. The media recognized that young people were no longer victims of the media but creators of media, especially the development of blogs and the willingness of young people to engage with the comments the general public made (despite the reality that some "adult" comments showed, at times, a real immaturity). Indeed, when the adult response showed a genuine acknowledgment, there was also recognition that activism is changing in the space of the adolescent liminal in ways that could be only dreamed about in the youth protests of the 1960s and 1970s. Indeed, one female teacher on Maia's Radical Youth blog summed up the potential that exists when adults acknowledge the agency of young people for what it is—not just about choice but also about resistance: "As for skipping school to protest—good on them. The school year has many interruptions, and I think a protest in which students are thinking critically and standing up for their rights is a much more valuable interruption than say a huge sports-showdown between schools. But then being a teacher, I do, funnily enough, value the ability to think over the ability to conform" (Suse in Maia 2006).

Conclusion

In this chapter, we have attempted to explore the ways in which young people in Aotearoa–New Zealand organizations performed agency. It has been an exploration of the activity of agency rather than the being of agency. Through looking at organizations such as Radical Youth and YOU, we can see evidence of an agency of resistance. YOU tended to have a male-dominated presence in the media and, on the Internet, tended to be spoken about in political blogs written and contributed to by males. Like the old politicians of yesteryear, these young activists were playing with the big boys and were praised and attacked by adults. Radical Youth had both male and female leaders, and both voices were heard. However, like other young female activists, the Internet forums of choice were social networking sites. Radical Youth received some acknowledgment from liberal adult activists and politicians but again found themselves attacked for their actions.

Although both organizations did bring about change in differing ways (YOU has been recognized by politicians as a voice of youth, and the Radical Youth campaign for youth pay rates did lead to changes in policy, with the worldwide McDonald's franchise leading the way), their success was limited, particularly in the ways in which adults read this agency. Rather than seeing these acts of resistance as youth-led performance, reacting adults saw them as adult led, immature, and ineffective. In effect, through the eyes of reacting adults, these young people were not demonstrating the type of transformative agency espoused by R. White and Wyn (1998). Instead, the young people involved themselves in a form of cultural agency (Wulff 1995b), that is, in activities that would challenge, rewrite, and reconstruct the culture of youth, the boundaries of liminality, and the reality of being.

In all of this discussion, there exists a paradox. New Zealand adults do not want young people to be placid, malleable, docile individuals who merely wait in a stage of adolescent becoming. Indeed, in Aotearoa–New Zealand, many adults want young people to be active agents, to be involved in decisions about their own lives, and to have a voice. The positive response YOU received during its visit to Parliament in 2007 illustrated this point. However, adults also want to define and regulate this agency, the parameters that surround it, and the outcomes that could be achieved. This fact was seen in the personal attacks heaped on many members of YOU when they made personal and political statements on blogs. The actions of Radical Youth in the protest march in a public space during school hours especially illustrated how threatening most of adult society found the actions of politicized young men and women. Furthermore, despite the continuous attempts by adults to seize and control what was happening, the youth voice continued to speak. In all of it, young people found a space to stand—a space of *tino rangatiratanga*.

These instances of *tino rangatiratanga* became transformative moments for the young people involved. They not only challenged adults but also gave the young people a sense of being in the now (being active agents) rather than being in the future (becoming agents). These young people may have used traditional means (media, protest, and so forth), but they found new and meaningful spaces to speak—in particular the Internet, the space of the blog, and social networking site. They effectively threw a challenge back to adults—give us these spaces, and recognize our voices. As Omar Hamed (2006), a founding member of Radical Youth, says, "We are young, we are angry and we are poor. And as the recent insurgency in France shows us, we are everywhere."

10

Imagining Papua New Guinean Cultural Modernities in Urban Australia

Youth, Cultural Schools, and Informal Education

JACQUELYN A. LEWIS-HARRIS

1999—Irene Barlow (eighteen years old) had just won the Miss Papua New Guinea contest in the Brisbane, Australia, beauty and fashion completion. Barlow had raised funds, given community speeches, and amassed an elaborate traditional dance costume in which she represented her people, the Motu-Koita, and in a larger sense, the people of Papua New Guinea. She and her mother were planning their trip to Pago Pago, America Samoa, where she would represent Papua New Guinea in the Miss Pacific beauty pageant.

2003—Kara (fourteen years old) tells ethnographer Lewis-Harris: "We had 'Culture Day' at our high school, and my sister and I decided to perform dances from Manus Island and also Kerama (the Papuan Gulf). Our mom got some tapa and helped us gather materials from people's gardens to make the costumes. Our classmates were copying dances from the telly while we performed our version of PNG [Papua New Guinean] dances. We were a big hit, but some of our classmates were jealous because of all the attention we got."

Defining Papua New Guinea in Oz

Young Australian–Papua New Guineans are at the forefront of imagining alternative cultural markers of modernity through their conscious decision to adopt and display facets of their Papua New Guinean cultural heritage and reframe them within an Australian context.

211

Both of the opening examples illustrate young Australian–Papua New Guineans' internalization of external influences in forming new senses of cultural identity and modernity in urban Australia. Barlow engaged in a beauty pageant, a prototypically "modern" event, but utilized a contemporary form of a customary Motu-Koita costume and dance, while Kara and her sister made a conscious decision to perform a modified form of traditional dance to distinguish themselves from the Australian norm. Both examples illustrate young women imagining their identity in terms combining Papua New Guinean and Australian ways of imagining identity framed by a racialized, postcolonial paradigm of Papua New Guinean females.

Appadurai's reflection on the influence of media and migration in relation to modernity, imagined selves, and the formation of diasporic public spheres is applicable to the youth experience In Australia. He notes, "This mobile and foreseeable relationship between mass-mediated events and migratory audiences defines the core of the link between globalization and the modern. . . . [T]he work of the imagination viewed in this context is neither purely emancipation nor entirely deciphered but is a space of contestation in which individuals and groups seek to annex the global into their own practices of the modern" (1996, 3). Through the use of electronic media and historical and cultural influences from both their Papua New Guinean and Australian heritage, young Australians of Papua New Guinean heritage have developed contemporary identities, imagining new kinds of selves and a place for themselves in urban Australia. Many have embraced portions of their family's indigenous PNG cultures as part of their identity development in reaction to the racialized, postcolonial environment of Australia. They have developed what Appadurai (1996) has described as diasporic public spheres through a "technoscape" of social networking sites like Facebook, YouTube, Myspace, and Bebo. This technoscape allowed them to imagine their lives in terms not explored before, as in the formation of personal web pages, websites, "techno-clans," and online families.

Why would these young people emphasize their foreign ethnicity when they could "pass" for a member of the dominant white ethnic group? Why imagine alternative modernities that challenge the hegemonic constructions of masculinity and femininity presented in Australian popular mass media and prescribed by customary gender roles? This chapter will attempt to address these questions and provide examples garnered from the cultural activities of young Australian–Papua New Guinean artists who are first- and second-generation descendants of Papua New Guinean migrants in Australia. I will focus primarily on females, as they are most active in the development and support of the imagined modernities and their actions often challenge the customary gender norms.

Methodology

The majority of this research was conducted in Brisbane, Melbourne, and Sydney, Australia, in 2000 with a return trip in 2003. The earlier part of the study involved participant observation, structured and semistructured interviews with a survey, and archival research. The most current research involved chat-room conversations, e-mail, and the use of social networking sites. I used social networking sites to gather information on people's presentation of self and communicate with many of the young people and their families. They use Facebook, Myspace, and Bebo accounts to post numerous photographs of their latest dance performances, clothing designs, and trips back to PNG as well as videos and music.

Racial, Gender, and Historical Precepts

I focus here on youth agency in relation to racial and ethnic authenticity and the interrelated issues of gender roles, hybridity, and reinvention. The majority of the young people discussed in this study are of mixed ethnicity, with the father being Australian of English ancestry and the mother from PNG. I argue that young Australians of Papua New Guinean descent formulate alternative conceptions of identity in reaction to the majority white Australian population's attitudes toward Australian–Papua New Guinean cultural, ethnic, or racial identity, which categorizes such iden tity as "primitive" and "premodern." My interviews and observations have revealed a correlation between external racialized, postcolonial attitudes and the forging of cultural identities within imagined alternative cultural modernities that implicitly include many aspects of Papua New Guinean sociality and identity into the modern Australian self.

The majority of Papua New Guineans in Australia have settled in the Brisbane, Sydney, Townsville, Darwin, Cairns, and Melbourne areas. By 2001, the first and second waves of Papuan immigrants, their children, and miscellaneous spouses of British and Australian men had increased the Papua New Guinean population to more than 23,600 (Australian Bureau of Statistics Census of Population and Housing 2003), with 75 percent of the population living in the states of New South Wales and Queensland.

When the first wave of Papua New Guineans migrated in the early 1970s, Australia was not known for its racial and ethnic tolerance; the majority of the citizenry had condoned the separation and suppression of the remaining Aboriginal population, and the government had restricted the immigration of Pacific and Asian neighbors (D. Bell 1993; Brock 1993; Dever 1997). The country had an established legacy of racist governmental policies in Australia and PNG (Thomson 1952; Burton-Bradley 1965; Fink 1965; Oram 1976) that continued in 2000 through the influence of the "One-Nation" national party. The general public still tended to look at the majority of Papua New Guineans as "former colony people," "Pacific Islanders," and "Aide Islanders." Facing the possibility of discriminatory treatment, many of the migrating families settled in urban centers, as they provided a more tolerant atmosphere for mixed-race unions and Pacific islanders in general.

In my conversations with white Australians, the terms *ethnicity* and *race* were often conflated, while many of the Australian–Papua New Guineans saw them as two distinctive concepts. It is important to define these terms, as they play such a significant role in the imagining of Australian–Papua New Guinean alternative modernities. According to sociologist Tracy Ore, "Race denotes a group of people who perceive themselves and are perceived by others as possessing distinctive hereditary traits. Ethnicity denotes a group of people who perceive themselves and are perceived by others as sharing cultural traits" (2006, 9). This definition is similar to the view adopted by Australian–Papua New Guinean youth as they imagined ethnic modern selves within a racialized Australian society. Ira Bashkow notes that the postmodern critiques of modernity have "sought to fragment it into a plurality of histories and discourses that reflect differences in positions of power." They "do not lead us into a deeper understanding of modernity as itself a racialized discourse" (2006, 10). In his study of Orokaiva modernity, *The Meaning of Whiteman,* Bashkow suggests that the Orokaiva people of PNG constructed concepts of modernity in reaction to Western racialized concepts. Bashkow untangled the Orokaiva association of white skin to notions of modernity: "Under colonialism, whites' persistent efforts to change Orokaiva habits, economy, religion and so on incorporated Orokaiva into the western paradigm of inequality in which whites, as instigators of progress, were active makers of history, while blacks were passive subjects: at best followers who could attain a second-hand civilization by imitating whites" (ibid.).

Young Australians of Papua New Guinean descent similarly implicitly recognize the inherent racism in ideas about modernity and attempt to define alternative modern identities that are less racist. The parents and grandparents of these young people had lived under a colonial Australian government and educational system similar to the one experienced by the Orokaiva, and their personal racialized and deculturalizing experiences consequently had an influence upon their children's perceptions. Several teens told me about their parents' deculturalizing experiences under colonial Australian rule and how this history made them more determined to claim ownership of their Papua New Guinean heritage. For example, a young teen in Canberra decided to learn her grandmother's customary dances, as her mother, who had attended boarding school, had been forbidden to participate in ceremonies.

Racism was particularly strong when directed at Papua New Guinean women. Scholars have well documented the subjugation of African and Pacific island women and the objectification of their bodies, whether through the arts, commercialization, or other forms of exploitation (Sharpley-Whiting 1999; Gottschild 2005). In *Staging Tourism,* Jane Desmond reflected, "From the beginning, this enabling discourse of the ideal native was 'raced' and 'gendered' in particular ways: female, not male, and 'brown' not 'black,' 'yellow,' or 'red.' Combined with ideologies of colonialism, these ideas can produce imaginaries that merge the feminine and the exotic. As Marianna Torgovnick notes, what is 'typical indeed of Western thinking about the primitive [is] the circularity between the concepts of "female" and "primitive"'" (1999, 5). Papua New Guinean women were doubly racialized because they were opposed not only to white women but also to "brown" Polynesian women. Through carefully crafted travel literature, Burns Philip commercial promotions, missionary tracts, and art photography publications, Papuan New Guinean women were described in a range of ways, from seductive "woodland nymphs" to savage "primitives," depending upon the darkness of their skin and physical characteristics (Stephen 1993). The Polynesian phenotype was favored over the darker Melanesian, as "the 'Polynesian' figure is one of attractive exoti-cism for many Caucasian visitors precisely because it represents difference perceived to be free of the domestic tensions and fears" (Desmond 1999, 140). Those Papuan New Guinean women with lighter brown skin, less kinky hair, and "finer features" were placed into the Polynesian category, while the darker women were placed in the Melanesian (former colonized black) category, which was associated with more negative descriptors of *kanaka* (literally "native"), "primitive," and "coarse."

These stereotypes and implied associations posed problems for Australian–Papua New Guineans as these perceptions carried over into late-twentieth-century Australia and generated disagreement as to how the offspring of mixed marriages were to be identified by the general public. Many of the young Australian–Papua New Guineans looked like Polynesians, but they assumed the dance, cultural attributes, and atti-tudes associated with the darker Melanesians. Young Australian women of Papua New Guinean descent thus faced an environment where the per-ception of Papua New Guinea women was quite negative, while there was a positive, romantic, image of Polynesian women and pressure for young women to play up to that image.

Young female and older artists inferred that the performance of their art was partially defined by Australians' perceptions of PNG and Melane-sian females. The influential Solien Besena and Papua New Guinean art-ist Wendi Choulai succinctly observed, "The result of indigenous people having idealized images about ourselves created for us, affects the way we see ourselves. This is reinforced through the demand of the tourist indus-try for dancing drum-beating natives in grass skirts. It is interesting to note that when I first 'called' the dancers to the Asia Pacific Triennial (in Brisbane) the women wanted to dance topless as they thought this what would be expected of them and would make them more authentic" (1997, 15). Whereas the older generation of dancers felt obliged to modify their cultural activities, to cater to the larger Australian society, young females were unwilling to dance topless and thought it was demeaning. Young female dancers also described instances in which festival sponsors had expected them to perform Tahitian- or Cook Island–style dances (involv-ing much hip shaking), since they looked more Polynesian than Papua New Guinean and catered to audience taste. They also gave examples of deliberate misinterpretations of their performance in festival programs and being asked to modify their choreography or to make it more exciting by adding risqué costume modifications.

Despite the pressure from a misguided public, I found that the young women's participation in cultural activities provided them with a sense of uniqueness that enhanced their personal image among their Australian and Australian–Papua New Guinean peers. Many of them actively participated in the construction of imagined, ethnically modern selves within the diasporic sphere. For example, in the opening example, two sisters in a suburban-based high school presented forms of customary dance for Culture Day and explained how their dance performance had their fellow students intrigued, jealous, and excited. Kara and her sister said they gained a newfound respect and had a higher status after performing in their traditional dress, with tapa cloth tops. Alison and Lauren Chan similarly discussed their gratitude in being able to participate in a 1996 Australian-based performance of a rare funerary dance, the Guma Roho. While professing to enjoy the Australian lifestyle and culture, the Chan sisters talked about their joy in learning more about their paternal heritage, meeting their distant PNG relatives, and being publicly recognized as being part of the Solien Besena clan.

Irene Barlow, an eighteen-year-old dancer and instructor in her mother's dance group, ran for and won the Miss Papua New Guinea contest, giving her the right to represent ideal PNG values and beauty in a Pan-Pacific venue. Feminist scholar Susan Dewey (2008b) has described pageants as manifestations of gender inequality through which bodies are modeled to fit a paradigm, while Cohen, Wilk, and Stoeltje, in their book on international beauty contests, stressed how the deportment, appearance, and style embody ideal values and goals of a nation, locality, or group (1996, 4). Barlow told me that the opportunity to present a positive representation of PNG femininity and culture was foremost on her mind. She did not see beauty pageants as exploitation but as a way to make a declaration about cultural identity both within the Australian–Papua New Guinea community as well as the PNG and Pan-Pacific communities.

Choice as a Key Aspect of Modernity

Australian perceptions of race and ethnicity constantly framed Australian–Papua New Guinean conversations about cultural retention. The cultural officer at the Papua New Guinean embassy in Canberra observed, "The first generation of mixed-race Papua New Guinean kids often pass for Spanish, Italian, or Polynesian, while the darker ones sometimes call themselves South Sea Islanders; as they get older and have children, some of them come here to get help in reclaiming their P.N.G. heritage" (Decklin, personal communication, 2000). Returning to my initial question, why does one group deny their ethnicity or race, owing to the pressures of racism, while another group actively seeks to advertise and reclaim their ancestral connections? Bruce Knauft's (2002) exploration of Gebusi personal agency and modernity provides insight into this issue. Knauft notes that for the Gebusi, one of the distinctive features of being modern was the mandate to explore personal roles that were not available in the past. The notion of personal choice as key to modernity is an important element in understanding how young Australian–Papua New Guinean youth imagine their identities. They had the choice to break free of the racial and ethnic stereotypes placed upon them by the Australian majority and to define their own ethnic or racial identity through their cultural activities; by doing so they were able to obtain a sense of belonging and explore their options to use their "PNG difference" to differentiate themselves from the Australian norm.

Many of the youth expressed a sense of needing to find a unique individual identity saying that Australians were lacking in the cultural resources to craft an authentic unique self, since they just copied Americans and Brits. This construction is interesting because it highlights the desire to craft a unique individual self, generally considered to be an ideology associated with "modernity," yet casts cultural traditions, freely chosen by the individual, as key to a modern individualistic identity. Young Australians of Papua New Guinean descent expressed the belief that Australian cultural identity was nebulous and only beginning to take shape, but that Australians were nevertheless highly opinionated about other cultures. Many of the girls said that white Australian culture was nothing compared to their PNG cultural experiences and their families' indigenous cultures. Alison and Lauren Chan stated, "We were attracted to our grandmother's P.N.G. culture because Australian culture is just an American copy" (personal communication, 2000). Others thought that many of their Australian friends had no real cultural identity, as they lacked focus, did not identify with the Aboriginal cultures, and looked to television and other foreign media for cultural clues. Helen Morton found a similar desire to take control of one's ethnic identity in her research on young Tongans residing in Melbourne, Australia. She says, "Confusion is not uncommon, and while some handle it by adroitly shifting between identities as contexts alter, others find themselves rejecting the cultural identity others would ascribe to them; I even found that one young man rejected the very concept of cultural identity" (2002, 243). One young woman described her schoolmates' culture: "Their music is from the U.S. and Britain, their fashion sense is from foreign magazines and MTV" (Turia, personal communication, 2000). Of course, Australian ethnicity and popular culture were more intricate than the young people's perceptions, but they did have many negative restrictions connected to their colonial past and rejection of Aboriginal and Koori cultures.

When discussing the effect of Australian perceptions upon young Australian–Papua New Guinean women, a number of my female teenage informants complained about young Papua New Guinean women who had recently moved to Australia and married Australian or British men but tried to pass as some other nationality or ethnicity. Several of the teens confronted these young women in public, telling them that they could not hide their PNG roots and could never be "white." They said that they were not trying to force the newcomers into group compliance but wanted to remind them not to deny their ethnicity and nationality, as it was very obvious to other Papuan New Guineans that the women's physical features and postures marked them as being from PNG.

During my interviews, female teens often made fun of the new arrivals, mimicking their speech affectations and their pretentiousness. They noted that these newly married immigrants believed that they had "turned Australian" because they had married and moved to Australia. The girls looked at these newcomers rather scornfully and felt that they had lost a positive part of their identity. It is interesting to note here that while these young women feel it is important for everyone to choose his or her identity, they also clearly feel that some choices are not appropriate. Young women who just wanted to be Australian were looked down upon, while those who tried to formulate some kind of dual identity were seen as making appropriate choices.

Safe Havens, Gendered Influences, and Modernity Incubators

Typically, in my interviews, young artists said that they had been exposed to some type of experience that sparked their interest in PNG culture.

Sometimes it was participation in a traditional ceremony, a festival display of PNG culture, or even a negative race-related incident. The combination of the young people's thirst for cultural knowledge along with the recognition that their cultural activities provided psychological protection from a racialized environment contributed to the development of new cultural identities. However, there was an interesting twist: unlike the Western notions of personhood, identity, and personal progress associated with Western modernities, they reflected Melanesian notions of personhood that stressed the importance of social relationality as an alternative to Western individuality (Knauft 2002, 245).

Papua New Guinean–Australian cultural associations and dance groups have existed in a limited form, since the initial migration wave into Australia in the 1970s. They provided a safe haven in which the women could meet and develop cultural classes for children and social events for the community. The Canberra-based Papua New Guinea Women's Association was one of the first to be established. It served as a social support network for wives of contract government workers, students, and local residents in the late seventies (Decklin, personal communication, November 2000). In 1981, with the aid of the PNG High Commission, this influential association promoted PNG culture through weekend children's classes and special presentations. They also sponsored a dance group that performed a mixture of PNG ceremonial dances for official Australian functions and national celebrations.

By the year 2000, each Australian state or territory, with the exception of Western Australia, had at least one PNG Association in the largest town or city. The number of associations in each city was dependent upon the overall population size and the number of early Papuan migrants who had settled there. Sydney, for example, had two official associations, the PNG-Australia Association, which was predominately comprised of Motu-Koita families who migrated before 1975, and the PNG Wantoks' Association, which comprised a mix of older and recent Papua New Guinean migrants and temporary residents. The PNG-Australia Association members often interacted as if they were one large village, still holding certain codes of behavior that would be expected within their PNG environment. For example, the protocol of respect between age groups was upheld, with the younger members acquiescing to the requests of the elders or by volunteering their children to carry out requested tasks. I also noticed this respectful interaction modeled between people from different areas of PNG, in social settings and when working on projects through the different associations.

In addition to providing social and cultural support for adults, the PNG associations' activities and weekend cultural schools supplied a positive atmosphere and education for the children. Association members were very concerned over the loss of cultural practices and knowledge as well as their children's lack of exposure to their indigenous culture. The majority of the organizers **and instructors** were women, thus providing a female-biased view of cultural history; men were not excluded, but there were more women immigrants than men. The associations usually incorporated more than one cultural group's history and discussed PNG culture as a whole. These schools were the incubators for imagined cultural markers of modernity and catalysts of current youth activities. Ranu Ingram James, one of the founding members of Drum Drum, a professional Papua New Guinean–Australian performance group, said of her experience with the PNG cultural schools held in Darwin, "We went to school during the week and we went to Papua New Guinea School on the weekends. And we learned about Papua New Guinea and did dancing and singing and cooking and all sorts of stuff about being Papua New Guinean. And we did that every day but it was a formal Papua New Guinean education thing that they did on a Saturday" (http://www.mont.org.au/oral_hist/james.html). The association schools' influence ebb and flowed, as they were dependent upon groups of volunteer teachers who were willing to develop and maintain the classes. In 2002, Brisbane, Melbourne, and Sydney were in the process of reviving their schools, but they were having difficulties, as the majority of the work fell upon the shoulders of a few women who were also involved in many other community projects, including the semiprofessional dance groups.

Association Dance Groups

Researchers have discovered that participation in the arts, culturally sensitive curricula, and other related activities provides young people with an alternative venue through which to sustain their identity development (Gibson and Ogbu 1991; E. Jones, Pang, and Rodriguez 2004). The weekend cultural schools were the cultural home for Australian–Papua New

Guinean dance groups, providing validation, instruction, and support for younger dancers who were searching for knowledgeable teachers and role models. Through these groups, young people began to understand and respect their mothers' or parents' cultural traditions while gaining a healthy dose of self-esteem through knowledge of their ancestry.

The dance groups were the most popular form of asserting and displaying PNG cultural identity to the general Australian population. The smaller dance troupes were multigenerational, while the large ones had children, teen, and adult groups; the majority of the young dancers interviewed for this paper participated in both peer-aged groups and multigenerational ensembles. Most dance groups performed only one cultural dance form, as in the case of the older Motu-Koita groups, and the dominant cultural group directed the choreography. In Brisbane, where there was a large Papua New Guinean population, there were eight dance groups in 2000. Three of these groups presented a facet of Motu-Koita and Solien Besena cultures, while other groups hailed from the New Guinea Highlands, Madang Province, and the outer islands. As seen in Hanna's (1987) research on urban dance groups, the dance troupes provided a cultural refuge for youth who found value in intermingling with extended family members and other members of the PNG community. Their participation gave the young artists the strength and assuredness to imagine culturally marked "modern" identities.

In 2000 and 2003, I carried out a short survey based upon initial informal discussions with dancers and cultural keepers to obtain a better understanding of the importance of the dance and cultural groups to young Australian–Papua New Guineans. Twenty-five young people aged fifteen to twenty-one listed cultural pride, personal grounding, and making a distinction between Australian and PNG culture as their primary reasons for participating in the cultural and dance groups. The majority of those persons interviewed unanimously agreed that the weekend classes and social gatherings were often more important than performing the dances, as the process of learning was important to building good relationships. Observation of traditional practices was given a high rating, as people saw these activities as keeping them culturally invested while residing within the dominant Australian culture. The young women, especially, also indicated that all of the cultural activities provided a sense of mental well-being, place, and pride in their ancestral culture, as well as supplying a valuable cultural commodity (dance) that they alone could control. A smaller subset of females, aged thirteen to twenty-three, thought that the cultural activities also helped them to define their identity.

All of the young artists seemed to have some form of nostalgia for PNG, but had a very realistic view that they would have a hard time living there, as they had been raised in Australia. Many of the young women credited their knowledge of PNG culture with helping them retain a certain personal balance not found in their daily existence. In fact, the topic of balance and cultural pride arose in everyone's conversations and interviews, regardless of their age or status within the groups.

The role of the individual in imaging modernity as noted in Appadurai (1996) and Knauft (2002) was quite evident among the teenage girls and some boys. Youth who did not actively participate in dance and cultural activities, for example, constructed unique imagined selves in which they were Australian with the option of being Papua New Guinean. This persona appeared to be very situational. They incorporated Papua New Guinean references in their language, using Tok Pisin or Motu, the PNG lingua franca, when they did not want outsiders in their conversations; they selected PNG foods such as sago, coconut-based dishes, and fresh fish, Papua New Guinean style, if it was advantageous in certain social situations. Some preferred textiles that reflected "Oceanian" designs or PNG designs, and on the personal side, some of the teens whom I interviewed had also decided to tattoo their clan designs on their arms or legs as a positive reinforcement of their commitment to their clans.

In the process of being Papua New Guinea in the context of Australia, the young people transformed Papua New Guinean identity. Their semiprofessional and professional groups were organized as multiethnic, multicultural groups that represented a national rather than tribal view of PNG. Hanna documented this phenomenon in urban-based customary dance groups as "linking more extensive and diverse groups and geographical areas, opening up more communication channels . . . and stimulating an accelerated, exponential pace of creativity" (1987, 204).

The founders of these groups often adopted several dance routines from different regional cultures, as they represented their version of PNG culture in Australia. An excellent example of an artistic group that arose from the cultural schools was Drum Drum, a music and dance ensemble based in Darwin, Northern Territory. The group was formed in 1993 when the then teenage siblings of the Ingram family were attending the University of the South Pacific. The initial group members primarily consisted of the children of Paia and John Ingram, a Motu-Australian family whose ancestors hailed from the Aroma clan of Gaba Gaba village in the Central Province. PNG Drum Drum began with the performance of Motu material and gradually developed a wider PNG repertoire along with its own compositions.

The Ingrams attributed their interest in Papua New Guinea culture to the staunch support of their parents and especially their mother, who encouraged them to attend weekend cultural schools. The group has become involved in writing and producing new music with several well-known PNG musicians from other areas of the country. They developed a website (http://www.drumdrum.com.au) and had a page with music samples on the Australian Broadcast Corporation Northern Territory web page. On their website one section is called Blak Beats, "Working in the Community, Spreading Words of Unity." In this section they state, "An important part of our work is done within the community. When we are not performing, rehearsing, recording or touring we spend our time working within our community through cultural development and educational programs spreading the philosophy of respect and unity." Drum Drum was the most professional Australian–Papua New Guinean group in Australia; they have produced albums; toured Australia, the United States, Singapore, and Europe; and been featured in the Manchester Commonwealth Games Festival.

Drum Drum has influenced other young artists and even established an internship to help other Australian–Papuan New Guinean youth hone their skills. Katrina Sonter, one of the founders of Sunameke, was one of those artists taken under the wing of Drum Drum. Sunameke is an Adelaide-based dance group formed around 1996 by four teenage sisters, Katrina and Samantha Sonter and Julia and Yolanda Gray (http://web.me .com/mageau/SUNAMEKE/HOME.html). The Sonter sisters trace their maternal heritage to Manus Island, while the Grays' mother comes from the Mekeo area of Central Province, west of Port Moresby. The Sonter sisters became interested in dance through weekend cultural classes and through visits to their mother's village on Manus Island.

Katrina Sonter related her excitement and enthusiasm to me about first seeing Drum Drum perform at a festival, when she was a young teen. She was enthralled with them, as they were the first professional PNG touring group she had seen in a national Australian arts festival. Sonter stated, "It was wonderful! I was so proud to see a group of young Papua New Guineans perform so well" (personal communication, 2000). After attending their performance in Adelaide, Katrina and Samantha met the members, who became their cultural mentors. Katrina later moved to Darwin for a short time and worked with the members of Drum Drum. On her return to Adelaide in 1996, she worked with Samantha and the Gray sisters to form Sunameke. Katrina observed, "Personally, I have been really surprised by the open welcome that I've received from the P.N.G. ladies back home (P.N.G.) or in Canberra when we came to perform there . . . and the welcome we get from some of the Pacific Island communities" (personal communication, January 9, 2001).

Sonter also complained that the Australian audiences were always drawn to the exotic and sexually suggestive Manus dances over their contemporary repertoire of the more subtle South Coast and Morobe dances (personal communication, 2000). As a construction of Papua New Guinean culture in Australia, Sunameke presents a hybrid representation of PNG culture shaped by the popular Australia expectations—a mix of South Coast, Trobriand, and Manus Island dance along with a contemporary production of PNG songs and interpretive modern dance. By 2001 they had recruited more young artists and evolved into a South Pacific ensemble based in Darwin, featuring dances from PNG and other western Pacific cultures, making it a Pan-Pacific group.

The Solien Besena: Imagining Alternative Modernities

The Solien Besena, a subclan of the Motu-Koita, were unique in their approach to fostering and maintaining ethnic and cultural identity while building social cohesion and legitimacy in Australia. The key proponents of the cultural development were women; unlike the earlier Motu-Koita families that migrated with males, the initial Solien Besena migration was primarily females. Initially, the female cultural experts had to play the male dance roles when teaching dance and cultural history. Eventually, they incorporated video recordings of male roles and flew elders in from PNG for important ceremonies (Barlow, personal communication, 2000).

The Solien Besena had a finely honed political sense, which placed them in the forefront of imagining Papua New Guinean identity in

Australia. Perhaps their mixed racial heritage—Motu-Koita, Malaysian, Javanese, and British—contributed to their creativity, since they had had to maneuver between multiple cultures and ethnicities over several geographic locations. This flexible identity is a good example of the imagined selves that Appadurai (1996) states as a typical by-product of modernity.

As mentioned previously, ethnicity was often understood by the general Australian public to mean the same as "race," and the Solien Besena were often perceived as yet another needy, tan-skinned Polynesian group. In reaction, the Solien Besena used ethnically oriented frames, schemas, and narratives to define themselves and establish their validity as a unique multiracial group that had its own ethnicity. Their performances were often promoted through such racist statements as "These artists were the children of tribal warriors" and "They are the first of their group to . . ." Much to the younger female artists' chagrin, the older dancers found it advantageous for festival booking to emphasize sensational choreography and the exotic to cater to their Australian audience. Contemporary Solien Besena artist Wendi Choulai noted, "There is a resistance to accepting the idea of anything creative, modern, intellectual or interpretive from a Papua New Guinea contemporary or traditional artist. This phenomenon is explained by Indonesian art critic Jim Supangkat as a perception similar to Orientalism where cultural backgrounds of the Third World were always seen as related to traditions and ethnicity; in a word, uniqueness" (1997, 9). Choulai was the first Solien Besena contemporary artist to rebuke these stereotypes and promote the idea that Papua New Guineans could be both ethnically distinct and thoroughly modern and creative. She was a major role model for many of the Solien Besena and Motu-Koita youth and helped to create venues in which the youth could experiment with and display contemporary art forms.

In their 1998 article on Papua New Guinea modernities, Errington and Gewertz argue that for middle-class Papua New Guineans, "on the collective level culture was, comparably, increasingly enacted as interest-group politics, as serving loosely to link persons pursuing provisionally shared self-interests" (1996, 115). Choulai's invitation to the Asia-Pacific Triennial of Contemporary Art in Brisbane and resulting performance in 1996 introduced young artists to the use of culture as a way to define an interest group. The exhibit and performance helped to legitimize Solien Besena as well as Motu-Koita traditional dance and cultures in a new venue for a large international audience, while specifically involving the youngest generations of Solien Besena and Motu-Koita dancers in the production and performance of the Guma Roho funerary ceremony. This performance also provided the under-twenty youth with roles that would later become a catalyst for youth-led initiatives.

Choulai's efforts sparked at least two projects that allowed young people to imagine their lives in terms they could not before. Zara Choulai-Kassman, the twenty-two-year-old niece of Wendi Choulai and Aaron Choulai, built a Solien Besena Facebook page after participating in her great-uncle's Guma Roho ceremony held in Papua New Guinea in 2008. On her page she stated:

> For All Those Who Know The Story Of The Two Nenehi Clan Sisters, Biria & Daihanai (And Jimmy Malay/Solien), And Are Descended From Either Sister—This Is A Group Where We Can Finally Begin To Link Everyone Up Virtually. As We've Moved On to the age where Facebook, Bebo & Other Social Networks Lead Us To Find More Of Our Relatives Online, We're Beginning To "See" Just How Big The Family Is & The Global Expansion Of This Besena. So Far, We Have "Official" Records Of Biria & Daihanai's Children, And The Generation Afterwards (Most Of Them Would Be Our Grandparents). From There, The Family Has Seemed To Have "Exploded" And Records, & Clan Connectivity Have Been Lost . . . After Compiling All The Information That We Hope To Obtain From These Groups (Bebo & Facebook) We Will Then Set Up A Website Solely For The Solien Besena, Where All The Information Will Be Available For Personal References And For Future Generations. (http://www.facebook.com/s.php?init=q&q=solien+besena&ref=ts&sid =61618633a449fbaf080b942c8b4d293c#/group.php?sid=61618633a449f baf080b942c8b4d293c&gid=4458686?489&ref=search)

Zara's attempt to unite her kin and collect material about her heritage has been successful in spawning at least two other rival websites, established by males. In establishing the first website and imitating the collection of genealogical information, she has challenged a customary male role. She also changed the way that lineage and clan identity were conceptualized for Papua New Guineans in Australia. Before completing this chapter, I received an e-mail stating that a Solien Besena male and another person related by marriage were requesting the same information to post on the Internet (anonymous, personal communication, 2009).

Aaron Choulai chose another route. As an accomplished musician who was awarded "Young Artist of the Year" at the 2006 Australian Jazz Awards and named as one of the most influential Melburnians in the *Age's Melbourne Magazine* in 2007, he decided to produce a jazz opera to highlight and promote his heritage. At age twenty-five he premiered *Ai Na Asi a Mavaru Kavamu, We Don't Dance for No Reason* at the Queensland Music Festival. It was later performed in Melbourne as well as Port Moresby, Papua New Guinea. This multimedia jazz opera featured a Papua New Guinean *Peroveta Anedia* (Prophet songs) choir, projected visual images of Tatana, and a jazz ensemble. The Australian press release, while praising the production, still worked within the popular stereotypes, seizing upon Aaron's exoticness: "Aaron Choulai is a human melting pot of cultures—he was born in Papua New Guinea to his Chinese/Motu mother and his Jewish/Polish/Australian father" (http://www.png.embassy.gov .au/pmsb/MR080226.html). The Australian Broadcasting Corporation interview captured the uniqueness of the production and gave insight into this Solien Besena cultural identity through an interview with Aaron: "The 24-year-old is in Brisbane for the Queensland Music Festival, which is featuring his show 'We don't dance for no reason.' For the performance, Aaron has brought with him a choir from his ancestral village, Tatana. . . . Aaron says, 'People that will come will get an insight into Motuan culture, and into a lot of the social problems in Papua New Guinea. First and foremost, though, you're going to hear incredible singing that's never been documented and never really been explored at all.'" "We don't dance for no reason" is *ai na asi a mavaru kavamu* in Motu. "Literally that means, 'we don't do silly dances,'" explains Aaron. "It comes from a side of my family that moved out of Tatana . . . and these people are song keepers of a traditional dance called 'reroipe,' which you do when someone dies, to signify the end of a mourning period" (http://www.abc.net.au/local /stories/2007/07/16/1979873.htm).

Aaron also kept a personal and recording company home page as well as Facebook and Myspace (http://www.myspace.com/aaronchoulai) pages. Aaron and Zara have used the technoscape effectively to disseminate their cultural information and shown the way for the next generation through the effective use of new modes of presentation.

Conclusion

As seen from these examples, external perceptions of race and gender were important concepts in framing Australian–Papua New Guinean youth's imagining of alternative modernities. White Australian stereotypes of Pacific women, racialized discourse, and cultural unawareness became a catalyst for young people's forming new senses of cultural identity and imagining cultural markers of modernity. The notion of personal choice, was also a strong element in how young people, especially females, have developed what Appadurai (1996) has described as diasporic public spheres through a "technoscape" of social networking sites.

This technoscape has allowed them to imagine their lives in terms not explored before. In the Australian–Papua New Guinean and Solien Besena situations, the fabrication of cultural identity reflected behaviors and situational flexibility that were a "production that is never complete, always in process, and always constituted within, not outside" (Hall and Jacques 1990, 222). It has been posited that cultural revivals have become a basic component in the demonstration and definition of Pacific identity within urban contemporary spheres (Linnekin and Poyer 1990; Nero 1992; Morton 2002; Herda 2002). This chapter explored the extraordinary role of young women in imagining alternative cultural identities and markers of modernity through their conscious decision to adopt and display facets of their Papua New Guinean cultural heritage and reframe them within a Western construct.

The demonstration of Australian–Papua New Guinean and Solien Besena dance in secular Australian celebrations and festivals provided a venue for the reaffirmation of cultural identity and validity, within the larger Australian community as well as the smaller PNG communities. These activities filled a gap in their lives that Australian culture could not provide. Members of the Australian–Papua New Guinean communities noted that the retention of their cultural practices and development of the new art forms provided youth with the environment and the grounding they needed to be themselves and sustain their culture. Implicitly realizing that racist dimension to mainstream Australian ideas about white moderns and brown primitives, young Australians of Papua New Guinean descent find ways to be both Papua New Guinean and fully Australian and modern.

11

Islanders among a Sea of Gangs

Diasporic Masculinities and Gang Culture
among Tongan American Youth

JOSEPH ESSER

On one of those overly humid afternoons in the Island Kingdom of Tonga, G-Money sits on a beat-up, old brown couch, reminiscing about his childhood experiences of gang life on the streets of Los Angeles. G-Money's arms, buff from prison-yard workouts, are marked with tattoos signifying his affiliation with one of LA's many Crip sets as well as his identification as a Tongan. Outside his rented house on the outskirts of the capital city, boys dressed in wraparound skirts and finely woven waist mats are beginning to return home from school. As they chase a robust pig digging for food in the middle of the muddy dirt road in front of the house, the disparity between G-Money's experiences as a Tongan youth in Los Angeles and the lives of the young men passing are intriguingly apparent. In his XXXL royal-blue T-shirt, khaki Dickies shorts, and matching Chuck Taylor shoes, G-Money embodies an LA gangsta, specifically, a Tonga Crip Gangsta (TCG). Unlike the lives of the bucolic youths in the street, G-Money's adolescence was one of excessive violence and ethnic loyalty:

> To be from a gang that you have so much pride. . . . Especially a gang that's supposed to represent your creed, your ethnicity. I'm a Tonga Crip. If someone says fuck Tonga Crips, they are like saying fuck my race and they are saying fuck the Crips. It gives you even more endurance, more motivation. It's like, man . . . I'm a patriot. Do I have pride or not? You have people with so much dedication and loyalty, you know. You throw "Tongan" up into it, and that's one more motivation to be like, man? That's like sayin' "Fuck my momma."

As a result of his involvement in gangs ,G-Money spent extended time in juvenile hall, leading to incarceration shortly after his eighteenth birthday, eventually resulting in G-Money's deportation back to Tonga and the people he had so actively sought to represent in the hood. His affiliation with TCG ran deeper than the bonds and security he found in the gang alongside other Tongan youth whose families had also migrated to the same violent landscape in inner-city South Los Angeles. The gang offered a platform through which G-Money and his peers were able to give voice and meaning to their experiences in the multiple cultural worlds they traversed.

As immigrant youth like G-Money experience racism, cultural marginalization, poverty, and urban decay, they articulate their shared experiences and negotiate culture and ethnicity through gangs and violent, hypermasculine identities. The proliferation of gangs, John Hagedorn states, "is clearly related to familiar economic and social changes now associated with globalization—urbanization, immigration and social marginalization" (2007, xxv). Through what Manuel Castells refers to as "resistance identities" (1997, 8), displaced, marginalized youth make powerful statements about gender, modernity, and globalization through enacting hypermasculine and racialized identities through gangs. One must, however, avoid essentializing such experiences and identities, since clearly gang members like G-Money inhabit multiple social worlds and multiple identities. G-Money holds both LA Crip and Tongan nationalist identities through the gang and is involved in the dynamic process of redefining each. "It is not just that collective identities and ways of life are created, but that they are internally contested, that their boundaries are porous and overlapping, and that people live in more than one at the same time" (Calhoun 1995, 47).

The cross-cultural popularity of gangsta culture rests in its ability to articulate shared experiences and to confront cultural and social marginalization (see Alonso 2004; Hagedorn 2007; and Quinn 2005). Eithne Quinn explains that while gangsta is a kind of dissident, everyday political culture, it is also a hypervisible commercial form, making it a powerful and compelling image in the lives of youth. "It both contains common subversions of authority predicated on a history of discrimination and offers a highly commodifiable brand of youth and race rebellion" (2005, 23). It is "a simplified code—young males' obsession with power and prowess,"

Ward Keeler further adds, that makes gangs, gang imagery, and gangsta music so appealing and transportable across cultural boundaries (2008). Gang culture is the embodiment of a violent masculinity, and owing to the bloodshed associated with gangs, it operates as both an extremely meaningful medium and, simultaneously, a destructive force in the lives of many youth.

My research examines the early and formative experiences and narratives of those migrant youths who "do not make it" in the United States: those youths who find themselves involved in gangs and in and out of the juvenile court system, serve time in jail and prison, and ultimately are forcefully removed from the United States through deportation to Tonga. In examining the construction of gang identities, masculinity, and youth culture among Tongan male adolescents, I seek to address how young people's positions in socially, racially, and economically marginalized communities in the United States are generative of certain discourses of masculine identity that make gang membership meaningful.

Tongan Migration to California

In 1979, thirteen-year-old Buddha boarded a Los Angeles–bound Polynesian Airlines flight with his older sisters, younger brother, and parents at Tonga's Fua'amotu Airport. Following a fifteen-hour flight, Buddha arrived at his new home of Los Angeles, California, to join his aunt, who had become an American citizen five years earlier. Torn between sadness about leaving and excited anticipation about arriving, Buddha had varied ideas about what life would have in store for him. He said, "The night before we went to the States, I remember I was sitting at Polynesian Airlines talking with my cousin. I remember telling him, 'Hey, we goin' to America. You just pick up money on the streets. It's like picking up leaves or something.' I don't remember where I got that idea, but I still remember it. I had ideas like that—it's gonna be better food, better clothing and toys, stuff like that."

South Los Angeles lived up to neither Buddha's thirteen-year-old imagination nor his father's. Although they had come to the United States on visitors' visas, his parents had no intention of returning to Tonga once there, because they wanted their children to be educated in the United States, and settled in one of Los Angeles's poorer neighborhoods. During the mid- to late 1970s, in fact, many immigrant families from the Pacific were settling throughout South Los Angeles, in Inglewood, Carson, Hawthorne, Compton, and Long Beach. During the 1970s and 1980s, the neighborhoods of South Los Angeles were witnessing an explosive rise in gang-related violence and a significant increase in crime, as gang members fought for control of the city's crack cocaine trade (Klein, Maxson, and Cunningham 1991, 623). By the time of the 1992 LA riots, South Central (now commonly referred to as South Los Angeles) had become synonymous with urban decay and street violence. The number of gang-related murders in Los Angeles County more than doubled from 1987 to 1992, from 387 to 803 (Howell 1999, 209). Unfortunately, some Tongan youths would witness and play a role in this crime, both as victims and as perpetrators. Indeed, the year that Buddha arrived in Los Angeles was the very same year that Crip gang founder Raymond Washington was murdered.

The devastating fact is that many Tongan youths like Buddha started their urban lives in the few places their families could afford, usually decaying areas of the city plagued by criminal activity. Many Tongan families entered the United States in the 1970s and 1980s just as skilled manufacturing jobs were beginning to be outsourced abroad (Small 1997, 7). While jobs were vanishing from major urban centers, new problems of widespread unemployment, poverty, and crime were beginning to flood these areas. Beginning in the 1970s, the city of Los Angeles suffered a major decline in its manufacturing base, resulting in massive loss of the union jobs that offered wages that could support a family on a long-term, sustainable basis. Street gangs like the Crips, Bloods, Los Sureños, La Mara 18s, and Mara Salvatrucha (MS-13) rose to notoriety in the hardest-hit areas.

Tongan migration to the United States dramatically increased following Congress's 1965 enactment of the Hart-Celler Act, which ultimately created a new immigrant demographic within the United States because it abolished national-origin quotas (Waldinger 1989). The newly adopted policy resulted in an unprecedented movement of Pacific islander immigrants to the United States. The United States set an annual limitation by country in 1968 for all immigrants allowed into the United States, but since the number of family-reunification visas remained unlimited, chain immigration became a significant means for early migrants from the Pacific to bring over their sizable sibling networks (Small 1997, 52).

When Buddha's family first arrived in Los Angeles, they stayed with his paternal aunt and her Samoan husband's family. Their neighborhood was located between Compton and Long Beach, where the few resident Tongans were closely related to Buddha's family. Most other Tongans were scattered throughout the Los Angeles basin, sometimes at great distances from each other. Crime rates in the area were among the highest in the city, with residents often too scared or disaffected to call the police or serve as witnesses. Buddha immediately knew he had to establish a network of support to survive in such a fraught new environment, noting:

> My first impression of the States was that I had to try and fit in. I didn't know gangstas then. Before I went to the States, I watched a couple movies before I went, but that's all. Getting dropped off in the borderline of Compton and Long Beach, that's all about macho stuff. It's gang-infested neighborhoods. It's Crip neighborhood, so it didn't take long to reach the level of what would play out the rest of my life. At the age of thirteen, that's where I was at. I was trying to figure out "how do I fit into this?" This is my new world. Nothing like what I had expected. . . . I had a few ideas what the States would be like. It was nothing like what we face. Years later during long days and nights in prison, I have thought about that time and how much I wanted to fit in.

Buddha's Tongan days as a carefree youth, swimming at the wharf, relaxing with peers on the waterfront, and playing pickup rugby games, abruptly terminated after his arrival in Los Angeles County. His family, like many others, left Tonga with the hopes of greater financial opportunities in prosperous urban centers, only to settle in the least-affluent and more peripheral areas of the cities. It is thus unsurprising that Buddha describes his first year in LA as a complete shock, using a particularly evocative example of the vast cultural difference he encountered in his new environment:

> In Tonga, we respect old people. One day me, my dad, and my dad's brother-in-law and some Tongans were hanging out across the street, and an old lady was walking with a walker. She barely could walk. She was carrying a purse, and two youngsters ran up and tried to yank it from her. She wouldn't let go, so they had to slam her on the ground to

take it. My uncle was going to run to stop it, but another Tongan guy said, "No, you gonna get shot!" But that's what we saw there. Seeing more of that happening over and over, you get used to it. You say, "Hey, ain't nothing wrong there. Everybody else is doing that." Compton and Long Beach, where we lived, was murder capital of the States for a minute [long period of time]! I think it played a part on not only me but my brother and them also. From skipping school to go swimming [in Tonga] to seeing all that [in LA], that's a whole different flip of the page in life.

Adolescence in Tonga

In Tonga, male adolescence (referred to as *taimi talavou*) is a formative time in the development of young men's identity as they move from boyhood to manhood (Marcus 1978). From the time boys reach puberty until they marry, most adolescent males in Tonga spend large amounts of their time away from their families' households and in the company of their peers in a separate quarters, called the boys' hut (Morton 1996, 110). This practice, referred to as *nofo huti*, offers adolescent boys a great degree of freedom and independence. Many young boys eagerly move to the boys' hut to be associated with friends, siblings, and older boys. During this adolescent period and throughout the stay in the boys' hut, peer socialization and youth culture become the "primary sites for the development of masculine identity" (ibid., 112). This process, Cowling argues, "encourages the development of strong bonds between male peers and between male siblings, but also helps to confirm the assumption of a masculine heterosexual identity and behavior" (1990, 172). The extended role of the village in Tonga often acts as a larger social-control mechanism to regulate the behavior of young males, who otherwise appear to have complete independence and lack supervision. The freedom of male youth has very different consequences in the anonymous space of an American city. Through migration, *nofo huti*, whereby young males find and define their identity, masculinity, and community, becomes "the hood."

Many families first encountered American life in California or Hawaii, which are often ports of entry to the United States from Tonga. Like other immigrants, these Tongan families later relocated to areas where their fellow family members and villagers had already established themselves, such as Inglewood, Long Beach, and Compton in Los Angeles; East Palo

Alto in the San Francisco Bay Area; and Glendale in Salt Lake City, Utah. Newly arrived families often live with relatives for short periods until they are able to find their own residence and stable employment. This time is often filled with frequent moves and can be an economically and emotionally turbulent time.

Many Tongan families are unprepared for the considerable costs associated with living and raising a family in the States. Poor and working-class immigrant parents commonly experience new financial stresses and challenges, having to work harder and longer hours to provide the basic necessities of food and shelter for their family. More often than not, both parents are required to work one or more full-time jobs. The struggle to provide for one's family can conflict with a parent's ability to provide guidance and supervision. The situation is compounded by the lack of an extended kin-support network to share in child rearing, as is common in the Pacific.

Although many families left Tonga with hopes of finding economic opportunities, they often faced downward mobility in low-status, minimum-wage jobs. Indeed, Tongans and Samoans have the lowest income per capita of any major racial or ethnic group in Southern California (Kawakami 2006). Most Tongan adults must hold multiple jobs in order to maintain their own households because of the increased cost of living and their social obligation to remit money to family members remaining in Tonga (Small 1997).

This precarious economic situation was compounded for Buddha's parents after their visitor visas expired and they became undocumented workers. Buddha's youthful experiences in urban America vastly differed from his father's upbringing in the islands. In rank- and status-oriented Tonga, *faka'apa'apa* (respect) and deference are largely defined by the values and associated behaviors of *'ofa* (love and generosity), *talangofua* (obedience), and *fetokoni'aki* (mutual assistance) (Morton 1996). Young people are expected and obligated to show respect and deference to those people older and higher ranking than them, often in embodied ways such as lowering their eyes, not speaking in the presence of superiors, and offering *tokoni* (help and assistance) without reservation.

Respect in the hood and the code of the streets were very different from the expectations structuring Tongan village life. As Elijah Anderson (1999) maintains, "street culture" and "the code of the street" are informal systems of governing the use of violence. Status, rank, and respect are largely attained through violent and tough identities. According to Anderson, responsibility for order and safety essentially devolves on the individual. Safety comes from having a violent reputation, toughness, and aggressiveness. Displaying a violent demeanor not only commands respect but also serves to discourage others from testing or challenging those individuals exhibiting the street-code style. Buddha told me:

> We had Tonga [referring to *anga fakatonga*] at home, but how much time do we spend at home? It didn't take long for me, for that not to mean anything because of the new culture that I was in. Most youth, how much do they spend at home? I don't know. It probably varies from different families. For me, I didn't spend much time at home, so I was robbed of that or whatever. So I created my own identity of what I thought makes me Tongan. Tongan is a warrior or all them other stuff; we don't bow down to nobody. I'm not scared of nobody. That came from stories we hear about Tonga, the little we heard here and there— there's Tongan war stories everywhere . . . how we whipped on Samoa, how we whipped on Fiji. We conquered the Pacific. Coming to a place where it's about being tough, that's like throwing kerosene on the fire, and it ignites just like that. It's a combination of different things. If you don't have much to live for . . . life don't mean nothin'. Why should I care? I ain't scared of nothin'.

Buddha describes himself as viewing a violent inner-city present through a vague lens of a Tongan warrior past. His tales of fierce Tongan battles help him to make sense of a fraught inner-city existence in which violence is one of the few ways young men believe they can achieve self-respect. Through this reified notion of tradition and culture, Buddha employed gang membership to create a violent, hypermasculine, but Tongan identity in which Pacific traditions of warfare and respect resonated with the somewhat different codes of violence and authority in street gangs to produce a potent new identity.

In this hostile environment, Buddha and his peers experienced ethnic self-segregation and personal difficulties connecting with fellow students, fueling a deeper anger and resentment that played itself out on the streets. Parents' attempts to shape their children's behavior into an obedient, respectful, and attentive ideal (*anga lelei*) often only increased adolescents' sense of isolation, feelings of frustration, and a lack of guidance. These young adults often could not turn to their parents to express their concerns, problems, and struggles in trying to learn and make sense of both cultures. Buddha told me:

> Our parents didn't understand our problems. They expected us to have Tongan problems. They didn't recognize that we weren't in Tonga and we had American ways now. In the Tongan way [*anga fakatonga*] we couldn't talk back to our dads and explain what was going on with us. A lot of my friends in high school had the same problem. Other students feared us in high school because we were violent and aggressive. You know what they say, misery loves company, and we were drawn together because of that, I guess. That's where I found my sense of belonging, through the gang, eh.

Tongan migrant parents expect young Tongan males to forge their identity and masculinity following a timeworn model of community interaction with peers and family. However, in a community plagued by drugs, gangs, and violence, the results can be destructive, and for some immigrant youth, identifying one's community, resisting cultural assimilation, and asserting one's own distinctive history is realized through gang membership. As Buddha explained, his eventual gang affiliation stemmed out of his own personal search for identity and community in an area already dominated by youth gangs.

In Buddha's Long Beach neighborhood, gang conflicts were beginning to escalate, and young men from the large Samoan community had established a large Crip-affiliated gang, called the Sons of Samoa (SOS). Too young to join SOS, Buddha and his cousin mimicked their older peers by calling themselves the Original Samoans, the irony of which was not lost upon him:

> It's funny when two Tongans started a gang called Original Samoans.... We were getting high already. The first year I got there was the first year I started smokin' weed. I started gettin' drunk. Back then, there was only a few Tongans that was hip to the gang. Tongans mostly just hung out; it wasn't no gang stuff. They would beat on people; it wasn't no gang.

It was mostly guys that just hang out together. The first year we were there, I went to a Samoan school. I think that's when that gangsta stuff kicked in. There was a lot of Samoans from SOS, a Crip gang, eh. There were no Tongans there, so that's when I started tryin' to fit in. Act and try to pick up their whole way of life, dress thing, Stacy Adams and Dickies [Crip-affiliated clothing brands], and all that greased-up stuff.

Buddha's struggle to fit in at school resulted in regular reprimands from both school officials and parents. Given the rough start Buddha was having in Long Beach, his parents decided to send their son to Monroe Jr. High School in nearby Inglewood, where there was a much larger Tongan student body.

Inglewood: Home of the Tonga "Crips"

Inglewood was one of a few areas in the city where Tongans had begun to establish themselves as a visible community. Apartment-complex managers and owners in Inglewood provided affordable rentals to Tongans without extensive background or credit checks and hefty security-deposit requirements, thus facilitating the growth of the Tongan community. A successful Fiji-born businessman owned a large East Inglewood building complex he called the Fijian Apartments and sympathized with the precarious status of many newly arrived Tongan families. He was also familiar with Tonga's culture and traditions, as indigenous Fijians and Tongans share a close and interwoven history as neighboring Pacific islanders. Many Tongan families moved straight from the islands to Inglewood, particularly the ones who, like the Fiji-born landlord, were members of the tightly connected Mormon Church in Tonga.

The Fijian Apartments were located on the east side of Inglewood on the western border of South Los Angeles, an area crowded with low-income rental properties. This community was nicknamed "Little Las Vegas" because of its reputation for drug sales, prostitution, and crack addiction. The west side of Inglewood had a much better reputation, with new apartment buildings under construction and relatively affordable single-family homes that many newly arrived families hoped to eventually inhabit in order to escape the criminal activity plaguing East Inglewood. This upward mobility through home ownership never took place for many migrant families, and consequently their children began their urban lives in a setting framed by gang violence.

The eastern district of Inglewood has remained the turf for rival Crip and Blood gangs as well as a growing number of Hispanic gang sets. To the west of the Fijian Apartments were a few Crip gangs, both small in size and territory: the Raymond Avenue Crips, Imperial Village Crips, and Osage Legend Crips. However, Blood gangs surrounded the rest of the neighborhood to the north, south, and east, outnumbering Crip sets in the area greatly. To the east was the turf of the Inglewood Family Gang, the largest Blood gang in the area that formed shortly before the Blood alliance forged in 1971. Since the gang's formation, the Inglewood Family has maintained an unbroken feud with all of the Inglewood's Crip gangs. The Crenshaw Mafia formed in the late 1970s as a spin-off of the Inglewood Family, with its turf spanning a six-block housing project known as the Bottoms. Their territory extends within a single block of the Fijian Apartments, and directly to the west is the Raymond Avenue Crips' turf. Coincidentally, the major apartment complex and area that Tongan families were moving to happened to be located in the center of the territory that the Raymond Crips, Crenshaw Mafia, and Inglewood Family gangs were battling over.

In 1978, Masi, a young teen from Tonga, arrived with his family at the Fijian Apartments in Inglewood. At that time a handful of Tongan families lived in the apartment complex. Families came together in the Fijian Apartments in a number of different configurations: recently married couples with young children, adult siblings raising their children together, and single-parent families. As the oldest Tongan youths in the apartment complex during that time, Masi and his peers would play an important role in defining Tongan youth culture and experiences in the area as they made sense of their new social environment.

During his first two years in Inglewood, Masi attended Monroe Jr. High School in Inglewood. There he met Buddha. Although Buddha and Masi had both grown up on the same island in Tonga, they attended different schools, belonged to different churches, and did not know each other until they arrived in the States. A handful of Tongan students attended the predominantly African American Monroe Jr. High School, and the two boys quickly bonded with each other through their shared language and cultural identity, despite the fact that Buddha lived in Long Beach rather than Inglewood. Buddha remembers traveling from Long Beach with his family on the weekends to attend weddings and events in Inglewood's Tongan community, noting, "In Long Beach, it was only Samoans other than our family. From what I remember, there was a lot of gang stuff happening then."

Yet in Inglewood gangs were more active in schools and in the neighborhood. Masi had befriended a number of the local neighborhood kids whose older brothers were already representing the Raymond Crips. Given the chance, Masi and the younger boys would hang out with the boys' older brothers in the Raymond Crips. Over time, Masi and the younger neighborhood boys were challenged to different tests. Masi quickly gained the respect of many of the older gang members by not shying away from dangerous and violent activities. As Masi's younger gang contemporary G-Money explained:

Once he affiliated himself with the Raymond Crips is when he did some pretty crazy shit to give himself a name. . . . [T]hat name made everybody, as far as Crips, respect all Tongans. He did crazy shit like cuttin' muthafucka's balls off and hanging fools up. The school I went to, they told me that when I went there . . . that that Tongan dude from Raymond Crips hung this Blood on the flag pole and stuff . . . cut his balls off. You know, shit like that and then ever since then, that opened doors to earn a lot of respect from [because of] him.

On the streets, Masi was known as Volcano. Volcano's excessive violence commanded respect from gang members and intensified fears from rival gangs. Like Buddha, Volcano was making a name for Tongans and, consequently, new enemies for young Tongan boys and men in the area. His excessive acts of violence led him in and out of juvenile hall. In 1986, at the age of nineteen, Volcano was given a twelve-year sentence for shooting at the police.

It was during this time that many Tongan youths in Los Angeles began to noticeably bond and identify around a common Crip identity. By the age of fifteen, Buddha founded the South Pacific Islanders along with his first cousins in Long Beach, affiliating themselves with Crip sets throughout the area. The Tonga Crip Gangstas also had recently formed and taken root in Inglewood, partly based in the need for mutual protection and partly in response to the isolation and cultural alienation the boys experienced. Initially comprising Volcano's younger brothers, cousins, and other Tongan boys from the area, TCG would become the largest Tongan gang in LA and an established part of the Inglewood gang turf, a new ally for the few Crip sets in a predominantly Blood neighborhood. All young male Tongan migrants, even the ones who purposely avoided gangs, were increasingly identified as having Crip affiliation owing to the brazen acts of a few who actively sought to create reputations in the streets. The most active TCG members during the mid-1980s found themselves engaged in the same street war as Volcano, some by choice and others as a consequence of newly racialized identities in the neighborhood. With Volcano's affiliation with the Raymond Crips, TCG allied itself with the Crip sets in the neighborhood, inheriting both allies and enemies. In the process, the young men inherited the decadelong history of violence that continued to ravage the neighborhood. A handful of young men actively represented the gang, claiming the two-block area around the Fijians Apartments as TCG's hood. As G-Money explained:

> The way I seen it, Tongans didn't know how to gangbang, you know. 'Cause I grew up around a lot of Raymond Crips, and they kind of paved the way. "If you're going to gangbang, this is how you gangbang." Then when I seen TCG formulate, they was comprised of a crazy-ass fool, and the rest of the guys affiliated themselves with this crazy-ass dude. But they weren't as crazy as Volcano. There would probably be one dude out of a bunch of guys that actually is arrestable, while the rest is just fuckin' homeboys bangin' at home. You know . . . dressed up and shit like that. They were like that for a while. . . . You had like one, two, three real dudes that were putting it down. Tongans back then was like, "If we run into a Blood, we're going to fuck him up. But if we don't, then we are just going to drink and have a good time."

Not everyone who affiliated with the early TCG took gangbanging to the level of the most active TCG members. Many affiliated themselves with Tonga Crips as teens and later left gang life by the wayside when they married and began to follow Tongan religious and cultural expectations for male heads of households. G-Money complained that this trend left the burden of mentoring responsibilities to younger gang members:

Our older peers weren't around . . . like how older OGs [Original Gang-stas] are supposed to be . . . to mold you, and tell you how it is. Some was locked up. Others got lost in marriage . . . with paternity, and all that. Then it's like they never gangbanged before in their life. It's a trip. That's the Tongan way, though. Like it never happened. It's like a part of their life that was a mistake, you know. And then they do a 360 turn. You go to the wife's family. You take care of the wife's family or however the fuck they do that shit. That's how it happens. I see a lot of dudes that call themselves gangbangers back then   and then they all gain weight with kids and shit. We just took the responsibility with ourselves.

TCG-Money Fam: The Next Generation

Malia, an unmarried mother of a young child, moved into the Fijian Apartments around the same time as Volcano and his family. Malia left Tonga following the birth of her son Paki, who would later be known on the streets as G-Money. The powerful social stigma attached to chil-dren born to unmarried parents prompted Malia's family to support her migration to the United States, an unusual move for a young unmar-ried Tongan woman. As her newborn grew up in Inglewood, Volcano and his older Tongan youth were in the process of establishing TCG. Too young to affiliate with TCG, G-Money watched on the sidelines as the older boys in his apartment complex and his church ward took to repre-senting the Tonga Crips. By the late eighties and early nineties, many of the most active TCGs were imprisoned or had left the area. A number of violent encounters with the Crenshaw Mafia, Inglewood Family Bloods, and Lennox 13 led to the arrest and incarceration of TCG members on aggravated assault, attempted murder, and manslaughter charges. TCG members were also incarcerated for selling crack and marijuana, carry-ing assault rifles and semiautomatic handguns, and committing armed robberies and auto theft.

By the time G-Money and his peers were entering adolescence and coming of gangsta age, the original TCG gang was scattered and leader-less. Despite the fact that only a few older gangstas were still around to show the new generation the ropes, the second generation of Tonga Crips built on the previous generation's reputation and escalated violence in the neighborhood. In a neighborhood where gangs were almost a way of life, even with the absence of many of the original TCGs, avoiding gang conflict in Inglewood was difficult. G-Money told me:

> When I started gangbanging . . . the only reason why was 'cause the Bloods would approach me at school because I was Tongan. They was like, "You a Crip?" [I said,] "No, I'm not a Crip. I don't even gangbang." It was a constant thing. I would come to school, and I had to put up with these fools constantly harassing me, like, "You'se a Crip!" They would lift up your shirt, looking for something blue . . . looking for a reason to punch me. Looking for a reason to jump you because of where we stayed. Just 'cause I stayed in that area and was identified with that group. I tried to tell my mom, "I gotta check out of my school." My mom was like, "Nah, just deal." I tried to tell my mom to check me out of that school because I'm not going to graduate. She didn't believe me.

By the time G-Money reached junior high school, many of his classmates began affiliating themselves with the gangs of their neighborhoods. In ninth grade, at the age of fifteen, G-Money and a circle of peers formed their own gang, calling themselves "Tonga Crip Gangstas, Money Fam" (TCG-Money Fam). These boys shared similar experiences growing up: breakdown in the family unit, cultural and social alienation, crowded living conditions, and threats from gangs in the area. The TCG-Money Fam also had long histories and tight bonds with one another, as neighbors at the Fijian Apartments and as classmates in elementary and junior high school. Others met only on Sundays at the Westchester Third (Tongan) Ward of the Latter-day Saints church in Inglewood. At that time, the Third Ward was the only LDS church in the area offering church services in the Tongan language. There, families in Inglewood would gather with other Tongan families from around the Los Angeles area to attend church services.

The boys gathered at church each Sunday with their families, greeting each other with "What up, Cuz! What up, Loc!" (Crip-affiliated terms of familiarity) before they sat for sacrament and sermons. After the formal services finished, church members broke up into smaller meeting groups based on their age and sex. By the ninth grade, G-Money and most of his peers had graduated to the Aaronic Priesthood church quorum where they congregated each week. Over the years, the church school had developed into a forum where the boys came to socialize, share experiences, and embrace their Tongan roots. It was at these weekly quorums that the TCG-Money Fam first "jumped" each other into their gang. The term *jumped in* refers to the ritual beating one receives to gain membership to the gang. It entails being kicked and punched until the gang member or leader calls for it to end. This action bonds the members together as a family and is a testament to new gang member's courage, strength, and character. In an almost organic act, the TCG-Money Fam began. G-Money recounted:

> In the Mormon church . . . you're a deacon, from deacon to priesthood, and then you work your way up. I was in my priesthood class, and we were all kickin' it at a park and then we just started telling each other, "Hey, let's jump each other in." I thought they were kidding, right. And then when the first one got jumped in, I was like fuck it. Then I got jumped in. We just socked up the first dude, and when they say it's enough, then the next dude get in. . . . [T]he other dude gets up, and then he joins in. We started naming everybody in our clique [by their first initial] . . . either the beginning of it or the end of it . . . that has their letter and the name that they represent. My homeboy was C-Money. And then he put me on, and he was like, you want to be G-Money? And everybody else had their cliques. They had the Rocs, the Nuts, the Locs. They put on they own homeboys. That's how it really started, like K-Roc, D-Loc, P-Money, T-Money. . . . My clique was the Money Fam clique.

Without a deeper understanding of the social and historical context in which these youth grew up, one might assume that the TCG-Money Fam gang might was formed out of boredom or in jest. But the gangs had deeper roots; the conflicts and reputations left in the streets by the older generation of Tonga Crip Gangstas had created real problems and hostilities in the neighborhood for the younger generation of Tongan boys coming of age. As a group, the TCG-Money Fam provided protection from harassment and attacks of gangs at school and around the neighborhood. G-Money told me:

> When you're a kid growing up . . . a kid is going to get picked on or is going to be the one picking on people. If he is going to be the neutral one . . . where he is the one getting along with everyone, there's still going to

be that one kid that is giving him problems. And then it's up to him to stand up for himself. If not, he is probably [going to] look to a group for kids, his friends, to have his back. If he has cousins, that's good; then he is going to follow his cousins. If he doesn't have cousins, that's cool; he's going to have little homies and stuff. And he is going to hang out with the little homies. And whatever the little homies are into, he will mess around with.

The formation of the TCG-Money Fam also filled a void, creating social solidarity and an important social network in which displaced and culturally isolated youth from around the city could connect. For those gang members who met only once a week in the LDS church ward, the TCG-Money Fam offered a new social space and structure around which to organize. The gang brought about a closeness and sense of family that was lacking in the home. By the early 1990s, the TCG-Money Fam were hanging out on the streets and at each other's homes in Inglewood away from the influences of church and school. Because most of the boys' parents and older family members worked multiple jobs, the boys were left with plenty of unsupervised time to skip school and hang out around the neighborhood. The clique regularly hung out around the neighborhood block their gang had claimed until the late hours of the night. G-Money said:

Everybody would go to the block that we all hang out at or wherever someone's house is at. We'd go post up and make it known that this block is our block! Some niggas would have rocks [crack], trying to make a couple dollars. Your homeboy would be selling rocks on the side. You'd just post up. It's like numbers to the clique. So then you just go there and see how many niggas there, see who is going to show up in the hood. It's like . . . who shows and who don't show, you know? Who's about it and who's not about it.

The streets offered gang members possibilities for both income and respect. The gangsta life with its fast money from drugs and robberies and the quick elevation of status and respect through violence on the street was alluring. Through the gang, money came easily and was often spent just as quickly. G-Money told me:

I would keep a hundred dollars' worth [of crack] on me, and then I would try to sell that hundred. Depending on if I want to stand in the hood, sell it all, and then go buy me some new shit . . . like a new shirt, new pants, new shoes. Or if I don't want to stay standing in the hood all day, I would stand there as long as I could sell fifty dollars' worth. Just to have money in my pocket. After that I would go stash. You could sell that shit hella fast 'cause where we stayed at because there were so many fuckin' hookers, crack heads . . . everywhere. The luckiest I got from ʄuⅽkin' ⅽⅾⅿⅾⅾⅾⅾⅾ ⅾⅾⅾ ⅾⅾⅾ ⅾⅾⅾⅾⅾⅾⅾⅾ. I ⅾⅾⅾⅾⅾ ⅾⅾⅾⅾ ⅾⅾⅾⅾⅾ ⅾⅾⅾ ⅾⅾⅾⅾⅾⅾⅾⅾ on fuckin' clothes. I didn't have no priorities. My priorities was trying to look good . . . clean. I was living with my mom. It was something to do.

At first, G-Money and the Money Fam clique were involved in minor gang activities: theft, graffiti, selling drugs, and threatening and strong-arming passersby. TCG graffiti clearly marked the gang's territory: "Beware of Tongans! TCG-Money Fam." The boys would strike out the *B*'s and *P*'s in their graffiti to show their disdain for Blood and Piru gang sets. As the Money Fam took to representing its clique, the gang's conflict transcended the history of previous generations' conflicts and took a violent turn. G-Money had an established "beef" with members of the Crenshaw Mafia going to school at Morningside. In junior high school, young boys trying to affiliate with Crenshaw Mafia bullied G-Money and his fellow Tongan classmates. Once the Money Fam banded together in junior high and high school, hostilities were unleashed, and conflict escalated from fighting in school to spilling out onto the streets. Eventually, it became too dangerous for G-Money and many others in the Money Fam clique to continue going to the school, which unfortunately was located in the rival gang's neighborhood. G-Money had missed so many classes resulting from his truancy and suspension that by his junior year of high school, he simply stopped going.

Without school to occupy their time, G-Money and two of his homeboys, P-Money and C-Money, took to representing the TCG-Money Fam as a full-time pursuit. The gang itself was composed of thirty to forty individuals, and, like any social organization, different members occupied different roles. G-Money and his two "ace" homeboys filled the role of soldiers, actively seeking to make a name and reputation for TCG through violence. Some of the gang members followed the boys' lead, while many of the Money Fam merely affiliated themselves socially. As gang conflicts continued to unfold in Inglewood, violence became the main vehicle to attaining respect. G-Money described the violence he experienced growing up as almost natural, or at least something to which he had become desensitized:

> It wasn't about, "Let's go kill muthafuckin' enemies," until me and my little partners . . . we came out. We were like, "We gotta try to put Tonga back on the map." Because me and my little homeboys were raised in Inglewood . . . I mean we was the only ones that actually stayed in Inglewood, while everybody else stayed on the outskirts all around. They would just come around. Because we stayed in Inglewood, we had to wake up every morning to what was going on in Inglewood. When we realized that we was going to gangbang, we started walking over into our enemies' neighborhood. Striking up on the wall, letting them know we here. Then when they started coming around, we just started having exchanges. The first time [shooting at someone], it was like, "Fuck it." I was shitting bricks. Until I did it, it was like, "Oh, we going to do that again." Who else do we got problems with, you know? But some people, it comes natural, some people would have to be under the influence, and some people . . . you tell them when, and they say, "Let's go." That's just how it is in the States, man . . . especially in low-budget, low-income areas.

As G-Money and the Money Fam put the Tonga Crips "back on the map," it became increasingly dangerous to move around the neighborhood and outside of their insular gang turf. Because the TCG-Money Fam gang was relatively small in comparison to the larger gangs surrounding the neighborhood, TCG had become *islanders* of a different sort. With a territory no larger than a two-block radius and surrounded by rival gangs to the east, north, and south, TCG were islanders among a sea of gangs.

Discussion

In the preceding narratives, Buddha, Masi, and G-Money's early experiences in US inner cities illustrate their attempts to balance on the delicate threshold between traditional Tongan family expectations and the realities they experience in the hood. Moving away from one's homeland to a new country can be exciting while at the same time a turbulent experience for immigrant youths and their families. Tongans, like other migrants, face difficulties with language, poor socioeconomic status on arrival, and changing family and community dynamics in the United States. Immigrants are also confronted with the long history of America's racializing narrative, in which they are under intense pressure to define themselves and respond to others' definitions. According to many gang theorists (see Vigil 2002), these factors along with the actual experiences immigrant youths initially have in the United States present risks for youths' involvement in gangs.

The narratives of young men such as Buddha, Masi, and G-Money furthermore chronicle a breakdown of the family unit occurring in each of their households. Under the stresses of migration, families and normative cultural practices may no longer function the same way they once did in Tonga, leaving children isolated from important parental and kin-based authority structures. In each of these young men's accounts, parents and family members in the United States have to work harder and longer hours to provide for their families. Without close relatives to aid in their supervision, children become latchkey keys and have to fend for themselves. Immigration to inner-city LA stresses the structures and functions of the family as they face urbanization. Without the existence of a parallel communal network and social structure like the village in Tonga, youth in the United States are expected learn to become men through communal socialization with peers and family, a strategy that seems highly dysfunctional within the confines of the impoverished ghetto and culture of the streets. The breakdown of these important social and familial controls that may have functioned to shape normative, lawful behavior in the past accounts for youths' gang involvement in the present. Cultural strains on rules and duties between first-generation parents and second-generation children often add to a family's stress (Vigil 1988, 2002). Schools tend to have a poor record of performance with poor, ethnic-minority populations, especially if there is a sharp cultural contrast between the majority and minority cultures. This point becomes apparent when little to no communication or ties between school and home occur. This void is made worse in the classroom when cultural and language differences present themselves as difficulties in poorly funded school districts. For the most marginalized and blocked-off segments of the populations, the social-control mechanisms commonly inculcated by family and school are all but absent (Hirschi 1969). The total effect at this point becomes overwhelming. It is important to note that despite the stresses of immigration and being closed off to mainstream institutions, many Tongan youth are able to avoid gangs altogether. Given the distressed social, historical, and economic environment of South Los Angeles into which many Tongan families relocate, predictably some of these youths would adopt gang life and define their peers, mirroring other disaffected youths in the city.

The experiences and encounters youths have upon arrival to the States may present some with risks toward gang involvement; however, the identities and cultural formations these youths construct through gangs should be viewed as a highly creative process and medium through which youth acclimate to change. Migration is a time in the lives of immigrant youths in which they must define themselves, their peers, their identity, and, ultimately, their own culture. In the context of the South Pacific islanders and the Tonga Crip Gang, culture, identity, and gender are shaped through a creative, albeit violent, process. In the complex process of articulating their experiences and place as immigrants and youths in the ghetto, Tongan youths express self, community, and cultural identity through the medium of the gang. The experiences and spaces through which migrant youths traverse are liminal spaces in which these youths are temporarily outside both the traditional Tongan community and the established hood: worlds often in conflict with each other.

References

Abbink, Jon. 2004. "Being Young in Africa: The Politics of Despair and Renewal." In *Vanguard or Vandals: Youth, Politics, and Conflict in Africa*, edited by Jon Abbink and Ineke Van Kessel, 1–34. Leiden: Brill.

Adler, Peter. 1998. *Peer Power: Preadolescent Culture and Identity*. New Brunswick, NJ: Rutgers Univ. Press.

Alarcón, Norma, Caren Kaplan, and Minoo Moallem. 1999. "Introduction: Between Woman and Nation." In *Between Woman and Nation: Nationalisms, Transnational Feminisms, and the State*, edited by Caren Kaplan, Norma Alarcón, and Minoo Moallem, 1–16. Durham, NC: Duke Univ. Press.

Alexander, Jocelyn. 1997. "The Local State in Post-war Mozambique: Political Practice and Ideas of Authority." *Africa* 67, no. 1: 1–26.

Ali, Syed Sajjad. 2009. "In Tripura, Dancing Fireworks and a Touch of Royalty." *Hindustan Times*, Mar. 3.

Allison, Anne. 2006. *Millennial Monsters: Japanese Toys and the Global Imagination*. Berkeley and Los Angeles: Univ. of California Press.

Alonso, Alejandro. 2004. "Racialized Identities and the Formation of Black Gangs in Los Angeles." *Urban Geography* 25, no. 7: 658–74.

Amit-Talai, Vered, and Helena Wulff, eds. 1995. *Youth Cultures: A Cross-Cultural Perspective*. New York: Routledge.

Anderson, Allan. 2001. *African Reformation: African Initiated Christianity in the 20th Century*. Trenton, NJ: African World Press.

Anderson, Benedict. 1983. *Imagined Communities: Reflections on the Origin and Spread of Nationalism*. London: Verso.

Anderson, Elijah. 1999. *Code of the Street: Decency, Violence, and the Moral Life of the Inner City*. New York: W. W. Norton.

Anderson-Levitt, Kathryn. 2003. *Local Meanings, Global Schooling: Anthropology and World Culture Theory*. New York: Palgrave Macmillan.

Ando, Y. 2004. "The Changing Transition to Adulthood in Japan: Timing and Order of Events in the Life Course." *Ningen Kagaku* 14: 227–49.

Anthias, Floya. 1989. "Women and Nationalism in Cyprus." In *Woman-Nation-State*, edited by Nira Yuval-Davis and Floya Anthias, 150–67. London: Palgrave Macmillan.

Anthias, Floya, and Nira Yuval-Davis. 1989. Introduction to *Woman-Nation-State*, edited by Nira Yuval-Davis and Floya Anthias, 1–15. London: Palgrave Macmillan.

Appadurai, Arjun. 1996. *Modernity at Large: Cultural Dimensions of Globalization*. Minneapolis: Univ. of Minnesota Press.

———. 2001. "Grassroots Globalization and the Research Imagination." In *Globalization: A Public Culture Book*, edited by Arjun Appadurai, 1–19. Durham, NC: Duke Univ. Press.

Archambault, Julie. 2009. "Being Cool or Being Good: Researching Mobile Phones in Southern Mozambique." *Anthropology Matters* 11: 1–9.

———. 2010. "La fièvre des téléphones portables: Un chapitre de la 'Success Story' Mozambicaine?" *Politique Africaine* 117: 83–105.

Aries, Phillipe. 1965. *Centuries of Childhood: A Social History of Family Life*. New York: Vintage.

Arnfred, Signe. 2001. *Family Forms and Gender Policy in Revolutionary Mozambique (1975–1985): Travaux et documents*. Bordeaux: Centre d'Études d'Afrique Noire.

Augé, Marc. 1995. *Non-places: Introduction to an Anthropology of Supermodernity*. Translated by John Howe. London: Verso Publications.

Australian Bureau of Statistics Census of Population and Housing. 2003. "Multicultural Australia: The Papua New Guinea–Born Community." http://www.immi.gov.au/statistics/infosummary/papuanewguinea.pdf.

Axelrod, Paul, and Michelle Fuerch. 1998. "Portuguese Orientalism and the Making of the Village Communities of Goa." *Ethnohistory* 45, no. 3: 439–76.

Bandyopadhyay, Ranjan, and Duarte Morais. 2005. "Representative Dissonance: India's Self and Western Image." *Annals of Tourism Research* 32, no. 4: 1006–21.

Barboza, David. 2005. "Upstart from Chinese Province Masters the Art of TV Titillation." *New York Times*, Nov. 28.

Barlow, T. 2000. "QFDA Dance Messages." Jan. No. 27.

Bashkow, Ira. 2006. *The Meaning of Whiteman: Race and Modernity in the Orokaiva Cultural World*. Chicago: Univ. of Chicago Press.

Batson-Savage, Tanya. 2007. "'Hol' Awn Mek a Answer mi Cellular': Sex, Sexuality, and the Cellular Phone in Urban Jamaica." *Continuum* 21, no. 2: 239–51.

Baudrillard, Jean. 1998. *The Consumer Society: Myths and Structures*. New York: Sage.

Bauman, Zygmunt. 1998. *Globalization: The Human Consequences*. New York: Columbia Univ. Press.

————. 2001. *Community: Seeking Safety in an Uncertain World*. Cambridge: Polity Press.

————. 2005. *Work, Consumerism, and the New Poor*. London: Open Univ. Press.

————. 2007. *Liquid Times: Living in an Age of Uncertainty*. Cambridge: Polity Press.

Beals, Fiona. 2008. *Reading Between the Lines: Representations and Constructions of Youth and Crime in Aotearoa/New Zealand*. Saarbrucken, Germany: Verlag Dr. Muller.

Beck, Ulrich. 1992. *Risk Society: Towards a New Modernity*. London: Sage.

Bell, B, L, 2005, "Children, Youth, and Civic (Dis)ungagement. Digital Technology and Citizenship." CRACIN Working Paper no. 2005-5, Canadian Research Alliance for Community Innovation and Networking (CRACIN), Toronto.

Bell, Diane. 1993. *Daughters of the Dreaming*. Minneapolis: Univ. of Minnesota Press.

Ben-Amos, I. K. 1995. "Adolescence as a Cultural Invention: Philippe Ariès and the Sociology of Youth." *History of the Human Sciences* 8: 69–89.

Besnier, Niko. 2002. "Transgenderism, Locality, and the Miss Galaxy Beauty Pageant in Tonga." *American Ethnologist* 29: 534–66.

————. 2004. "Consumption and Cosmopolitanism: Practicing Modernity at the Second-Hand Marketplace in Nuku'alofa, Tonga." *Anthropological Quarterly* 77: 7–45.

————. 2009. "Modernity, Cosmopolitanism, and the Emergence of Middle Class in Tonga." *Contemporary Pacific* 21, no. 2: 1043–88.

Beston, A. 2006. "1000 March on 'School Strike.'" *Waikato Times*, Mar. 21.

Bhabha, Homi. 1984. "Of Mimicry and Men: The Ambivalence of Colonial Discourse." *October* 28: 127.

————. 1992. Freedom's Basis in the Indeterminate." *October* 61: 46–57.

Blackshaw, Tony. 2005. *Zygmunt Bauman*. New York: Routledge.

Bourdieu, Pierre. 1984. *Distinction: A Social Critique of the Judgment of Taste*. London: Routledge.

————. 1991. *Language and Symbolic Power*. Cambridge, MA: Harvard Univ. Press, 1984 (originally 1979).

Brennan, Denise. 2004. *What's Love Got to Do with It? Transnational Desires and Sex Tourism in the Dominican Republic*. Durham, NC: Duke Univ. Press.

Brison, Karen J. 1999. "Hierarchy in the World of Fijian Children." *Ethnology* 38: 97–120.

————. 2003. "Imagining Modernity in Rural Fiji." *Ethnology* 42: 335–48.

————. 2007a. "The Empire Strikes Back: Pentecostalism in Fiji." *Ethnology* 41, no. 1: 21–41.

———. 2007b. *Our Wealth in Loving Each Other: Self and Society in Fiji.* Lanham, MD: Lexington Books.

Broadbent, K. 2001. "Shortchanged? Part-Time Workers in Japan." *Japanese Studies* 21, no. 3.

Brock, Peggy. 1993. *Outback Ghettos: Aboriginals, Institutionalization, and Survival.* Cambridge: Cambridge Univ. Press.

Brosius, Christiane, and Melissa Butcher, eds. 1999. *Image Journeys: Audiovisual Media and Cultural Change in India.* Delhi: Sage.

Brubaker, R. 2002. "Ethnicity Without Groups." *Archives Européenes de Sociologie* (May): 1–35.

Bucholtz, Mary. 2002. "Youth and Cultural Practice." *Annual Review of Anthropology* 31: 525–52.

Burke, Timothy. 1996. *Lifebuoy Men, Lux Women: Commodification, Consumption, and Cleanliness in Modern Zimbabwe.* Durham, NC: Duke Univ. Press.

Burton-Bradley, B. 1965. *Port Moresby Mixed Race Class.* Sydney: Univ. of Sydney.

Butcher, Melissa. 2003. *Transnational Television, Cultural Identity, and Change: When STAR Came to India.* Thousand Oaks, CA: Sage.

Butler, Judith. 1999. *Gender Trouble: Feminism and the Subversion of Identity.* New York: Routledge.

Calhoun, Craig. 1995. *Critical Social Theory.* Oxford: Blackwell.

Campoamor, Leigh. 2008. "Pity, Performance, and the Production of Value(s) among Working Children in Lima, Peru." Paper presented at the annual meeting of the American Anthropological Association, San Francisco, Nov. 19.

Caputo, Virginia. 1995. "Anthropology's Silent 'Others': A Consideration of Some Conceptual and Methodological Issues for the Study of Youth and Children's Cultures." In *Youth Cultures: A Cross-Cultural Perspective,* edited by Vered Amit-Talai and Helena Wulff, 19–42. New York: Routledge.

Carpini, M. X. D. 2000. "Gen.com: Youth, Civic Engagement, and the New Information Environment." *Political Communication* 17, no. 4: 341–49.

Carrier, James. 1990. "Reconciling Commodities and Personal Relations in Industrial Society." *Theory and Society* 19, no. 5: 579–98.

Casinader, J. 2008. "Think Globally, Act Sometimes." *New Zealand Herald,* Mar. 23.

Cassia, P. S. 2005. *Bodies of Evidence: Burial, Memory, and the Recovery of Missing Persons in Cyprus.* New York: Berghahn Books.

Castells, Manuel. 1997. *The Power of Identity.* Oxford: Blackwell.

Centre of Business Development Ability Association (Chûo Shokugyô Nôryoku Kaihatsu Kyôkai). 2010. "Report of the Experience Ability Appraisal Study" [Keiken Nôryoku Hyôka Kijun (Kashô) Kentô Hôkokusho]. http://www.mhlw.go.jp/houdou/2007/09/h0927-3a.html.

Cha, Ariana Eunjung. 2009. "In Crisis, China Vows Openness; Government Also Says It Will 'Dramatically Increase' Stimulus Program." *Washington Post,* Mar. 5.

Chambers, Erve. 1999. *Native Tours: The Anthropology of Travel and Tourism.* Long Grove, IL: Waveland Press.

Chatani, K. 2008. "From Corporate-Centred Security to Flexicurity in Japan." Employment Sector: Employment Working Paper no. 7. Geneva: International Labour Organisation.

Chatterjee, Partha. 1986. *Nationalist Thought and the Colonial World: A Derivative Discourse?* Minneapolis: Univ. of Minnesota Press.

Chen, Lingchei Letty. 2006. *Writing Chinese. Reshaping Chinese Cultural Identity.* New York: Palgrave Macmillan.

Cheng Naishang. 2009. "Zhongxing mei shi chuncui nuxing xinli de shenmei" [Androgynous beauty is a purely women's view of beauty]. http://blog.sina.com.cn/s/blog_4aba2161010005mq.html.

Children's Rights in Goa. 2006. *Child Sexual Abuse in Goa: A Case Study.* Mapusa, Goa: Children's Rights in Goa.

China Digital Times. 2009. "Super Voice Girls and Democracy." http://chinadigital times.net/2005/08/super-voice-girls-and-democracy-eswn/.

Ching, Yang. 2008. "Performing Contradictions, Performing Bad-Girlness in Japan." In *Gender and Globalization in Asia and the Pacific,* edited by Kathy E. Ferguson and M. Mironesco. Honolulu: Univ. of Hawaii Press.

Choulai, Aaron. 2005. Press release. http://www.png.embassy.gov.au/pmsb/MR 080226.html.

―――. 2007. http://www.abc.net.au/local/stories/2007/07/16/1979873.htm2007.

―――. 2009. http://www.myspace.com/aaronchoulai.

Choulai, Wendy. 1997. "Indigenous Oceanic Design in Today's Market: A Personal Perspective." Master's thesis, Royal Melbourne Institute of Technology.

Christiansen, Catrine, Mats Utas, and Henrik Vigh, eds. 2006. *Navigating Youth, Generating Adulthood: Social Becoming in an African Context.* Uppsala: Nordic African Institute.

Christodoulou, Demetrios. 1992. *Inside the Cyprus Miracle: The Labors of an Embattled Mini-Economy.* Minneapolis: Univ. of Minnesota Press.

Christou, Miranda. 2002. "Fragments of Memory, Visions of Struggle: Political Imagination in a Greek Cypriot High School." PhD diss., Harvard Univ.

―――. 2006. "A Double Imagination: Memory and Education in Cyprus." *Journal of Modern Greek Studies* 24, no. 2: 285–306.

―――. 2007. "The Language of Patriotism: Sacred History and Dangerous Memories." *British Journal of Sociology of Education* 28, no. 6: 709–22.

CNNIC. 2005. "16th Statistical Survey on the Internet Development in China, July." *China Internet Network Information Center.* http://www.cnnic.net.cn /en/index/0O. Accessed Apr. 14, 2009.

Cockburn, Cynthia. 2004. *The Line: Women, Partition, and the Gender Order in Cyprus*. New York: Zed Books.

Cody, Edward. 2005. "In Chinese Cyberspace, a Blossoming Passion." *Washington Post,* July 19, A15.

Coe, Cati. 2005. *Dilemmas of Culture in African Schools*. Chicago: Univ. of Chicago Press.

Cohen, Colleen, Richard Wilk, and Beverley Stoeltje, eds. 1996. *Beauty Queens on the Global Stage: Gender, Contests, and Power*. New York: Routledge.

Cole, Jennifer. 2004. "Fresh Contact in Tamatava, Madagascar: Sex, Money, and Intergenerational Transformation." *American Ethnologist* 31, no. 4: 573–88.

Cole, Jennifer, and Deborah Durham. 2007. "Introduction: Age, Regeneration, and the Intimate Politics of Globalization." In *Generations and Globalization: Youth, Age, and Family in New World Economy,* edited by Jennifer Cole and Deborah Durham, 1–28. Bloomington: Indiana Univ. Press.

Coleman, S. 2005. *Remixing Citizenship: Democracy and Young People's Use of the Internet (Research Report)*. London: Carnegie Young People's Initiative.

Comaroff, Jean, and John Comaroff. 1991. *Of Revelation and Revolution*. Vol. 1, *Christianity, Colonialism, and Consciousness in South Africa*. Chicago: Univ. of Chicago Press.

———. 2005. "Reflections on Youth: From Past to Postcolony." In *Makers and Breakers: Children and Youth in Postcolonial Africa,* edited by Alcinda Honwana and Filip de Boeck. Trenton, NJ: Africa World Press.

Condry, Ian. 2001. "A History of Japanese Hip-Hop: Street Dance, Club Scene, Pop Market." In *Global Noise: Rap and Hip-Hop Outside the USA,* edited by Tony Mitchell, 222–47. Hanover, NH: Wesleyan Univ. Press.

———. 2006. *Hip Hop Japan: Rap and the Paths of Cultural Globalization*. Durham, NC: Duke Univ. Press.

Cook, T. 2004. "Beyond Either/Or." *Journal of Consumer Culture* 4, no. 2: 147–53.

Corsaro, William A. 1985. *Friendship and Peer Culture in the Early Years*. London: Ablex.

———. 1997. *The Sociology of Childhood*. London: Pine Forge Press.

———. 2003. *We're Friends, Right? Inside Kids' Culture*. Washington, DC: Joseph Henry Press.

Cowling, Wendy. 1990. "On Being Tongan: Responses to Concepts of Tradition." PhD diss., Macquarie Univ.

———. 1995. "The Lives of Boys and Men." Unpublished paper.

Cyprus Minister of Education and Culture. 2009. "Welcoming Letter to Students." http://www.schools.ac.cy/dde/circular/data/Doc4501.pdf.

Dai Xiaolin. 2005. "'Chaoji nvsheng' ruxuan shida wenhua liuxingyu" ["Super girl" is included in the ten most popular cultural terms]. *Beijing Chenbao* [Beijing Morning Post], July 19.

Dai Zhikang. 2008. "Wangluo shequ xin chaoliu: Shejiao hua, xifen hua, yule hua" [New trends of Internet communities: Socialization, segmentation, entertainment]. *Chengxu Yuan* [Programmer] 12.

D'Andrea, Anthony. 2007. *Global Nomads: Techno and New Age as Transnational Countercultures in Ibiza and Goa.* New York: Routledge.

Dasgupta, Romit. 2003. "Creating Corporate Warriors: The 'Salaryman' and Masculinity in Japan." In *Asian Masculinities: The Meaning and Practice of Manhood in China and Japan,* edited by Kam Louie, 118–34. London and New York: Routledge.

———. 2004. "'Crafting' Masculinity: Negotiating Masculine Identities in the Japanese Workplace." PhD diss., Curtin Univ. of Technology.

de Boeck, Filip, and Alinda Honwana. 2005. *Makers and Breakers: Children and Youth in Postcolonial Africa.* Oxford: James Currey.

de Cillia, R., M. Reisigl, and R. Wodak. 1999. "The Discursive Construction of National Identities." *Discourse and Society* 10: 149–73.

Desai, Nishtha. 2001. *See the Evil: Tourist-Related Pedophilia in Goa.* Mumbai: Vikas Adhyayan Kendra.

Desmond, Jane. 1999. *Staging Tourism: Bodies on Display from Waikiki to Sea World.* Chicago: Univ. of Chicago Press.

Deutsch, N. L., and E. Theodorou. 2009. "Aspiring, Consuming, Becoming: Youth and Identity in a Culture of Consumption." *Youth and Society* 20, no. 10: 1–26.

Dever, Maryanne, ed. 1997. *Australia and Asia Cultural Transactions.* Honolulu: Univ. of Hawaii Press.

Devine, Peter. 2004. "The Ink of Life: Tattoos in Fiji." Undergraduate thesis, Union College.

Dewey, Susan. 2008a. *Hollow Bodies: Institutional Responses to Sex Trafficking in Armenia, Bosnia, and India.* Sterling, VA: Kumarian Press.

———. 2008b. *Making Miss India Miss World: Constructing Gender, Power, and the Nation in Postliberalization India.* Syracuse, NY: Syracuse Univ. Press.

Diversi, M. 2006. "Street Kids in Nikes: In Search of Humanization Through the Culture of Consumption." *Cultural Studies Critical Methodologies* 6, no. 3: 370–90.

D'Mello, Ashley. 2004. "No Lessons Learnt from Goa." *Times of India,* Sept. 7, 8.

Doezema, Jo. 2000. "Loose Women or Lost Women? The Re-emergence of the Myth of White Slavery in Contemporary Discourses of Trafficking in Women." *Gender Issues* 18, no. 1: 38–54.

Dolby, Nadine. 2000. "The Shifting Ground of Race: The Role of Taste in Youth's Production of Identities." *Race, Ethnicity, and Education* 3, no. 1: 7–23.

Do Nascimento, J. 2005. "Jalons pour une théorie de l'appropriation des NTIC en Afrique." In *Société Numérique et Développement en Afrique: Usages et politiques publiques,* edited by J.-J. Gabas, 229–54. Paris: Karthala.

Donner, J. 2008. "Research Approaches to Mobile Use in the Developing World: A Review of the Literature." *Information Society* 24: 140–59.

Drum Drum website. n.d. http://www.drumdrum.com.au. Accessed Mar. 2009.

Durham, Deborah. 2000. "Youth and the Social Imagination in Africa: Introduction to Parts 1 and 2." *Anthropological Quarterly* 73, no. 3: 113–20.

———. 2004. "Disappearing Youth: Youth as a Social Shifter in Botswana." *American Ethnologist* 31: 589–605.

———. 2005. "'They Are Only Playing': Songs, Choirs, and Youth in Botswana." In *Makers and Breakers: Children and Youth in Postcolonial Africa,* edited by Alcinda Honwana and Filip de Boeck, 150–66. Oxford: James Currey.

———. 2007. "Empowering Youth: Making Youth Citizens in Botswana." In *Generations and Globalization: Youth, Age, and Family in the New World Economy,* edited by Jennifer Cole and Deborah Durham, 102–31. Bloomington: Indiana Univ. Press.

Dwyer, Rachel. 2000. *All You Want Is Money, All You Need Is Love: Sex and Romance in Modern India.* London: Frank Cassell.

Economic News Daily. 2005. "Chaonü fengbao guajin xianggang gushi" [Super Girl storm sweeps Hong Kong stock market]. *Meiri jingji xinwen,* Sept. 5.

ECPAT. 2002. *Report on the Implementation of the Agenda for Action Against the Commercial Sexual Exploitation of Children.* Bangkok: End Child Prostitution, Child Pornography, and Trafficking of Children for Sexual Purposes International.

Edwards, K. 2007. "From Deficit to Disenfranchisement: Reframing Youth Electoral Participation." *Journal of Youth Studies* 10, no. 5: 539–55.

Enloe, Cynthia. 1989. *Bananas, Beaches, and Bases: Making Sense of International Politics.* Berkeley and Los Angeles: Univ. of California Press.

Erikson, Erik. 1968. *Identity: Youth and Crisis.* New York: W. W. Norton.

Errington, F., and Deborah Gewertz. 1996. "The Individuation of Tradition in a Papua New Guinea Modernity." *American Anthropologist* 98, no. 1: 114–26.

Fairclough, Norman. 1995. *Critical Discourse Analysis: The Critical Study of Language.* London: Longman.

Felgate, W. S. 1982. "The Tembe Thonga of Natal and Mozambique: An Ecological Approach." Department of African Studies, Occasional Publications no. 1. Durban: Univ. of Natal.

Felski, Rita. 1995. *The Gender of Modernity.* Cambridge, MA: Harvard Univ. Press.

Ferguson, James. 1999. *Expectations of Modernity: Myths and Meanings of Modern Life in the Zambian Copperbelt.* Berkeley and Los Angeles: Univ. of California.

Ferguson, Kathy E., and Monique Mironesco. 2008. "Advancing Feminist Thinking on Globalization." In *Gender and Globalization in Asia and the Pacific: Method, Practice, Theory,* edited by Kathy E. Ferguson and Monique Mironesco, 335–58. Honolulu: Univ. of Hawaii Press.

Fernandes, L. 2000. "Nationalizing 'the Global': Media Images, Cultural Politics, and the Middle Class in India." *Media, Culture, and Society* 22, no. 5: 611–28.

Fernando, Jude. 2001. "Children's Rights: Beyond the Impasse." *Annals of the American Academy of Political and Social Science* 575: 8–24.

Fine, Gary Alan. 1987. *With the Boys: Little League Baseball and Preadolescent Culture.* Chicago: Univ. of Chicago Press.

Fink, R. 1965. "Moresby's Race Relations." *New Guinea and Australia, the Pacific and Southeast Asia* 1, no. 2: 42–46.

First, R., M. Forjaz, and A. Manghezi. 1998. *O Mineiro Moçambicano: Um Estudo Sobre a Exportação de Mão de Obra em Inhambane.* Maputo: O Centro Universidade Eduardo Mondlane.

Fisher, William. 1997. "Doing Good? The Politics and Antipolitics of NGO Practices." *Annual Review of Anthropology* 26: 439–64.

Fiske, John. 1982. *Introduction to Communication Studies.* London and New York: Routledge.

Fornäs, Johan. 1995. "Youth, Culture, and Modernity." In *Youth Culture in Late Modernity,* edited by Johan Fornäs and Goran Bolin, 1–15. Thousand Oaks, CA: Sage.

Freedman, A. 2006. "Stories of Boys and Buildings: Ishida Ira's *4-Teen* in 2002 Tokyo." *Japan Forum* 18, no. 3: 381–98.

"'Freeters' Shun Traditional Work in Japan." 2003. *News from Japan,* http://www.ajstas.netfirms.com/page_5.htm.

Friedman, Jonathan. 1991. "Consuming Desire: Strategies of Selfhood and Appropriation." *Cultural Anthropology* 6, no. 2: 154–63.

———. 1994. *Cultural Identity and Global Process.* London: Sage.

Funaki, I., and L. Funaki. 2002. "A Compromise Identity: Tongan Americans in the United States." In *Pacific Diaspora,* edited by Paul Spickard, Joanne Rondilla, and Debbie Wright. Honolulu: Univ. of Hawaii Press.

Furlong, Andy. 2008. "The Japanese Hikikomori Phenomenon: Acute Social Withdrawal among Young People." *Sociological Review* 56, no. 2: 309–25.

Furlong, Andy, and Fred Cartmel. 1997. *Young People and Social Change: Individualization and Risk in Late Modernity.* Philadelphia: Open Univ. Press.

Gable, E. 2000. "The Culture Development Club: Youth, Neo-Tradition, and the Construction of Society in Guinea-Bissau." *Anthropological Quarterly* 73: 195–203.

Gage, A. J., and C. Bledsoe. 1994. "The Effects of Education and Social Stratification on Marriage and the Transition to Parenthood in Freetown, Sierra Leone." In *Nuptiality in Sub-Saharan Africa,* edited by C. Bledsoe and G. Pison, 148–64. Oxford: Clarendon Press.

Gal, Susan. 1979. *Language Shift.* New York: Academic Press.

Gamburd, Michelle Ruth. 2000. *The Kitchen Spoon's Handle: Transnationalism and Sri Lanka's Migrant Households*. Ithaca, NY: Cornell Univ. Press.

Garsten, C. 1999. "Betwixt and Between: Temporary Employees as Liminal Subjects in Flexible Organizations." *Organization Studies* 20, no. 4: 601–17.

Geffray, Christian. 1990. *La cause des armes au Mozambique: Anthropologie d'une guerre civile*. Paris: Karthala.

Gellner, Ernest. 1983. *Nations and Nationalism*. Ithaca, NY: Cornell Univ. Press.

Genda, Y. 2005. *A Nagging Sense of Job Insecurity: The New Reality Facing Japanese Youth*. Tokyo: International House of Japan.

———. 2007. "Jobless Youths and the NEET Problem in Japan." *Social Science Japan Journal* 10, no. 1: 23–40.

Gerke, Solvay. 2000. "Global Lifestyles under Local Conditions." In *Consumption in Asia: Lifestyles and Identities*, edited by Chua Beng-Huat, 131–48. London: Routledge.

Gerth, Karl. 2003. *China Made: Consumer Culture and the Creation of the Nation*. Cambridge, MA: Harvard Univ. Press.

Ghosh, Shohini. 1999. "The Troubled Existence of Sex and Sexuality: Feminists Engage with Censorship." In *Image Journeys: Audio-Visual Media and Cultural Change in India*, edited by Christiane Brosius and Melissa Butcher, 233–59. New York: Sage.

Gibson, Margaret, and John Ogbu. 1991. *Minority Status and Schooling*. New York: Garland.

Gilligan, Carol. 1982. *In a Different Voice: Psychological Theory and Women's Development*. Cambridge, MA: Harvard Univ. Press.

Gmelch, George. 2003. *Behind the Smile: The Working Lives of Caribbean Tourism*. Bloomington: Indiana Univ. Press.

Goldman, Laurence. 1998. *Child's Play: Myth, Mimesis, and Make-Believe*. Oxford: Berg.

Goodwin, Marjorie Harness. 1991. *He-Said-She-Said: Talk as Social Organization among Black Children*. Bloomington: Indiana Univ. Press.

Gottschild, Brenda Dixon. 2005. *The Black Dancing Body*. New York: Palgrave Macmillan.

Griffin, C. 2001. "Imagining New Narratives of Youth: Youth Research, the 'New Europe,' and Global Youth Culture." *Childhood* 8, no. 2: 147–66.

Grixti, J. 2006. "Symbolic Transformations: Youth, Global Media, and Indigenous Culture in Malta." *Media, Culture, and Society* 28, no. 1: 105–22.

Guo Muhua. 2008. "Zhongguo dianshi dansheng 50 nian" [Fifty years of Chinese television]. *Jing Bao* [Express News], May 8.

Hadjipavlou, Maria. 2006. "No Permission to Cross: Cypriot Women's Dialogue Across the Divide." *Gender, Place, and Culture: A Journal of Feminist Geography* 13, no. 4: 329–51.

Hagedorn, John M. 2007. *Gangs in the Global City: Alternatives to Traditional Criminology.* Urbana: Univ. of Illinois Press.

Hahn, H. P. 2009. "Mobile Phones and the Transformation of the Society: New Forms of Criminality and the Mastering of the New Technologies in Burkina Faso." Paper presented at the European Conference on African Studies, Leipzig, Germany.

Hahn, H. P., and L. Kibora. 2008. "The Domestication of the Mobile Phone: Oral Society and New ICT in Burkina Faso." *Journal of Modern African Studies* 46: 87–109.

Hall, Granville Stanley. 1905. *Adolescence.* Reprint, New York: Arno Press, 1969.

Hall, Margaret, and Tom Young. 1997. *Confronting Leviathan.* London: Hurst.

Hall, Stuart. 1993. "What Is This 'Black' in Black Popular Culture?" *Social Justice* 20, nos. 1–2: 104–11.

Hall, Stuart, and Michael Jacques. 1990. *New Times: The Changing Face of Politics in the 1990s.* New York: Verso.

Hamed, O. 2006. "New Zealand: Pay Revolt Heats Up." *Green Left Weekly.* http://www.greenleft.org.au/2006/662/7054.

Hanlon, Joseph. 1996. *Peace Without Profit: How the IMF Blocks Rebuilding in Mozambique.* Oxford: James Currey.

———. 2007. "Is Poverty Decreasing in Mozambique?" Paper presented at the inaugural conference of the Instituto de Estudos Sociais e Económicos, Maputo, Mozambique.

Hanna, Judith. 1987. *To Dance Is Human: A Theory of Nonverbal Communication.* Chicago: Univ. of Chicago Press.

Hansen, Karen Tranberg, with Anne Line Dalsgaard, Katherine V. Gough, Ulla U. Madsen, Karen Valentin, and Norbert Wildermuth. 2008. *Youth and the City in the Global South.* Bloomington: Indiana Univ. Press.

Harris, Anita. 2008. "Young Women, Late Modern Politics, and the Participatory Possibilities of Online Cultures." *Journal of Youth Studies* 11, no. 5: 481–95.

Harris, Anita, Janice Wyn, and S. Younes. 2007. "Young People and Citizenship: An Everyday Perspective." *Youth Studies Australia* 26, no. 3: 19–27.

Harris, Judith. 1999. *The Nurture Assumption.* New York: Basic Books.

Hartmann, Walfram, Patricia Hayes, and Jeremy Silvester. 1999. *Colonising Camera: Photographs in Making of Namibian History.* Athens: Ohio Univ. Press.

Harvey, David. 2006. *Spaces of Global Capitalism: A Theory of Uneven Global Development.* London: Verso.

Hayes, Patricia. 2007. "Efundula and History: Female Initiation in Pre-colonial and Colonial Northern Namibia." Posted on the *University of the Western Cape.* http://www.gwsafrica.org/knowledge/patricia.efprint.htm.

Heald, Suzette. 1999. *Manhood and Morality: Sex, Violence, and Ritual in Gisu Society.* London: Routledge.

Hebdige, Dick. 1998. *Hiding in the Light: On Images and Things*. London: Routledge.

Heine, C., & Friends. 2006a. "High School Troubles." http://clintheine.blogspot .com/search?q=radical+youth, Mar. 22.

———. 2006b. "Revolution, One Child at a Time." http://clintheine.blogspot .com/2006/03/revolution-one-child-at-time.html.

Helms, Elissa. 2003. "Women as Agents of Ethnic Reconciliation? Women's NGOs and International Intervention in Postwar Bosnia-Herzegovina." *Women's Studies International Forum* 26, no. 1: 15–33.

Henshall, Kenneth. 1999. *Dimensions of Japanese Society: Gender, Margins, and Mainstream*. New York: St. Martin's Press.

Herda, Phyllis. 2002. "Cook Islands Tivaevae: Migration and the Display of Culture in Aotearoa/New Zealand." In *Pacific Art, Persistence, Change, and Meaning*, edited by Anita Herle, Nick Stanley, Karen Stevenson, and Robert Welsch, 136–46. Honolulu: Univ. of Hawaii Press.

Hil, R., and J. Bessant. 1999. "Spaced-Out? Young People's Agency, Resistance, and Public Space." *Urban Policy and Research* 17, no. 1: 41–49.

Hirano, K. 2005. "'Freeters': Free by Name, Nature; Exploitative Corporate Culture Breeds Nomadic Workers." *Japan Times,* Jan. 29. http://www.japan times.co.jp/text/nn20050129f1.html.

Hirschfeld, Laurence. 2002. "Why Don't Anthropologists Like Children?" *American Anthropologist* 104, no. 2: 611–27.

Hirschi, Travis. 1969. *Causes of Delinquency*. Berkeley and Los Angeles: Univ. of California Press.

Hogan, D. P., and N. M. Astone. 1986. "The Transition to Adulthood." *Annual Review of Sociology* 12: 109–30.

Hogan, D. P., and T. Mochizuki. 1988. "Demographic Transitions and the Life Course: Lessons from Japanese and American Corporations." *Journal of Family Issues* 13, no. 3: 291–305.

Holloway, Sarah, and Gill Valentine. 2000. *Children's Geographies: Playing, Living, Learning*. London: Routledge.

Honda, Y. 2004. "The Formation and Transformation of the Japanese System from School to Work." *Social Science Japan Journal* 7, no. 1: 103–15.

Honwana, Alcinda, and Filip de Boeck. 2005. Preface to *Makers and Breakers: Children and Youth in Postcolonial Africa*, edited by J. Currey, ix–x. Oxford: James Currey.

Hooper, Beverly. 2000. "Globalization and Resistance in Post-Mao China: The Case of Foreign Consumer Products." *Asian Studies Review* 24, no. 4: 439–70.

Horiguchi, Sachiko. 2011. "Coping with Hikikomori: Socially Withdrawn Youth and the Japanese Family." In *Home and Family in Japan: Continuity and*

Transformation, edited by Ronald Ronald and Allison Alexy. London and New York: Routledge.

Horst, Heather A., and Daniel Miller. 2006. *The Cell Phone: The Anthropology of Communication.* Oxford and New York: Berg.

Howell, James C. 1999. "Youth Gang Homicides: A Literature Review." *Crime Delinquency* 45: 208–41.

Howland, Leela, and Wendy Olphert. 2002. *Logged Off: How ICT Can Connect Young People and Politics.* London: Demos.

———. 2005. *I Am Crazy about "Super Girl."* Beijing: Zhongxin Chubanshe.

Inui, A. 2005. "Why Freeter and NEET Are Misunderstood: Recognizing the New Precarious Conditions of Japanese Youth." *Social Work and Society* 3, no. 2: 244–51.

Isaacman, Allen. 1978. *A Luta Continua: Creating a New Society in Mozambique.* Binghamton: Fernand Braudel Center for the Study of Economies, Historical Systems, and Civilizations, State Univ. of New York.

Ishii-Kuntz, Masako. 2003. "Balancing Fatherhood and Work: Emergence of Diverse Masculinities in Contemporary Japan." In *Men and Masculinities in Contemporary Japan: Dislocating the Salaryman Doxa,* edited by James E. Roberson and Nobue Suzuki, 198–216. London and New York: RoutledgeCurzon.

Iwabuchi, Koichi. 2001. "Uses of Japanese Popular Culture: Trans/nationalism and Postcolonial Desire for 'Asia.'" *Emergences* 11, no. 2: 206.

Iwao, Sumiko. 1993. *The Japanese Woman: Traditional Image and Changing Reality.* New York: Free Press.

Jacobs, Andrew. 2009. "Memo from Beijing: Chinese Learn Limits of Online Freedom as the Filter Tightens." *New York Times,* Feb. 4.

Jakes, Susan. 2005. "Li Yuchun: Loved for Being Herself." *Time Asia,* Oct. 10, 15.

James, Allison. 2007. "Giving Voice to Children's Voices." *American Anthropologist* 109, no. 2: 261–72.

James, I. 2004. "Online Interview." http://www.ABC.net.au.

James, R. 2004. "Online Interview." http://www.mont.org.au/oral_hist/james.html.

Japan Ministry of Internal Affairs and Communication, Statistics Bureau. n.d. http://www.stat.go.jp/english/data/roudou/qa-1.htm#Q05.

Jones, Carla. 2003. "Dress for Sukses: Fashioning Femininity and Nationality in Urban Indonesia." In *Re-orienting Fashion: The Globalization of Asian Dress,* edited by Sandra Niessen, Ann Marie Leshkowich, and Carla Jones, 185–213. New York: Berg.

Jones, E., V. Pang, and J. Rodriguez. 2004. "Promoting Academic Achievement and Identity Development among Diverse High School Students." *High School Journal* 87, no. 3: 44–53.

Jones, S. 1990. "Is There a 'Place' for Children in Geography?" *Area* 22, no. 3: 278–83.

Juluri, Vamsee. 2002. "Music Television and the Invention of Youth Culture in India." *Television and New Media* 3, no. 4: 367–86.

Junod, Henri. 1966. *The Life of a South African Tribe.* Vol. 1. New York: University Books.

Kaplan, Caren, Norma Alarcón, and Minoo Moallen. 1999. *Between Woman and Nation: Nationalisms, Transnational Feminisms, and the State.* Durham, NC: Duke Univ. Press.

Kavoori, Anandam, and Aswin Punathambekar. 2008. *Global Bollywood.* Oxford: Oxford Univ. Press.

Kawakami, Laurie. 2006. "Transforming Tongan Identity: Tongan American Parents Struggle to Raise Children with an Increasingly American Outlook." *APASS* (Apr).

Keane, Michael, Anthony Fung, and Albert Moran. 2007. *New Television, Globalization, and the East Asian Cultural Imagination.* Hong Kong: Hong Kong Univ. Press.

Kedourie, E. 2005. "The Cyprus Problem and Its Solution." *Middle Eastern Studies* 41, no. 5: 649–60.

Keeler, Ward. 2009. "What's Burmese about Burmese Rap? Why Some Expressive Forms Go Global." *American Ethnologist* 36, no. 1: 2–19.

Kelly, John D., and Martha Kaplan. 2001. *Represented Communities: Fiji and World Decolonization.* Chicago: Univ. of Chicago Press.

Kempadoo, Kamala. 1999. *Sun, Sex, and Gold: Tourism and Sex Work in the Caribbean.* Lanham, MD: Rowman and Littlefield.

Kemper, Steven. 2001. *Buying and Believing: Sri Lankan Advertisers and Consumers in a Transnational World.* Chicago: Univ. of Chicago Press.

Kessen, Walter. 1983. *The Child and Other Cultural Inventions.* New York: Praeger.

Kitazume, T. 2005. "Weak Work Ethic Holding Back a Generation of Freeters." *Japan Times.*

Kjeldgaard, D., and S. Askegaard. 2006. "The Globalization of Youth Culture: The Global Youth Segment as Structures of Common Difference." *Journal of Consumer Research* 33: 231–47.

Klein, Malcolm W., Cheryl L. Maxson, and Lea C. Cunningham. 1991. "Crack, Street Gangs, and Violence." *Criminology* 29, no. 4: 623–50.

Knauft, Bruce. 2002. *Exchanging the Past: A Rainforest World of Before and After.* Chicago: Univ. of Chicago Press.

Kohli-Khandekar, Vandana. 2006. *The Indian Media Business.* Delhi and London: Response Books.

Kosugi, Reiko. 2003. *Furiitaa to iu Ikikata* [Freeters' Way of Living]. Tokyo: Keisou Shobou.

———. 2005. *The Transition from School to Work in Japan: Understanding the Increase in Freeter and Jobless Youth.* Tokyo: Japan Institute for Labor Policy and Training.

———. 2008. *Escape from Work: Freelancing Youth and the Challenge to Corporate Japan.* Translated by Ross Mouer. Melbourne: Trans Pacific Press.

Kovats-Bernat, J. Christopher. 2008. *Sleeping Rough in Port-au-Prince: An Ethnography of Street Children and Violence in Haiti.* Gainesville: Univ. Press of Florida.

Kulick, Don. 1992. *Language Shift and Cultural Reproduction.* Cambridge: Cambridge Univ. Press.

Lanclos, Donna. 2003. *At Play in Belfast: Children's Folklore and Identities in Northern Ireland.* New Brunswick, NJ: Rutgers Univ. Press.

Lancy, David. 1996. *Playing on the Mother-Ground: Cultural Routines for Children's Development.* New York: Guilford.

———. 2008. *The Anthropology of Childhood: Cherubs, Chattel, Changelings.* Cambridge: Cambridge Univ. Press.

Landreth, Jonathan. 2005. "China: Changing Channels." *Hollywood Reporter,* Aug. 30.

Larkin, Brian. 2008. *Signal and Noise: Media, Infrastructure, and Urban Culture in Nigeria.* Durham, NC: Duke Univ. Press.

Lesko, Nancy. 1996. "Past, Present, and Future Conceptions of Adolescence." *Educational Theory* 46, no. 4: 453–72.

———. 2001. *Act Your Age! A Cultural Construction of Adolescence.* New York: Routledge Falmer.

Levine, Robert. 2007. "Ethnographic Studies of Childhood: A Historical Overview." *American Anthropologist* 109, no. 2: 247–60.

Li, Hongmei. 2008. "Branding Chinese Products: Between Nationalism and Transnationalism." *International Journal of Communication* 2: 1125–63.

Liechty, Mark. 1995. "Media, Markets, and Modernization: Youth Identities and the Experience of Modernity in Kathmandu, Nepal." In *Youth Cultures: A Cross-Cultural Perspective,* edited by Vered Amit-Talai and Helena Wulff. London: Routledge.

———. 2002. *Suitably Modern: Making Middle Class Culture in a New Consumer Society.* Princeton, NJ: Princeton Univ. Press.

Ling, Yan. 2006. *Kejian yu bu kejian: 90 niandai yilai zhongguo dianshi wenhua yanjiu* [Visible and invisible: A study of Chinese television culture since 1990s]. Beijing: Zhongguo Chuanmei Daxue Chubanshe.

Linnekin, Joyce, and Lin Poyer, eds. 1990. *Cultural Identity and Ethnicity in the Pacific.* Honolulu: Univ. of Hawaii Press.

Lipsitz, George. 2001. *Time Passages: Collective Memory and American Popular Culture.* Minneapolis: Univ. of Minnesota Press.

LiPuma, Edward. 2001. *Encompassing Others: The Magic of Modernity in Melanesia.* Ann Arbor: Univ. of Michigan Press.

Liu, Kang. 1998. "Is There an Alternative to (Capitalist) Globalization? The Debate about Modernity in China." In *The Cultures of Globalization,* edited by Fredric Jameson and Masao Miyoshi, 164–88. Durham, NC: Duke Univ. Press.

Loudon, T. 2006. "Who Is Radical Youth?" Jan. 20. http://newzeal.blogspot.com/2006/03/who-is-radical-youth.html.

Louie, Kam. 2003. *Asian Masculinities: The Meaning and Practice of Manhood in China and Japan.* London and New York: Routledge.

Lu Jun. 2005. "Dazhong gouzao de "Chaonü' shenhua" [The mass-constructed "super girl" myth]. *Zhongguo Shehui Daokan* [China Society Periodical] 9: 11–13.

Lukács, G. 2010. *Scripted Affects, Branded Selves: Television, Capitalism, and Subjectivity in 1990s Japan.* Durham, NC: Duke Univ. Press.

———. 2012. "Employment as Lifestyle in 1990s Workplace Dramas." In *Global Futures in East Asia,* edited by Ann Anagnost, Andrea Arai, and Hai Ren. Stanford, CA: Stanford Univ. Press.

Lukose, R. 2005. "Consuming Globalization: Youth and Gender in Kerala, India." *Journal of Social History* 38, no. 4: 915–35.

Maccoby, Elinor. 1998. *The Two Sexes: Growing Apart, Coming Together.* Cambridge, MA: Harvard Univ. Press.

Mackie, Vera. 1995. "Feminism and the State in Modern Japan." In *Feminism and the State in Modern Japan,* edited by Vera Mackie. Melbourne: Japanese Studies Centre.

Maia. 2006. "Radical Youth Are My Heros." Blog, Jan. 20. http://capitalismbad.blogspot.com/2006/03/radical-youth-are-my-heros.html.

Mai Jieying and Fang Nan. 2005. "Xiaxin: Chaonü xingxiang daiyan zhugong nianqing yonghu" [Xiaxin: Using the "super girl" to target young consumers]. *Nanfang Doushi Bao* [Southern Metro Daily], Dec. 21.

Mains, D. 2007. "Neoliberal Times: Progress, Boredom, and Shame among Young Men in Urban Ethiopia." *American Ethnologist* 34, no. 4: 659–73.

Maira, Sunaina, and Elizabeth Soep. 2005. *Youthscapes: The Popular, the National, the Global.* Philadelphia: Univ. of Pennsylvania Press.

Malcolm, Rick. 2007. "Rick Malcolm: Parliament Beckons." Blog, Jan. 20. http://newzblog.wordpress.com/2007/12/31/rick-malcolm-parliament-beckons/.

Mallan, Kerry, and Sharyn Pearce. 2003. *Youth Cultures: Texts, Images, and Identities.* New York: Praeger.

Mankekar, Purnima. 2000. *Screening Culture, Viewing Politics: Television, Womanhood, and Nation in Modern India.* Oxford: Oxford Univ. Press.

————. 2008. "Media and Mobility in a Transnational World." In *The Media and Social Theory*, edited by David Hesmondhalgh and Jason Toynbee. London and New York: Routledge.

Mannheim, Karl. 1952. "The Problem of Generations" [1928]. In *Essays on the Sociology of Knowledge*, edited by Paul Kecskemeti, 276–320. New York: Oxford Univ. Press.

Manuel, Peter. 1993. *Cassette Culture: Popular Music and Technology in North India*. Oxford: Oxford Univ. Press.

Manuel, S. 2008. *Love and Desire: Concepts, Narratives, and Practices of Sex Amongst Youths in Maputo*. Dakar: Codesrin.

Marathettis, M. I. 1992. *The Greek Cypriot Educational System*. Nicosia, Cyprus: Theopress.

Marcus, George E. 1978. "Status Rivalry in a Polynesian Steady-State Society." *Ethos* 6, no. 4: 242–69.

Marshall, Judith. 1993. *Literacy, Power, and Democracy in Mozambique: The Governance of Learning from Colonization to the Present*. Boulder, CO: Westview Press.

Marshall-Fratani, Ruth. 1998. "Mediating the Global and the Local in Nigerian Pentecostalism." *Journal of Religion in Africa* 28: 278–315.

Martin, Phyllis M. 1994. "Contesting Clothing in Colonial Brazzaville." *Journal of African History* 35, no. 3: 401–26.

Massey, Doreen, John Allen, and Phil Sarre. 1999. "The 'Nature' of Human Geography: Issues and Debates." In *Human Geography Today*, edited by Doreen Massey, John Allen, and Phill Sarre, 1–21. Cambridge: Polity.

Mathews, Gordon. 2003. "Can 'a Real Man' Live for His Family? *Ikigai* and Masculinity in Today's Japan." In *Men and Masculinities in Contemporary Japan: Dislocating the Salaryman Doxa*, edited by James E. Roberson and Nobue Suzuki, 109–25. London and New York: RoutledgeCurzon.

————. 2004. *"The Generation Gap" and Its Implications: Young Employees in the Japanese Corporate World Today*. Hong Kong: Hong Kong Institute of Asia-Pacific Studies.

Mathews, Gordon, and Bruce White. 2004. "Introduction: Changing Generations in Japan Today." In *Japan's Changing Generations: Are Young People Creating a New Society?*, edited by Gordon Mathews and Bruce White. London and New York: Routledge.

Matsumiya, K. 2006. *Furii-ta-Hyouryuu* [Drifting Freeters]. Tokyo: Junpousha.

Mazumdar, Ranjani. 2007. *Bombay Cinema: An Archive of the City*. Minnesota: Univ. of Minnesota Press.

Mbembe, Achille. 1988. *Afriques indociles: Christianisme, pouvoir et état en société postcoloniale*. Paris: Karthala.

McDowell, Linda. 2003. *Redundant Masculinities? Employment Change and White Working Class Youth.* Oxford: Blackwell.

McKittrick, Meredith. 2002. *To Dwell Secure: Generation, Christianity, and Colonialism in Ovamboland.* Oxford: James Currey.

McRobbie, Angela. 1994. "Youth Culture and Femininity." In *Postmodernism and Popular Culture.* London: Routledge.

McVeigh, Brian J. 2002. *Japanese Higher Education as Myth.* Armonk, NY: M. E. Sharpe.

Mehta, Nalin. 2008. *Television in India: Satellites, Politics, and Cultural Change.* London and New York: Routledge.

Menon, Nivedita, and Aditya Nigam. 2007. *Power and Contestation: India since 1989.* London: Orient and Longman.

Meyerhoff, Miriam. 2003. "Claiming a Place: Gender, Knowledge, and Authority as Emergent Properties." In *Handbook of Language and Gender,* edited by Janet Holmes and Miriam Meyerhoff, 302–26. Oxford: Blackwell.

Miettinen, Kari. 2005. *On the Way to Whiteness: Christianization, Conflict, and Change in Colonial Ovamboland, 1910–1965.* Helsinki: Suomalaisen Kirjallisuuden Seura.

Mills, D., and R. Ssewakiryanga. 2005. "No Romance Without Finance: Commodities, Masculinities, and Relationships Amongst Kampalan Students." In *Readings in Gender in Africa,* edited by Andrea Cornwall, 90–95. Oxford: James Currey.

Ministry of Health, Labour, and Welfare. 2003. "White Paper on the Labour Economy, 2003: Economic and Social Change and Diversification of Working Styles." http://www.mhlw.go.jp/english/wp/wp-l/index.html. Accessed June 2008.

———. 2004. "White Paper on the Labour Economy, 2004: Trends and Features of the Labour Economy in 2003." http://www.mhlw.go.jp/english/wp/l-economy/2004/index.html. Accessed June 2008.

———. 2007a. "Report of the Experience Ability Appraisal Study [Keiken Nôryoku Hyôka Kijun (Kashô) Kentô Hôkokusho]. Centre of Business Development Ability Association [Chûo Shokugyô Nôryoku Kaihatsu Kyôkai]. http://www.mhlw.go.jp/houdou/2007/09/h0927-3a.html. Accessed Feb. 2010.

———. 2007b. "Transition and Features of Labour Economics" [Rôdô Keizai no Suii to Yokuchô]. Chap. 1 of "White Paper on Work-Life Balance and Employment Systems" [Wa-ku Raifu Baransu to Koyô Shisutemu]. http://www.mhlw.go.jp/wp/hakusyo/roudou/07/index.html. Accessed Feb. 2010.

———. 2007c. "White Paper on Work-Life Balance and Employment Systems." http://www.mhlw.go.jp/wp/hakusyo/roudou/07/index.html. Accessed Feb. 2010.

Ministry of Internal Affairs and Communications. 2008. "Population." Chap. 2 of "Statistical Handbook of Japan." http://www.stat.go.jp/English/data /handbook/c02cont.htm#cha2_4. Accessed Jan. 2009.

———. n.d. "Q&A Concerning Labour Force Survey in General: Question 7, 'Are "Freeters" Regarded as Employed or Unemployed?'" http://www.stat .go.jp/english/data/roudou/qa-1.htm. Accessed Feb. 2010.

Ministry of Youth Development. n.d. "Celebrating Everyday Young New Zealanders: Southern South Island Profiles: Dan Luoni." http://www.myd.govt .nz/EventsConferences/celebratingeverydayyoungnewzealanders/profiles /southernsouthislandprofiles.aspx.

Molony, Thomas. 2008. "Nondevelopmental Uses of Mobile Communication in Tanzania." In *Handbook of Mobile Communication Studies,* edited by James E. Katz, 339–51. Cambridge, MA: MIT Press.

Monahan, K. 2006. "How Much Is Enough?" *Waikato Times,* Apr. 8.

Montgomery, Heather. 2001. *In Modern Babylon? Prostituting Children in Thailand.* Oxford: Bergahn Books.

Morton, Helen. 1996. *Becoming Tongan: An Ethnography of Childhood.* Honolulu: Univ. of Hawaii Press.

———. 2002. "Creating Their Own Culture: Diasporic Tongans in Pacific Diaspora." In *Pacific Diaspora,* edited by Paul Spickard, Joanne Rondilla, and Debbie Wright. Honolulu: Univ. of Hawaii Press.

Munshi, Shoma. 2001. *Images of the "Modern Woman" in Asia: Global Media, Local Meanings.* London: RoutledgeCurzon.

Murphy, Sean D. 2004. "Enactment of Protect Act Against Sex Tourism." *American Journal of International Law* 98, no. 1: 182.

Nair Sen, Sankar. 2005. *Trafficking in Women and Children in India.* Delhi: Orient Blackswan.

Ndebele, Njabulo. 1995. "Recovering Childhood: Children in South African National Reconstruction." In *Children and the Politics of Culture,* edited by Sharon Stephens, 321–33. Princeton, NJ: Princeton Univ. Press.

Nero, Karen. 1992. "Introduction: Challenging Communications in the Contemporary Pacific." *Pacific Studies* 15, no. 4: 1–13.

Newitt, Malyn. 2002. "Mozambique." In *A History of Postcolonial Lusophone Africa,* edited by Patrick Chabal, 185–235. London: Hurst

Newman, Robert. 1984. "Goa: The Transformation of an Indian Region." *Pacific Affairs* 57, no. 3: 429–49.

New Zealand Electoral Commission. 2005. "Briefing to the Incoming Minister, 2005." http://www.elections.org.nz/news/2005-media-releases/ec-bim-2005 .html.

Neyzi, L. 2001. "Object or Subject? The Paradox of 'Youth' in Turkey." *International Journal of Middle East Studies* 33: 411–32.

Ni, Ching-ching. 2005. "Chinese Youth Discover the Thrill of Voting—for a Favorite Artist." *Los Angeles Times*, Oct. 18.

Nielinger, O. 2006. *Information and Communication Technologies (ICT) for Development in Africa.* Frankfurt: Peter Lang.

Noronha, Frederick. 1997. "Goa: Fighting the Bane of Tourism." *Economic and Political Weekly* 32, no. 51: 3253–56.

O'Brien, Donal B. Cruise. 1996. "A Lost Generation: Youth Identity and State Decay in West Africa." In *Postcolonial Identities in Africa*, edited by Richard Werbner and Terence Ranger, 55–74. London: Zed Books.

Ochs, Elinor. 1988. *Culture and Language Development.* Cambridge: Cambridge Univ. Press.

O'Connell Davidson, Julia. 2005. *Children in the Global Sex Trade.* London: Polity Press.

Odzer, Cleo. 1995. *Goa Freaks: My Hippie Years in Goa.* Crested Butte, CO: Blue Moon Books.

Offit, Thomas. 2010. *Conquistadores de la Calle: Child Street Labor in Guatemala City.* Austin: Univ. of Texas Press.

Oliver, Kelly. 2007. *Women as Weapons of War.* New York: Columbia Univ. Press.

One News and Radio New Zealand, prod. 2006. *Youth Pay Protest Turns Riotous.* Wellington and Auckland, New Zealand: One News, Television New Zealand.

Oram, Nigel. 1976. *Colonial Town to Melanesian City: Port Moresby, 1884–1974.* Canberra: Australian National Univ. Press.

Ore, Tracy. 2006. *The Social Construction of Difference and Inequality.* Boston: McGraw-Hill.

Orlove, Ben. 2005. "Editorial: Time, Society, and the Course of New Technologies." *Current Anthropology* 46: 699–700.

Osborn, Michelle. 2008. "Fuelling the Flames: Rumour and Politics in Kibera." *Journal of Eastern African Studies* 22: 315–27.

O'Toole, T., M. Lister, D. Marsh, S. Jones, and A. McDonagh. 2003. "Turning Out or Left Out? Participation and Non-participation among Young People." *Contemporary Politics* 9, no. 1: 45–61.

Page, David, and William Crawley. 2001. *Satellites over South Asia: Broadcasting Culture and Public Interest.* Delhi: Sage.

Page, E. 2006. "Marching in His Father's Footsteps." *Sunday Star Times*, Mar. 26.

Parreñas, Rhacel Salazar. 2005. *Children of Global Migration: Transnational Families and Gendered Woes.* Stanford, CA: Stanford Univ. Press.

Pfeiffer, J. 2002. "African Independent Churches in Mozambique: Healing the Afflictions of Inequality." *Medical Anthropology Quarterly* 16: 176–99.

Phillips, Joan. 1999. "Tourism-Oriented Prostitution in Barbados: The Case of the Beach Boy and the White Female Tourist." In *Sun, Sex, and Gold: Tourism and Sex Work in the Caribbean,* edited by Kamala Kempadoo, 183–99. Lanham, MD: Rowman and Littlefield.

Pilkington, Hilary, and Richard Johnson. 2003. "Peripheral Youth: Relations of Identity and Power in Global Local Context." *European Journal of Cultural Studies* 6, no. 3: 259–83.

Pilling, D. 2005. "Japan's Wageless Recovery: Creating an Underclass of Part-Time Workers." *Japan Focus.* http://japanfocus.org/products/details/1829.

Piot, Charles. 1999. *Remotely Global: Village Modernity in West Africa.* Chicago: Univ. of Chicago Press.

Platt, Steven R. 2007. *Provincial Patriots: The Hunanese and Modern China.* Cambridge, MA: Harvard Univ. Press.

Plunket, S., B. English, G. Young, and N. Singh. 2006. "Student Protest in Support of Scrapping Youth Pay Rates." In *Morning Report.* Wellington, New Zealand: Radio New Zealand.

Prensky, M. 2006. *Don't Bother Me Mom—I'm Learning!* St. Paul, MN: Paragon House.

Pribilsky, Jason. 2007. *La Chulla Vida: Gender, Migration, and the Family in Andean Ecuador and New York City.* Syracuse, NY: Syracuse Univ. Press.

Prout, A., and A. James. 1990. "A New Paradigm for the Sociology of Childhood? Provenance, Promise, and Problems." In *Constructing and Reconstructing Childhood,* edited by A. Prout and A. James, 7–32. London: Falmer Press.

Puri, Jyoti. 2008. "Sexualities and Complicities: Rethinking the Global Gay." In *Gender and Globalization in Asia and the Pacific: Method, Practice, Theory,* edited by Kathy E. Ferguson and Monique Mironesco, 59–79. Honolulu: Univ. of Hawaii Press.

Qian Qing. 2005. "'Chaoji nüsheng' huobao yingping de mimi? 5 chengshi guanzhong diaocha" [Why is "super girl" so hot? A survey of audiences in 5 cities]. *Shichang yanjiu* [Marketing Research] 9.

Quinn, Eithne. 2005. *Nuthin' but a "G" Thang: The Culture and Commerce of Gangsta Rap.* New York: Columbia Univ. Press.

Radical Youth. 2005. "Radical Youth Responds to Gang Violence." *Independent Media,* Nov. 2.

———. 2007a. "Radical Youth: Free the Urewera 18!" *Scoop,* Oct. 27.

———. 2007b. "Radical Youth to Re-launch the 'End Youth Rates.'" *Scoop,* May 1.

———. n.d. "Radical Youth: Myspace Profile." http://www.myspace.com/radical youth_aotearoa.

Rajadhyaksha, Ashish. 2008. "The Bollywoodization of the Indian Cinema: Cultural Nationalism in a Global Area." In *Global Bollywood,* edited by Anandam P. Kavoori and Aswin Punathambekar, 17–40. Oxford: Oxford Univ. Press.

Raqs Media Collective. 2003. "Call Centre Calling: Technology, Network, and Location." *Sarai Reader.*

Rasmussen, S. J. 2000. "Between Several Worlds: Images of Youth and Age in Tuareg Popular Performances." *Anthropological Quarterly* 73: 133–44.

Renold, Emma. 2005. *Girls, Boys, and Junior Sexualities: Exploring Children's Gender and Sexual Relations in the Primary School.* New York: Routledge Falmer.

Ren Woying. 2005. "Chaonü shi minzhu, Furong shi ziyou" ["Super Girl" is democracy, "Sister Hibiscus" is freedom]. *Shijie Shangye Pinglun* [World Business Review], Aug. 26.

Reuters. 2005. "Democracy Idol: A Television Show Challenges the Authorities." *Economist* 376, no. 8443: 42.

Reynolds, Pamela. 1995. *Traditional Healers and Childhood in Zimbabwe.* Athens: Ohio Univ. Press.

"The Rise and Fall of Mauli Dave." 2007. Sept. 12. http://www.aspisdrift.com/2007/09/rise-and-fall-of-mauli-dave.html.

Roberson, J. E. 1995. "Becoming *Shakaijin*: Working-Class Reproduction in Japan." *Ethnology* 34, no. 4: 293–313.

Roberson, J. E., and N. Suzuki. 2003. Introduction to *Men and Masculinities in Contemporary Japan: Dislocating the Salaryman Doxa*, edited by J. E. Roberson and N. Suzuki. London and New York: RoutledgeCurzon.

Roesch, O. 1992. "Renamo and the Peasantry in Southern Mozambique: A View from Gaza Province." *Canadian Journal of African Studies* 26: 462–84.

Rofel, Lisa. 1999. *Other Modernities: Gendered Yearnings in China after Socialism.* Berkeley and Los Angeles: Univ. of California Press.

Rogoff, Barbara. 1983. *Apprenticeship in Thinking.* Berkeley and Los Angeles: Univ. of California Press.

Rohlen, T. 1983. *Japan's High Schools.* Berkeley and Los Angeles: Univ. of California Press.

Roscoe, Jane. 2004. "Big Brother Australia." In *The Television Studies Reader,* edited by Robert C. Allen and Annette Hill. London: Routledge.

Rosen, David. 2005. *Armies of the Young: Child Soldiers in War and Terrorism.* New Brunswick, NJ: Rutgers Univ. Press.

Rousseau, Jean-Jacques. 2003. *Émile; or, Treatise on Education* [1762]. New York: Prometheus Books.

Routledge, Paul. 2000. "Consuming Goa: Tourist Site as Dispensable Space." *Economic and Political Weekly* 35, no. 30: 2647–56.

———. 2002. "Travelling East as Walter Kurtz: Identity, Performance, and Collaboration in Goa, India." *Environment and Planning D: Society and Space* 20, no. 4: 477–99.

Said, Edward. 1978. *Orientalism*. New York: Basic Books.

Saldanha, Arun. 2007. *Psychedelic White: Goa Trance and the Viscosity of Race.* Minneapolis: Univ. of Minnesota Press.

Salo, Elaine. 2003. "Negotiating Gender and Personhood in the New South Africa: Adolescent Women and Gangsters in Menenberg Township on the Cape Flats." *European Journal of Cultural Studies* 6, no. 3: 345–65.

Sandhu, Amandeep. 2008. Review of *In an Outpost of the Global Economy: Work and Workers in India's Information Technology Industry,* by Carol Upadhya and A. R. Vasavi. *Biblio* 13.

Sassen, Saskia. 2001. *The Global City: New York, London, Tokyo.* Princeton Univ. Press.

Scheper-Hughes, Nancy, and Carolyn Sargent, eds. 1999. *Small Wars: The Cultural Politics of Childhood.* Berkeley and Los Angeles: Univ. of California Press.

Schor, Juliet. 1998. *The Overspent American: Why We Want What We Don't Need.* New York: Basic Books.

Schwartzman, Helen B. 1979. *Transformations: The Anthropology of Children's Play.* New York: Plenum Press.

Sharan, Anita, and Saurabh Turakhia. 2008. "Welcome to the Real World." *Hindustan Times,* Mar. 3.

Sharma, Nandita. 2005. "Anti-trafficking Rhetoric and the Making of a Global Apartheid." *National Women's Studies Association Journal* 17, no. 3: 88–111.

Sharpley-Whiting, T. 1999. *Black Venus: Sexualized Savages, Primal Fears, and Primitive Narratives in French.* Durham, NC: Duke Univ. Press.

Sheldon, K. E. 2002. *Pounders of Grain: A History of Women, Work, and Politics in Mozambique.* Portsmouth, NH: Heinemann.

Silberschmidt, M. 2004. "Masculinities, Sexuality, and Socio-economic Change in Rural and Urban East Africa." In *Re-thinking Sexualities in Africa,* edited by S. Arnfred, 233–48. Stockholm: Almqvist and Wiksell Tryckeri.

———. 2005. "Poverty, Male Disempowerment, and Male Sexuality: Rethinking Men and Masculinities in Rural and Urban East Africa." In *African Masculinities: Men in Africa from the Late Nineteenth Century to the Present,* edited by L. Ouzgane and R. Morrell, 189–203. New York: Palgrave Macmillan.

Silverstone, R., and E. Hirsch, eds. 1992. *Consuming Technologies: Media and Information in Domestic Space.* London: Routledge.

Sina. 2009. "Zhongguo zuimei 50 ren Li Yuchun zanlie diyi" [Li Yuchun topped the list of the fifty most beautiful people in China]. http://ent.sina.com .cn/s/m/2008-11-25/11362266033.shtml.

Skillman, Teri. 1986. "The Bombay Hindi Film Song Genre: A Historical Survey." *Yearbook for Traditional Music* 18: 133–44.

Slater, D., and J. Kwami. 2005. *Embeddedness and Escape: Internet and Mobile Use as Poverty Reduction Strategies in Ghana.* Adelaide, Australia: Information Society Research Group.

Sloane, Patricia. 1998. *Islam, Modernity, and Entrepreneurship among the Malays.* New York: St. Martin's Press.

Small, Cathy A. 1997. *Voyages: From Tongan Villages to American Suburbs.* Ithaca, NY: Cornell Univ. Press.

Smith, A. D. 1998. *Nationalism and Modernism.* London: Routledge.

Smith, C. 2006. "After Affluence: Freeters and the Limits of New Middle Class Japan." *Department of Anthropology* (Yale Univ.).

Smith, F. 1998. "Between East and West: Sites of Resistance in East German Youth Cultures." In *Cool Places: Geographies of Youth Cultures,* edited by T. Skelton and G. Valentine, 290–305. London and New York: Routledge.

Society of China Television Broadcasting. 2006. "Statistics of China Television Broadcasting in 2005." In *China Television Broadcasting Yearbook.* Beijing: Society of China Television Broadcasting.

Solien Besena family website. 2009. http://www.facebook.com/s.php?init=q&q=so lien+besena&ref=ts&sid=61618633a449fbaf080b942c8b4d293c#/group.php ?sid=61618633a449fbaf080b942c8 b4d293c&gid=44586867489&ref=search.

Sommer, D. 2006. *Cultural Agency in the Americas.* Durham, NC: Duke Univ. Press.

Southern Metro Daily. 2005. "Shenzhou diannao: Baiwan daiyan fei huocu qianyue Li Yuchun" ["Divine vehicle" computer: A million advertising dollars to get Li Yuchun's contract fast]. *Nanfang Doushi Bao,* Nov. 24.

Stambach, Amy. 2000. *Lessons from Mount Kilimanjaro: Schooling, Community, and Gender in East Africa.* New York: Routledge.

Stephen, A. 1993. *Pirating the Pacific.* Sydney: Powerhouse.

Stephens, S. 1995. "Children and the Politics of Culture in 'Late Capitalism.'" In *Children and the Politics of Culture,* edited by S. Stephens, 3–48. Princeton, NJ: Princeton Univ. Press.

Strachen, Ian. 2003. *Paradise and Plantation: Tourism and Culture in the Anglophone Caribbean.* Charlottesville: Univ. Press of Virginia.

Strathern, Marilyn. 1988. *The Gender of the Gift: Problems with Women and Problems with Society in Melanesia.* Berkeley and Los Angeles: Univ. of California Press.

Sugimoto, Y. 2003. *An Introduction to Japanese Society.* Cambridge: Cambridge Univ. Press.

Sunameke website. 2009. http://web.me.com/mageau/SUNAMEKE/HOME.html.

Sutton, B. 2007. "Poner el Cuerpo: Women's Embodiment and Political Resistance in Argentina." *Latin American Politics and Society* 49, no. 3: 129–62.

Swain, Jim. 2005. "Masculinities in Education." In *Handbook of Studies on Men and Masculinities,* edited by Michael Kimmel, J. Hearn, and R. W. Connell, 213–39. Thousand Oaks, CA: Sage.

Swedenburg, T. 2007. "Imagined Youths." *Middle East Report* 245. http://www .merip.org/mer/mer245/swedenburg.html.

Szczelkun, Stefan. 1993. *The Conspiracy of Good Taste: William Morris, Cecil Sharp, Clough Williams-Ellis, and the Repression of Working Class Culture in the Twentieth Century.* London: Working Press.

Sznaider, N. 2000. "Consumerism as a Civilizing Process: Israel and Judaism in the Second Age of Modernity." *International Journal of Politics, Culture, and Society* 14, no. 2: 297–314.

Taga, F. 2003. "Rethinking Male Socialization: Life Histories of Japanese Male Youth." In *Asian Masculinities: The Meaning and Practice of Manhood in China and Japan,* edited by K. Louie and M. Low, 137–54. London and New York: Routledge.

Tang Delong. 2005. "Chaoji nusheng: Yige yule shenhua de faji" [Super Girl: The birth of a myth in the entertainment industry]. *Zhongguo Shehui Daokan* [China Society Periodical] 9: 9–10.

Teng Wei. 2006. "Xunzhao ziwo yu xiangxiang minzhu: Jiedu 2005 nian 'chaoji nüsheng' qiguan" [Seeking self and imagining democracy: Decoding the spectacle of the 2005 Super Girl]. In *Topic 2005,* edited by Sa Zhishan and Yang Zao, 1–42. Beijing: Sanlian Shudian.

Thomson, R. 1952. *Mixed-Blood Inquirer for the Australian Government* (government document).

Toivonen, T. 2008. "Introducing the Youth Independence Camp: How a New Social Policy Is Reconfiguring the Public-Private Boundaries of Social Provision in Japan." *SocioLogos* 32: 40–57.

Tomlinson, J. 1991 *Cultural Imperialism: A Critical Introduction.* Baltimore, MD: Johns Hopkins Univ. Press.

Tönjes, Hermann. 1996. *Ovamboland.* Windhoek: Namibia Scientific Society the Laws of Ondonga.

Toren, Christina. 1990. *Making Sense of Hierarchy: Cognition as Social Process in Fiji.* London: Berg.

———. 1993. "Making History: The Significance of Childhood Cognition for a Comparative Anthropology of Mind." *Man* 28, no. 3: 461–78.

———. 1999. "Compassion for One Another: Constituting Kinship as Intentionality in Fiji." *Journal of the Royal Anthropological Institute* 5, no. 2: 265–80.

———. 2004. "Becoming a Christian in Fiji: An Ethnographic Study of Ontogeny." *Journal of the Royal Anthropological Institute* 9, no. 4: 709–27.

———. 2007. "Sunday Lunch in Fiji: Continuity and Transformation in Ideas of the Household." *American Anthropologist* 109, no. 2: 285–95.

Trudgill, Peter. 1983. *On Dialect: Social and Geographical Perspectives.* New York: New York Univ. Press.

Uberoi, Patricia. 2001. "A Suitable Romance? Trajectories of Courtship in Indian Popular Fiction." In *Images of the "Modern Woman" in Asia: Global Media, Local Meanings,* edited by Shoma Munshi, 169–87. New York: RoutledgeCurzon.

United Nations. 2000. "UN Convention on the Rights of the Child." http://www .unhchr.ch/html/menu3/b/k2crc.htm.

United Nations Statistics Division. 2006. "Estimates of Population and Its Percentage Distribution, by Age and Sex and Sex Ratio for All Ages for the World, Major Areas and Region, 2006." http://unstats.un.org/unsd/demographic /products/dyb/dyb2006/Table02.pdf.

Unnikrishnan, Chaya. 2005. "Idol Chat." *Screen* (Mar. 4).

Vassiliadou, M. 2002. "Questioning Nationalism: The Patriarchal and National Struggles of Cypriot Women Within a European Context." *European Journal of Women's Studies* 9, no. 4: 459–82.

Veblen, T. 1965. *The Theory of the Leisure Class* [1899]. New York: A. M. Kelley.

Venter, N. 2006. "Upsize Me." *Dominion Post,* May 6, E1–E2.

Vigh, H. E. 2006. "Social Death and Violent Life Chances." In *Navigating Youth, Generating Adulthood: Social Becoming in an African Context,* edited by C. Christiansen, M. Utas, and H. E. Vigh, 31–60. Uppsala: Nordic African Institute.

Vigil, James. 1988. *Barrio Gangs: Street Life and Identity in Southern California.* Austin: Univ. of Texas Press.

———. 2002. *A Rainbow of Gangs: Street Cultures in the Mega-City.* Austin: Univ. of Texas Press.

Vishwanathan, Shiv. 2006. "Shop till You Drop." *Times of India,* Dec. 25.

Waldinger, Roger. 1989. "Immigration and Urban Change." *Annual Review of Sociology* 15: 211–32.

Wang Shuang. 2005. "Is Super Girl a Force for Democracy?" *Beijing Today* 222 (Sept. 2): 9.

Wang Xiaofeng. 2005. "Chaonü, yici minzhu yishi de qimeng" ["Super Girl": Enlightenment of democracy awareness]. Aug. 14. http://lydon.ycool.com /post.830866.html.

Weathers, C. 2009. "Nonregular Workers and Inequality in Japan." *Social Science Japan Journal* 12, no. 1: 143–48.

Wei Hong. 2005. "Yuchun yuzhao wangshang chuan, yici jia lai yici zhen" [Yuchun's online pictures, some fake and some authentic]. *E-Shidai Zhoubao* [E-Time Weekly], Aug. 17.

Welker, James. 2006. "Beautiful, Borrowed, and Bent: 'Boys' Love' as Girls' Love in *Shôjo Manga.*" *Signs: Journal of Women in Culture and Society* 31, no. 3: 841–70.

Wen Zhongsi. 2007. "Wangluo yanlun ziyou shi ge hao dongxi" [Online freedom of speech is a good thing]. http://www.scol.com/cn/comment/cqsj/2007 08130917.

West, H. G. 2005. *Kupilikula: Governance and the Invisible Realm in Mozambique.* Chicago: Univ. of Chicago Press.

West, H. G., and J. Fair. 1993. "Development Communication and Popular Resistance in Africa: An Examination of the Struggle over Tradition and Modernity." *African Studies Review* 361· 91–114.

White, Bob W. 2008. *Rumba Rules: The Politics of Dance Music in Mobutu's Zaire.* Durham, NC: Duke Univ. Press.

White, Merry. 1994. *The Material Child: Coming of Age in Japan and America.* Berkeley and Los Angeles: Univ. of California Press.

White, R. 1996. "No Go in the Fortress City: Young People, Inequality, and Space." *Urban Policy and Research* 14, no. 1: 37–50.

White, R., and J. Wyn. 1998. "Youth Agency and Social Context." *Journal of Sociology* 34, no. 3: 314–27.

Williams, C., J. Edlin, and F. Beals. 2010. "Looking from the Outside." In *A Handbook of Children's Participation: Perspectives from Theory and Practice,* edited by B. Percy-Smith and N. Thomas. New York: Routledge.

Williams, Linda. 1998. "Melodrama Revised." In *Refiguring American Film Genres: History and Theory,* edited by Nick Browne, 42–88. Berkeley and Los Angeles: Univ. of California Press.

Willis, Paul. 1977. *Learning to Labor: How Working-Class Kids Get Working-Class Jobs.* New York: Columbia Univ. Press.

Wodak, R., R. de Cillia, M. Reisigl, and K. Liebhart. 2000. *The Discursive Construction of National Identities.* Translated by A. Hirsch, R. Mitten, and J. W. Unger. Edinburgh: Edinburgh Univ. Press.

Wulff, Helena. 1995a. "Inter-racial Friendship: Consuming Youth Styles, Ethnicity, and Teenage Femininity in South London." In *Youth Cultures: A Cross-Cultural Perspective,* edited by Vered Amit-Talai and Helena Wulff, 63–80. New York: Routledge.

———. 1995b. "Introducing Youth Culture in Its Own Right: The State of the Art and New Possibilities." Introduction to *Youth Cultures: A Cross-Cultural Perspective,* edited by Vered Amit-Talai and Helena Wulff, 1–18. New York: Routledge.

Wyn, Johanna, and Rob White. 1997. *Rethinking Youth.* New York: Sage.

Xiao Gang. 2009. "This Is Our Freedom Declaration . . ." http://kaieconblog .spaces.live.com/blog/cns!B4C829CC97B9EDD8!2468.entry#comment.

Xiao Hui. 2006. "Ziwo chuyan, gexing jingji: Jiedu quanqiuhua yujing xia de 'Chaoji nüsheng' he 'Furong jiejie' xianxiang" [Chinese pop culture icons in an age of globalization]. In *Quanqiuhua yu "Zhongguo xing": Dangdai wenhua de houzhimin jiedu* [Globalization and "Chineseness": Postcolonial readings of contemporary culture], edited by Song Geng, 213–32. Hong Kong: Hong Kong Univ. Press.

Xiubo Shanren. 2009. "Cheng Naishan: Fukua zhongxingmei wei naban?" [Cheng Naishan: Why do you praise the "androgynous beauty"?]. http://blog.sina.com.cn/s/blog_462b02d2010006xi.html.

Xu Jilin. 2005. "Chuochuan 'Chaonü minzhu' de shenhua." [Poking through the myth of "super girl" democracy]. *Nanfang Doushi Bao* [Southern Metro Daily], Aug. 29.

Xu Wei, and Tang Delong. 2005. "'Chaonü' jiujing dianfu le shenme?" [What did the "super girl" show subvert?]. *Zhongguo Shehui Daokan* [China Society Periodical] 9: 8.

Yamakawa, Sayumi. 2007. "The Interrelationship of *Ohango* Ritual, Gender, and Youth Status among the Owambo of North-Central Namibia." In *Unravelling Taboos: Gender and Sexuality in Namibia*, edited by S. LaFont and D. Hubbard, 69–85. Windhoek: Legal Assistance Centre.

Yang, Mayfair Mei-Hui. 1999. "From Gender Erasure to Gender Difference: State Feminism, Consumer Sexuality, and Women's Public Sphere in China." In *Spaces of Their Own: Women's Public Sphere in Transnational China*, edited by Mayfair Mei-Hui Yang, 35–67. Minneapolis: Univ. of Minnesota Press.

Young, C. 2006. "Report from the Protest." In *Checkpoint*. Wellington, New Zealand: Radio New Zealand.

Youth Organised and United. 2007a. Blog, Jan. 20. http://www.kiwiblog.co.nz/2007/11/youth_organised_and_united.html.

———. 2007b. "Who What." http://www.nzyou.org.nz/client/about.

———. 2008. "Youth Organised and United." *Scoop*, Apr. 6.

Yuval-Davis, Nira. 1997. "Gender and Nation." In *Women, Ethnicity, and Nationalism*, edited by R. Wilford and R. L. Miller, 23–35. London: Routledge.

Zentella, Ana Celia. *Growing Up Bilingual*. Malden: Blackwell, 1997.

Zhang, Zhen. 2000. "Mediating Time: The 'Rice Bowl of Youth' in Fin de Siecle Urban China." *Public Culture* 12, no. 1: 93–113.

Zhao Jin. 2009. "Woguo wangmin shu jiejin 3 yi" [Chinese Internet-using population is nearly 300 million]. *Jingji Ribao* [Economic Daily], Jan. 14.

Zhao Yu. 2005. "Women weishenme xihuan Li Yuchun?" [Why do we like Li Yuchun?]. *Sanlian Shenghuo Zhoukan* [Sanlian Life Weekly], Sept. 15.

Zhou Rui. 2005. "Xiri junnan jinri bianxing xiangdang 'Chaonü'" [A handsome man wants to be a "super girl" after transgender surgery]. *Chongqing Chenbao* [Chongqing Morning Post], Sept. 10.

Zhu, Ying. 2009. "Transnational Circulation of Chinese-Language Television Dramas." In *TV China,* edited by Ying Zhu and Chris Berry, 221–41. Bloomington: Indiana Univ. Press.

Zimmerman, Bonnie. 1992. "Lesbians Like This and That: Some Notes on Lesbian Criticism for the Nineties." In *New Lesbian Criticism: Literary and Cultural Readings,* edited by Sally Munt, 1–15. New York: Columbia Univ. Press.

Index